LinguaForum

| 기획 | 링구아포럼 기획편집팀 |
|---|---|
| 지은이 | 링구아포럼 리서치센터 연구팀 |
| 본문디자인 | 주보민 |
| 표지디자인 | 구수연 |
| 편집인 | 최선주 |
| 발행인 | 이길호 |
| 발행처 | 링구아포럼 |
| 1판1쇄 | 2010. 9. 7 |
| 교재문의 | 02) 3480-6627  대표전화 02) 3480-6614 |
| 등록번호 | 제2000-000335호  등록일자 2000. 5. 17  ISBN 978-89-5563-617-8 (14740)  가격 13,000원 |

Copyright © 2010 by LinguaForum

**No unauthorized photocopying.**

All rights reserved. No part of this book may be reproduced or transmitted in any form or by any means, electronic or mechanical, including photocopying, recording, or any other information storage and retrieval system without the written permission of the publisher.

이 책은 링구아포럼이 독창적으로 개발하였습니다. 이 책의 내용, 사진 등 일부 혹은 전체 내용을 어떠한 방법으로도 무단 복사, 복제, 전재하는 것은 저작권법에 의해 금지되어 있습니다.

*Printed in the Republic of Korea*

R/N(CReTFRneG): 09071030KB

### 머리말

링구아포럼 *i*BT eTOEFL Reading은 초급 학습자 수준에 맞추어 개발된 토플 독해 교재이다. 토플은 전 세계적으로 인정받는 공신력 높은 시험으로서, 비영어권 국가 사람들에게 바람직한 영어 학습 방향을 제시해 주는 역할을 하고 있다. 그러므로 토플에서 요구되는 독해 능력을 학습하는 것은 학생들의 기초 실력을 튼튼히 다지는 데 큰 보탬이 될 것이다.

*i*BT eTOEFL Reading은 실제 토플 시험과 동일한 문제 유형으로 구성되어 있으나, 어휘와 문법은 초급 수준으로 눈높이를 낮춘 교재이다. 그리하여 학생들이 어려워하지 않으면서 자연스럽게 토플 유형에 익숙해질 수 있으며, 나아가 토플 시험에서 요구하는 공부 방식을 습득할 수 있다.

또한 새로운 디자인과 구성으로 TOEFL *i*BT에 보다 철저히 대비한 것이 본 개정판의 특징이다. *i*BT에 출제되는 모든 문제 유형을 7개 Chapter로 구성하여 상세히 분석하였다. 특히, 새로 등장한 문장 재구성 문제(Sentence Simplification Questions), 정보 분류 문제(Classifying, Categorizing, and Organizing Information Questions), 지문 요약 문제(Prose Summary Questions)에 각각 하나의 Chapter를 할애하여 집중적인 학습이 이루어지도록 하였다.

본 교재는 토플 시험 대비용 교재에 머물지 않고, 학생들의 진정한 독해력 향상을 돕기 위해 개발된 교재이다. 실전 문제를 풀기 위한 준비 과정인 Building Skills와 Basic Drills를 통해 학생들이 단순히 문제 푸는 요령만을 배우는 것이 아니라, 근본적인 독해 실력을 향상시킬 수 있다. 학생들이 본 교재를 통해 물고기보다는 '물고기 잡는 법'을 터득할 수 있었으면 하는 것이 연구진의 바람이다.

LinguaForum Research Center

독해 연구팀

## 각 장의 구성

### Word Preview

학습자가 반드시 알아야 할 중요 어휘를 미리 맛볼 수 있다.
이 어휘들은 Basic Drills, Reading Practice, iBT Practice에 반복되어,
해당 Chapter가 끝나면 자연스럽게 그 의미를 습득한다.

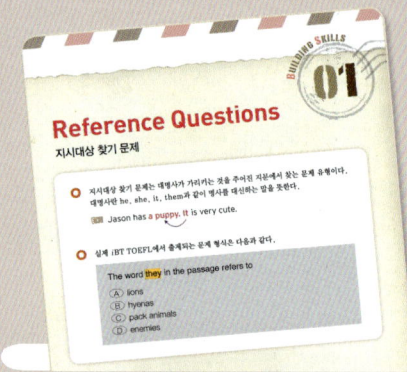

### Building Skills

문제 유형에 대한 정보와 실제 TOEFL iBT에 출제 형식을 익힌다.
또한 문제를 공략하기 위한 실질적이고 유용한 전략을 습득한다.

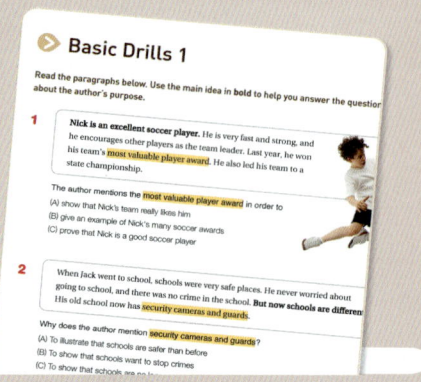

### Basic Drills

짧고 쉬운 지문과 함께, 기초 실력을 다질 수 있는 문제를 학습한다.
또한 중요 어휘의 영어 의미를 통해 능동적으로 어휘를 학습한다.

## Reading Practice

재미있는 지문과 함께 실제 토플 문제와 같은 유형의 문제를 풀어봄으로써, 해당 문제 유형을 집중 학습한다.

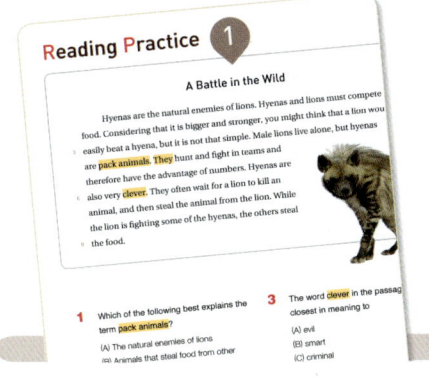

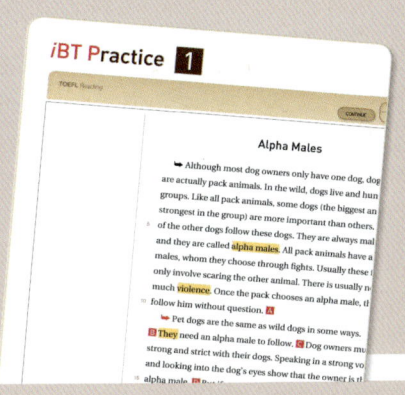

## iBT Practice

실제 TOEFL iBT 화면처럼 구성된 문제를 풀며 자신의 실력을 테스트해 보고 실전 감각을 익힌다.

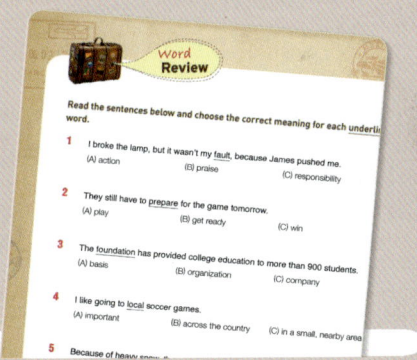

## Word Review

Word Preview에서 학습했던 어휘들을 중심으로 중요 어휘의 의미를 확실히 익힌다.

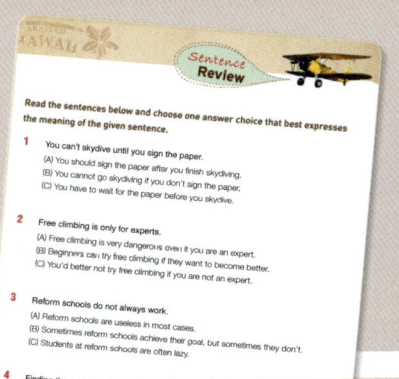

## Sentence Review

Paraphrasing 훈련과 문장 완성 문제를 통해 지문에서 까다로웠던 구문을 정확히 이해하고 넘어간다.

# Contents

**Chapter 1** — **Reference and Words** — 8
- 01 지시대상 찾기 문제 Reference Questions — 11
- 02 어휘 문제 Vocabulary Questions — 14
- 03 중요 용어의 의미 파악 문제 Essential Term Questions — 16
- Reading Practice — 18
- iBT Practice — 22
- Word Review — 26
- Sentence Review — 27

**Chapter 2** — **Fact and Negative Fact** — 28
- 04 세부사항 찾기 문제 Factual Information Questions — 31
- 05 잘못된 세부사항 찾기 문제 Negative Fact Questions — 37
- Reading Practice — 41
- iBT Practice — 45
- Word Review — 49
- Sentence Review — 50

**Chapter 3** — **Sentence Simplification** — 52
- 06 문장 재구성 문제 Sentence Simplification Questions — 55
- Reading Practice — 60
- iBT Practice — 64
- Word Review — 68
- Sentence Review — 69

## Chapter 4  Inference and Purpose  70

**07** 내용 추론 문제 Inference Questions  73
**08** 수사학적 의도 파악 문제 Rhetorical Purpose Questions  77
Reading Practice  81
*i*BT Practice  85
Word Review  91
Sentence Review  92

## Chapter 5  Insert Text  94

**09** 문장 삽입 문제 Insert Text Questions  97
Reading Practice  102
*i*BT Practice  106
Word Review  112
Sentence Review  113

## Chapter 6  Classifying, Categorizing, and Organizing Information  114

**10** 정보 분류 문제 Classifying, Categorizing, and Organizing Information Questions  117
Reading Practice  122
*i*BT Practice  126
Word Review  132
Sentence Review  133

## Chapter 7  Prose Summary  134

**11** 지문 요약 문제 Prose Summary Questions  137
Reading Practice  142
*i*BT Practice  146
Word Review  152
Sentence Review  153

## Mini Test 1-3  154
## Answer Key

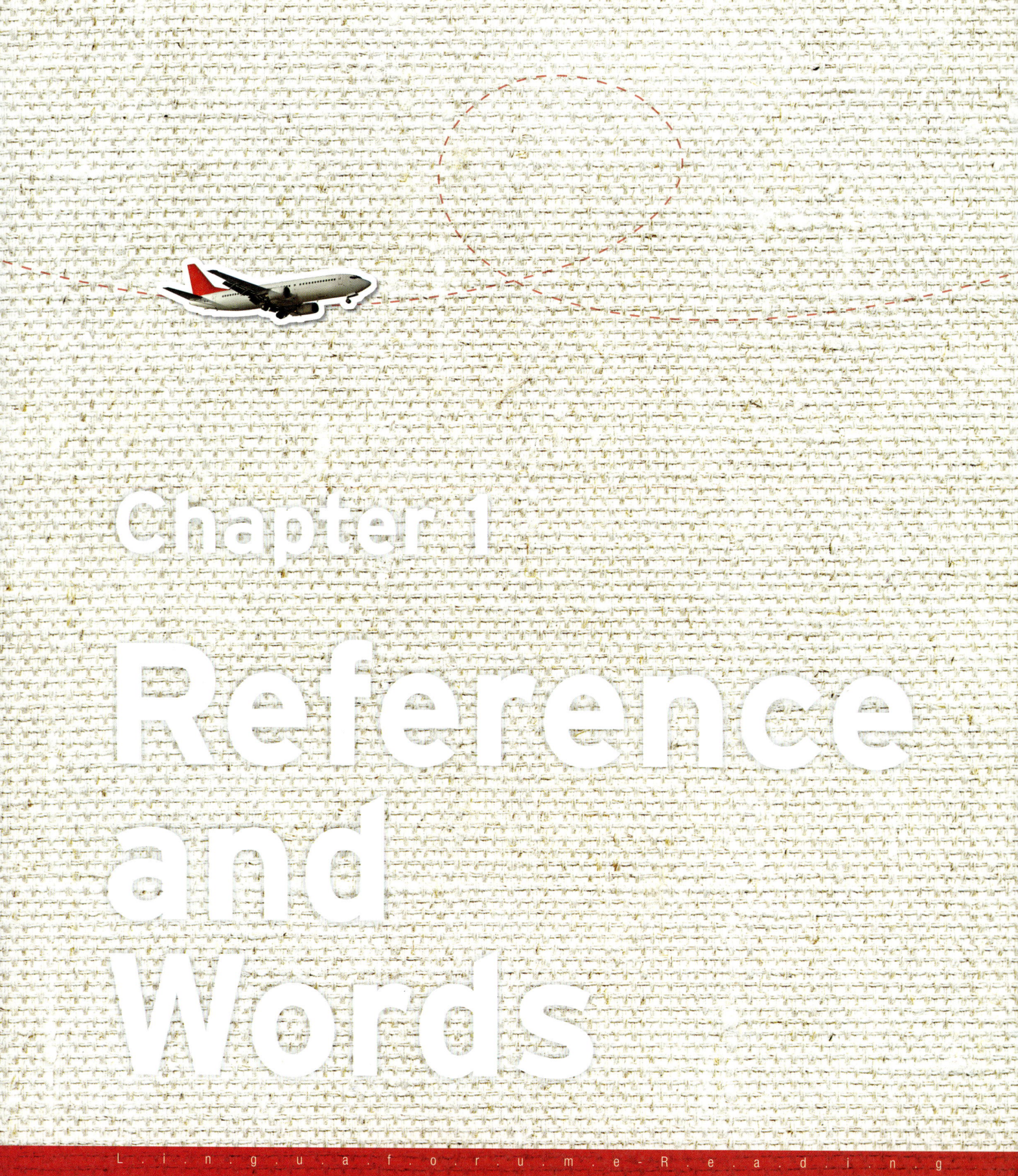

# Chapter 1
# Reference and Words

# Chapter 1
## Reference and Words

**01** **지시대상 찾기 문제**
Reference Questions
대명사가 지시하는 대상을 찾는 문제

**02** **어휘 문제**
Vocabulary Questions
특정 어휘의 의미를 묻는 문제

**03** **중요 용어의 의미 파악 문제**
Essential Term Questions
글의 내용을 통해 생소한 어휘의 의미를 파악하는 문제

# Word Preview

- **condition**

  When we bought the car, it was in good **condition**. But now it is very old.

- **fault**

  I broke the lamp, but it wasn't my **fault**. Derrick pushed me.

- **foundation**

  The Ford **Foundation** was established in 1936 by Henry Ford.

- **honorary**

  Mr. Smith is an **honorary** member of the club. He is treated as a member of the club but does not really belong to it.

- **huge**

  I know I've made a **huge** mistake. I'm terribly sorry.

- **injury**

  The player will miss the match because of an ankle **injury**.

- **local**

  There aren't any **local** hospitals here. The nearest hospital is 45 km away.

- **nervous**

  Tina was very **nervous** before the big test.

- **prepare**

  I have to do many things to **prepare** for our trip. I have to buy food, pack my clothes, and look at a map.

- **refer**

  The "you" in the song **refers** to the singer's ex-girlfriend.

# Reference Questions
## 지시대상 찾기 문제

- 지시대상 찾기 문제는 대명사가 가리키는 것을 주어진 지문에서 찾는 문제 유형이다. 대명사란 he, she, it, them과 같이 명사를 대신하는 말을 뜻한다.

  **Ex.** Jason has **a puppy. It** is very cute.

- 실제 iBT TOEFL에서 출제되는 문제 형식은 다음과 같다.

  > The word **they** in the passage refers to
  > Ⓐ lions
  > Ⓑ hyenas
  > Ⓒ pack animals
  > Ⓓ enemies

### 문제풀이 전략

❶ **주어진 대명사의 앞부분을 살핀다.**
일반적으로 대명사는 앞에서 사용된 명사를 가리킨다. 주어진 대명사의 앞 부분에 해당하는 지문을 살펴보도록 한다.

❷ **대명사의 단·복수/사람·사물/여성·남성 여부를 확인한다.**
주어진 대명사가 ① 사람을 나타내는지, 사물을 나타내는지, ② 형태가 단수인지 복수인지, ③ 여성인지 남성인지 살펴본다. 예를 들어, 주어진 대명사가 단수 그리고 여성이라면, 보기 중 복수 그리고 남성을 나타내는 단어는 답에서 제외될 수 있다.

Chapter 1. Reference and Words   **11**

# Basic Drills

Read the following paragraphs and answer the questions.

**1**
> Australia has wonderful beaches. Many people go to Australia for their summer vacations. Many of them are surfers. The beaches of Australia have excellent waves for surfing.

The word them in the paragraph refers to

(A) beaches    (B) people    (C) vacations    (D) Australia

**2**
> Ice climbing is a very dangerous sport. In ice climbing, people climb huge walls of ice on the sides of mountains. They need special equipment, like ice axes and special boots, to climb the ice walls. However, if it gets too warm, the ice can break, and the climbers can get hurt or even die.

The word They in the paragraph refers to

(A) Walls    (B) Sides    (C) Mountains    (D) People

**3**
> Kelly has a big test in her Spanish class tomorrow. Spanish is her most difficult class in school. Last night she studied for three hours. She thinks she is ready for it, but she is still nervous.

The word it in the paragraph refers to

(A) test    (B) class    (C) school    (D) Spanish

---

**WoRds**  Look at the paragraphs again, and find words with the same meaning.

- Extremely good or of very high quality       _excellent_
- A holiday, especially when you are traveling away from home   _____
- Worried         _____

**4** Most professional sports teams have a full-time doctor. Athletes often get small injuries during the sports season. It is the team doctor's job to make sure they do not become serious injuries.

The word they in the paragraph refers to

(A) sports teams　　(B) team doctors　　(C) athletes　　(D) small injuries

**5** You cannot start camp fires in most parks. This is because you could start a forest fire. Even if you are very careful with your camp fire, the wind could carry a small spark into the forest. It could then start a fire.

The word It in the paragraph refers to

(A) Camp fire　　(B) Wind　　(C) Spark　　(D) Forest

**6** Jack's favorite season is summer. The sun is always bright, and the weather is hot. Jack thinks it is the best part of the year.

The word it in the paragraph refers to

(A) season　　(B) summer　　(C) sun　　(D) weather

**WoRds** Look at the paragraphs again, and find words with the same meaning.

- A person who does a sport _____
- Very bad or dangerous _____
- A large area of land covered with trees _____

Chapter 1. Reference and Words  **13**

# Vocabulary Questions
어휘 문제

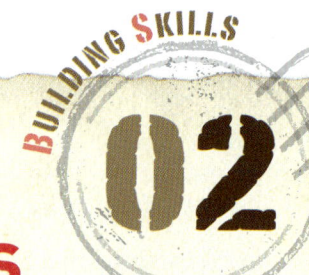

- 어휘 문제는 주어진 지문 내에서 어떤 단어가 갖는 의미와 비슷한 의미의 단어를 보기에서 고르는 문제 유형이다.

- iBT TOEFL에서는 어휘 문제가 지문당 4-6개 출제되어 그 비중이 매우 높다. 실제 시험에서 출제되는 문제 형식은 다음과 같다.

> The word **grant** in the passage is closest in meaning to
> Ⓐ cure
> Ⓑ live
> Ⓒ give
> Ⓓ buy

### 문제풀이 전략

❶ **한 단어가 여러 가지 의미를 가질 수 있음에 유의한다.**
어떤 단어들은 여러 가지 의미를 갖고 있기 때문에 주어진 지문에서의 적절한 의미를 고를 수 있어야 한다.
   The bed in the hotel is too **hard**.
여기에 사용된 단어 hard는 difficult와 not soft의 의미를 가질 수 있는데, 이 문장에서는 not soft의 의미로 사용되었다.

❷ **문맥(context)을 통해 유추한다.**
단어의 뜻을 모르는 경우에는 당황하지 말고 문맥을 통해 단어의 뜻을 짐작해 보도록 노력한다. 주어진 단어의 앞뒤에는 답을 찾을 수 있는 힌트(clue)가 숨어 있다. 이러한 힌트를 통해 단어의 뜻을 유추해 낼 수 있다.

## Basic Drills

Read the following paragraphs and answer the questions.

**1**

> Weight lifting is a difficult sport. Weight lifters get three **attempts** to lift the weight. If they can't lift the weight by the third time, they are out of the competition.

The word **attempts** in the paragraph is closest in meaning to

(A) games      (B) minutes      (C) tries      (D) pulls

**2**

> Skydiving is very exciting. For a few minutes, you can feel as free as a bird. However, skydiving is also dangerous. If you want to go skydiving, you will have to take a class first. The skydiving company will also ask you to sign a piece of paper. The paper says that it is not the company's fault if you get hurt. This is **required**. You can't skydive until you sign the paper.

The word **required** in the paragraph is closest in meaning to

(A) important      (B) necessary      (C) dangerous      (D) exciting

**3**

> The Internet is very useful for many reasons. You can use the Internet to find information or to chat with a friend. Moreover, there are many other things you can do on the Internet. For example, you can pay your cell phone **bill** on the Internet. This is faster and easier than paying it in person.

The word **bill** in the paragraph is closest in meaning to

(A) cash      (B) money      (C) fee      (D) pay

---

**WoRds**    Look at the paragraphs again, and find words with the same meaning.

- To raise; move something from a lower to a higher position    _____
- To write your signature on something to show that you agree with it    _____
- A mistake    _____

# Essential Term Questions
중요 용어의 의미 파악 문제

○ 중요 용어의 의미 파악 문제는 지문에서 중요하게 다루어지는 용어의 의미를 이해하는 문제 유형이다. 이를 위해서는 여러 문장, 또는 글 전체를 통해 해당 용어에 대한 정보를 얻어야 한다.

○ 실제 *i*BT TOEFL에서 출제되는 문제 형식은 다음과 같다.

| Based on the information in the passage, which of the following best explains the term ditching? <br><br>Ⓐ Not studying hard in school <br>Ⓑ Staying home from school because you are sick <br>Ⓒ Not going to school and going somewhere else <br>Ⓓ Quitting school | In many American high schools, ditching is a big problem. When students ditch school, they miss important classes. There are other problems too. No one knows where these students are. In an emergency, no one would be able to contact these students. Finally, many students go out into the city when they ditch school, and the city can be a dangerous place for students. |

### 문제풀이 전략

❶ 글의 소재(topic)를 찾는다.
'이 글이 무엇에 대한 것인가?' 하는 질문을 스스로에게 던져 보자. 중요 용어는 글의 소재(topic)와 일치하거나, 직접적인 관련이 있다. 위의 예제에서 "ditching"은 곧 글의 소재이다. 글 전체가 "ditching"을 설명하고 있으므로 글을 읽으면 자연히 그 의미를 파악할 수 있다. 정답은 "Not going to school and going somewhere else"이다.

❷ 성급하게 답을 고르지 않고 한 번 더 생각한다.
글의 첫 부분만 읽고 성급하게 답을 고르지 않도록 한다. 후반부에 용어에 대한 중요한 정보가 나오기도 한다.

# Basic Drills

Read the following paragraphs and answer the questions.

**1**
> Rock climbing is becoming a very popular sport in many countries. There are many kinds of rock climbing. Even beginners can do some climbing, but free climbing is only for experts. Free climbing is the most dangerous kind of rock climbing because there are no second chances. Usually, your rope will catch you if you fall while you are climbing. However, you have no ropes or safety equipment in free climbing.

Which of the following best explains the term free climbing?

(A) Rock climbing without paying for it
(B) Falling while climbing a rock
(C) Rock climbing without any ropes
(D) A very popular sport

**2**
> In most countries, young criminals do not go to jail. Instead, they go to reform schools. The goal of reform schools is to teach these young people to be better people and to follow the rules of their community. They have guards and walls, but the conditions are much better than in a real jail.

Which of the following best explains the term reform schools?

(A) Prisons for dangerous criminals
(B) Schools with walls and guards
(C) Schools that try to change young criminals into better people
(D) Jails with good conditions

**Words** Look at the paragraphs again, and find words with the same meaning.

- Liked by a lot of people
- A set of tools
- Purpose

# Reading Practice 1

## A Battle in the Wild

Hyenas are the natural enemies of lions. Hyenas and lions must compete for food. Considering that it is bigger and stronger, you might think that a lion would easily beat a hyena, but it is not that simple. Male lions live alone, but hyenas are pack animals. They hunt and fight in teams and therefore have the advantage of numbers. Hyenas are also very clever. They often wait for a lion to kill an animal, and then steal the animal from the lion. While the lion is fighting some of the hyenas, the others steal the food.

**1** Which of the following best explains the term pack animals?

(A) The natural enemies of lions
(B) Animals that steal food from other animals
(C) Animals that live in groups
(D) Animals that are fast and clever

**2** The word They in the passage refers to

(A) Lions
(B) Hyenas
(C) Animals
(D) Enemies

**3** The word clever in the passage is closest in meaning to

(A) evil
(B) smart
(C) criminal
(D) strong

# Reading Practice 2

## Hunting for Stars

Record companies are always looking for the next superstar, but finding the next Britney Spears or Justin Timberlake is not easy. Record companies hire head-hunters to find new musicians for them. Head-hunters travel around the world looking for new singers. They go to singing contests and small, local concerts. When they find someone with talent, they bring that person to the record company. The record company gives them singing and dance lessons to prepare them to be superstars. Of course, not all of these young singers become superstars. Still, it is the job of a head-hunter to find the one singer who will.

**1** Which of the following best explains the term head-hunters?

(A) People who want to be superstars
(B) People who find new singers for record companies
(C) People who teach singers to be superstars
(D) People who travel a lot

**2** The word them in the passage refers to

(A) musicians
(B) head-hunters
(C) Britney Spears or Justin Timberlake
(D) record companies

**3** The word talent in the passage is closest in meaning to

(A) ability
(B) songs
(C) music
(D) personality

# Reading Practice 3

## The Wish-Makers

There are many children around the world with terminal illnesses. For these children, time is short. They may only have a few years or even months to live. The Make-A-Wish Foundation tries to help these children by making their last wishes possible. Some children may want to visit a special place or meet a famous person.

The Make-A-Wish Foundation started with one little boy, Chris Grecius. Chris dreamed of being a police officer, but he was very sick. Before he died, an Arizona police department and many other people worked hard to grant him his wish. They made him an honorary police officer and made a special uniform for him. Chris died shortly after that, but not before he got his greatest wish.

**1** Which of the following best explains the term terminal illnesses?

(A) Very sick children
(B) Illnesses which cannot be cured
(C) Very serious illnesses
(D) Illnesses which last for a long time

**2** The word They in the passage refers to

(A) Make-A-Wish Foundation
(B) Children
(C) Terminal illnesses
(D) Years

**3** The word grant in the passage is closest in meaning to

(A) cure
(B) live
(C) give
(D) buy

# Reading Practice 4

## Keeping the City Green and Clean

How many trees are there in your neighborhood? In some cities, there are almost no trees. This is a big problem. Not only does it make the city less beautiful, but it also makes the air worse. We need trees because they produce oxygen*. Cities with too few trees have very bad air.

To fix this problem, many cities are now making green zones. The green zones are like giant parks. No new roads or buildings can be built in them. Usually the green zones are just outside of the city. This causes another problem; cities need room to grow, but they cannot spread into the green zones. Finding the correct balance between allowing a city to grow and keeping enough trees is very difficult.

★ oxygen: a gas that is necessary for most animals to live

**1** The word produce in the passage is closest in meaning to

(A) have
(B) require
(C) create
(D) use

**2** Which of the following best explains the term green zones?

(A) Large parks in the city
(B) Areas where no new buildings can be built
(C) Areas with many trees
(D) Amusement parks

**3** The word them in the passage refers to

(A) buildings
(B) cities
(C) green zones
(D) new roads

# iBT Practice 1

## Alpha Males

➡ Although most dog owners only have one dog, dogs are actually pack animals. In the wild, dogs live and hunt in groups. Like all pack animals, some dogs (the biggest and the strongest in the group) are more important than others. All of the other dogs follow these dogs. They are always males, and they are called **alpha males**. All pack animals have alpha males, whom they choose through fights. Usually these fights only involve scaring the other animal. There is usually not much **violence**. Once the pack chooses an alpha male, they will follow him without question. **A**

➡ Pet dogs are the same as wild dogs in some ways. **B** **They** need an alpha male to follow. **C** Dog owners must be strong and strict with their dogs. Speaking in a strong voice and looking into the dog's eyes show that the owner is the alpha male. **D** But if your dog thinks it is the alpha male, it will be very hard to control.

**1** According to paragraph 1, which of the following best explains the term alpha males?

- A Very strong animals
- B The leaders in a group of pack animals
- C Animals which are very scary
- D The smartest dogs in a pack

Paragraph 1 is marked with an arrow [➡].

**2** According to paragraph 1, pack animals choose an alpha male by

- A looking into each other's eyes
- B a series of fights
- C choosing the best hunter
- D following their owners

Paragraph 1 is marked with an arrow [➡].

**3** The word violence in the passage is closest in meaning to

- A death
- B force
- C blood
- D anger

**4** The word They in the passage refers to

- A Wild dogs
- B Pet dogs
- C Dog owners
- D Pack animals

**5** According to paragraph 2, dog owners should be strict with their dogs because

- A their dogs will see them as the alpha male
- B their dogs are bad
- C their dogs will learn tricks
- D their dogs will not look in their eyes

Paragraph 2 is marked with an arrow [➡].

**6** Look at the four squares [■] that indicate where the following sentence could be added to the passage.

**Dog owners should remember this fact.**

Where would the sentence best fit? Click on a square [■] to add the sentence to the passage.

# iBT Practice 2

## The Father of Modern Medicine

➥ Hippocrates, a physician in Greece around 430 B.C., was the father of modern medicine. There were physicians before Hippocrates, but his ideas about medicine and the body were very different from those of the other doctors of his time. At the time, it was believed that diseases were caused by angry gods or spirits. Hippocrates, however, believed that there were natural causes for every disease. He was also the first doctor to study the human body in detail. From his studies, he identified many diseases, and he was the first doctor to claim that our thoughts come from our brains. Before that, people believed that our thoughts and feelings came from our hearts.

➥ Hippocrates's greatest accomplishment was the Hippocratic Oath. Hippocrates understood that doctors held great power over their patients. He worried that some doctors would not use this power properly. So, he developed a promise. It said that doctors would only work to help their patients, never to hurt them. He made all of his students take his oath. Even today, all new doctors take the Hippocratic Oath.

**1** The word physician in the passage is closest in meaning to

   A doctor
   B warrior
   C patient
   D scientist

**2** According to paragraph 1, Hippocrates was different from other physicians because

   A he used modern medicine
   B he only wanted to help his patients
   C he did not believe spirits caused disease
   D he was famous

Paragraph 1 is marked with an arrow [➡].

**3** According to the passage, all of the following are true EXCEPT:

   A Hippocrates learned about medicine by studying the human body.
   B Hippocrates found cures for many diseases.
   C Hippocrates identified many diseases.
   D Hippocrates believed our brains control our thoughts.

**4** According to paragraph 2, which of the following best explains the term Hippocratic Oath?

   A The power a doctor has over his patient
   B The proper use of power by a doctor
   C Hippocrates' promise to his students
   D A doctor's promise not to hurt his patient

Paragraph 2 is marked with an arrow [➡].

**5** According to paragraph 2, why did Hippocrates create the Hippocratic Oath?

   A He wanted to know his patients.
   B He was worried some doctors would use their power improperly.
   C He was a good teacher.
   D He felt that doctors were dishonest.

Paragraph 2 is marked with an arrow [➡].

**6** The word them in the passage refers to

   A doctors
   B students
   C patients
   D promise

# Word Review

Read the sentences below and choose the correct meaning for each underlined word.

**1** I broke the lamp, but it wasn't my <u>fault</u>, because James pushed me.
(A) action  (B) praise  (C) responsibility

**2** They still have to <u>prepare</u> for the game tomorrow.
(A) play  (B) get ready  (C) win

**3** The <u>foundation</u> has provided college education to more than 900 students.
(A) basis  (B) organization  (C) company

**4** I like going to <u>local</u> soccer games.
(A) important  (B) across the country  (C) in a small, nearby area

**5** Because of heavy snow, the roads were in poor <u>condition</u>.
(A) state  (B) weather  (C) health

**6** Mike and his wife survived the accident with only slight <u>injuries</u>.
(A) surgery  (B) cost  (C) damage

**7** Tony Gwinn went to his final All-Star game as an <u>honorary</u> player.
(A) guest  (B) best  (C) senior

**8** The French word "rendez-vous" <u>refers to</u> a date or an appointment.
(A) changes  (B) means  (C) makes

Read the sentences below and choose one answer choice that best expresses the meaning of the given sentence.

**1** You can't skydive until you sign the paper.

(A) You should sign the paper after you finish skydiving.
(B) You cannot go skydiving if you don't sign the paper.
(C) You have to wait for the paper before you skydive.

**2** Free climbing is only for experts.

(A) Free climbing is very dangerous even if you are an expert.
(B) Beginners can try free climbing if they want to become better.
(C) You'd better not try free climbing if you are not an expert.

**3** Reform schools do not always work.

(A) Reform schools are useless in most cases.
(B) Sometimes reform schools achieve their goal, but sometimes they don't.
(C) Students at reform schools are often lazy.

**4** Finding the next Britney Spears or Justin Timberlake is not easy.

(A) People with enough talent to become superstars are hard to find.
(B) People who look like Britney Spears or Justin Timberlake are hard to find.
(C) It was not easy to find Britney Spears or Justin Timberlake.

**5** Chris died shortly after, but not before he got his greatest wish.

(A) Chris's greatest wish was to die.
(B) Chris's greatest wish came true shortly after he died.
(C) Chris saw his greatest wish come true before he died.

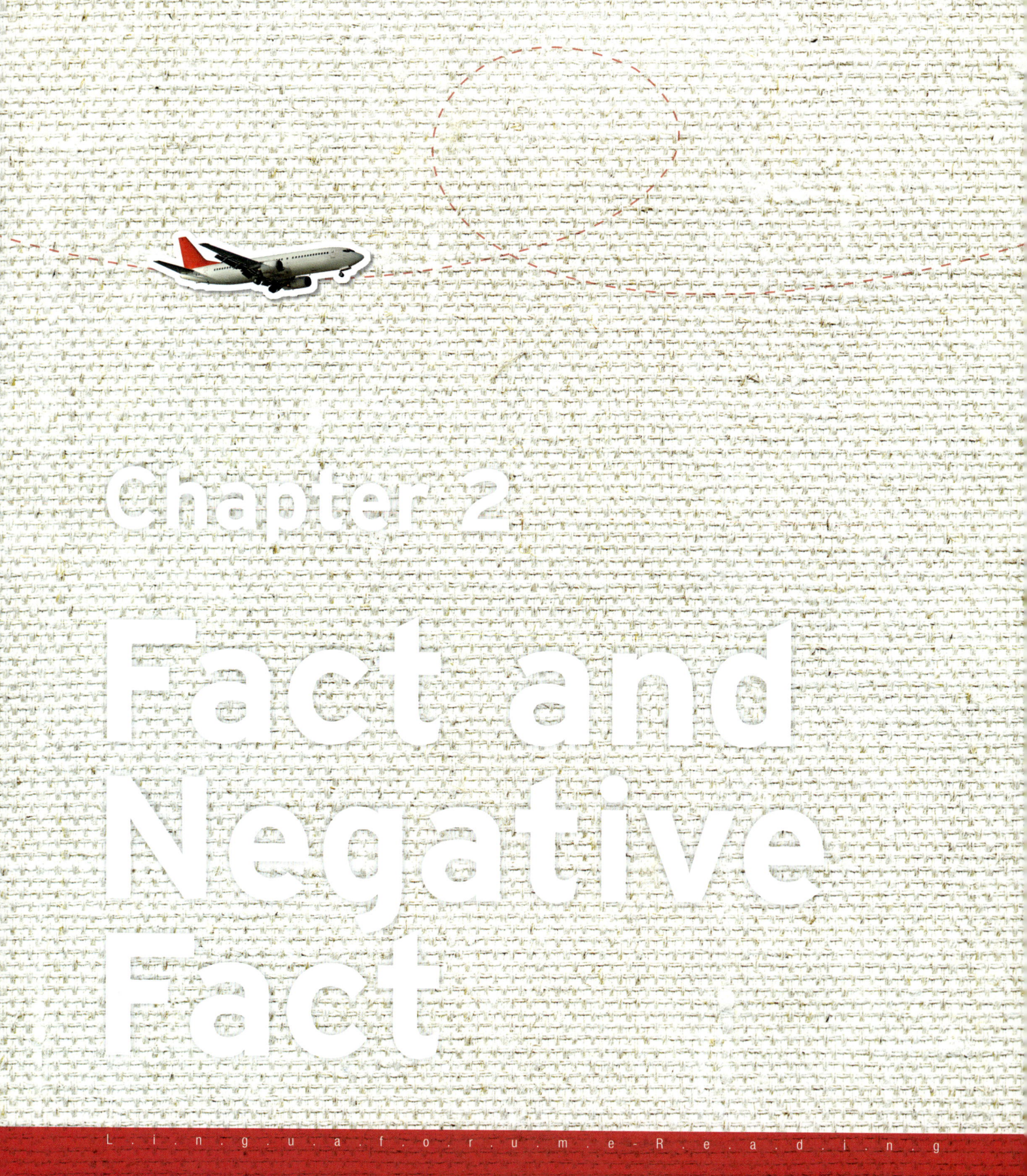

# Chapter 2
# Fact and Negative Fact

# Chapter 2
## Fact and Negative Fact

**04** **세부사항 찾기 문제**
Factual Information Questions

세부적인 내용을 정확히 이해했는지 확인하는 문제

**05** **잘못된 세부사항 찾기 문제**
Negative Fact Questions

글의 내용과 다르거나 관련 없는 내용을 찾는 문제

# Word Preview

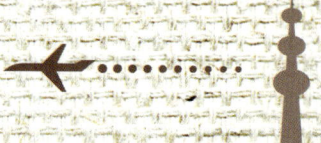

## ✠ culture
People from different countries have different ways of thinking and acting. They have different **cultures**.

## ✠ damage
The child broke his neighbor's window, so his parents had to pay for the **damage**.

## ✠ degree
It is very cold outside. It is only four **degrees**.

## ✠ law
Every country has **laws**. If you break the **laws**, you go to jail.

## ✠ modern
Tokyo is a very **modern** city. It has many new buildings.

## ✠ negative
Don't be **negative**. Try to think positively.

## ✠ powerful
Most sports cars are very **powerful**. They have very big engines.

## ✠ prevent
The teacher tried to **prevent** students from being noisy, but he could not stop them.

## ✠ solve
None of the students could **solve** the math problem, because it was too hard.

## ✠ southern
Australia, India, Brazil, and Indonesia are all in the **southern** part of the world.

# Factual Information Questions

세부사항 찾기 문제

○ 세부사항 찾기 문제는 지문에 제시된 정보를 파악하는 능력을 평가하는 문제 유형이다. 찾아야 하는 정보가 지문 내에 직접적으로 제시되어(directly stated) 있기 때문에 비교적 쉬운 문제 유형에 속한다.

○ 실제 *i*BT TOEFL에서 출제되는 문제 형식은 다음과 같다.

> According to the passage, the highest mountains in the world are in
>
> Ⓐ Asia
> Ⓑ Europe
> Ⓒ Australia
> Ⓓ North America

### 문제풀이 전략

❶ **Scanning과 key word 찾기**
문제에서 key word(이름, 지명, 숫자, 또는 길고 특이한 단어)를 골라 지문에서 검색한다. 이러한 과정을 **scanning**이라고 한다. 해당 부분을 찾아 그 부분을 자세히 읽으면 답을 찾는 데 걸리는 시간을 절약할 수 있다.

❷ **주어진 문장의 올바른 paraphrase를 찾는다.**
세부사항 찾기 문제의 보기는 지문에 사용된 표현을 그대로 되풀이하지 않지만 같은 내용을 담고 있다. 이처럼, 원래 문장과 다른 표현으로 같은 내용을 전달하는 것을 **paraphrase**라고 한다. 다음은 paraphrase의 예이다.

Jessica cleaned the pots and pans before she started her homework.
→ Jessica began her homework after she washed the dishes.

# Basic Drills 1

Read the following paragraphs and answer the questions. The correct answer will be a paraphrase of information from the paragraph.

**1**
> Earthquakes are always dangerous, but they can be very dangerous when they happen under the sea. When an earthquake happens under the sea, it can make giant waves, or tsunamis. The waves in a tsunami can be very high, sometimes up to 30 meters. When a tsunami hits land, it causes lots of damage. The water destroys trees, buildings, and anything else in its way.

What is a tsunami?

(A) An earthquake under the sea
(B) A large, dangerous wave
(C) An earthquake that destroys buildings

**2**
> Do you know what day March 21st is? It's Earth Day! Earth Day was started by John McConnell in 1970 as a way to bring people's attention to the problems of the environment. Earth Day started in San Francisco, but now countries all over the world celebrate Earth Day.

Why did John McConnell start Earth Day?

(A) He wanted to solve the world's problems.
(B) He loved the Earth.
(C) He wanted to make people aware of problems in nature.

EARTH DAY

---

**Words** Look at the paragraphs again, and find words with the same meaning.

- Harm
- To ruin completely
- The air, water, and land on Earth
- To enjoy a special event or occasion

# Basic Drills 2

Read the following questions. Use the words in **bold** to scan for the answers in the passage on the next page. DO NOT actually read the passage; just scan for the words in **bold**.

**1** Why do some people choose to live like their **ancestors**?

(A) They are very poor.
(B) They want to honor their ancestors.
(C) They want to keep their culture and way of life.

**2** How do most **Inuit** make their living?

(A) By farming
(B) By hunting and fishing
(C) By working in large companies

**3** Where do the **Aborigines** live?

(A) In Canada
(B) In Greenland
(C) In Australia

**4** Why are the ways of life of the Aborigines and Inuit in **danger**?

(A) Because modern people kill them and take their land
(B) Because the younger people don't want to live in the traditional way
(C) Because their people are dying from hunger

**5** How does **pollution** damage their way of life?

(A) It makes the people very sick.
(B) They can't catch enough animals for food.
(C) It makes their land very ugly.

Most people around the world live modern lives. They drive cars and work in offices. Their lives are very different from the lives of their ancestors. But some people do not live modern lives. They live like their ancestors because they want to keep their culture and way of life.

The Inuit are a good example of this. The Inuit live in the most northern parts of Canada and in parts of Greenland. Most Inuit live in small communities and make their living by hunting and fishing. The Aborigines of Australia are another example. The Aborigines live much like their ancestors did thousands of years ago. They live in the same kinds of homes and hunt in the same ways.

However, the ways of life of both the Inuit and the Aborigines are in danger. There are many reasons for this. The biggest reason may be that younger Inuit and Aborigines no longer want to live in the traditional way. When the young people leave for modern cities, there is no one to continue the traditional way of life. Pollution also damages the way of life of these people. Most traditional peoples make their living by hunting, and pollution makes it hard for them to catch enough animals for food. It is very sad, but in a few years, there may be no traditional cultures left in the world.

**WoRds** Look at the passage again, and find words with the same meaning.

- Belonging to the present time
- People who lived a long time ago
- The beliefs, way of life, art, and customs of a society
- Existing for a long time
- The process of making air, water, soil, etc. dirty

# Basic Drills 3

Read the following questions. Choose key words to scan for. Then scan for those words in the passage on the next page to help you answer the questions.

**1** How do bees help plants grow?

(A) They kill other insects.

(B) They spread pollen.

(C) They eat the fruit from plants.

**2** Why did scientists mix normal bees and African bees?

(A) They wanted to make bigger bees.

(B) They wanted the bees to make more honey.

(C) They wanted the bees to spread more pollen.

**3** How can killer bees kill a person?

(A) Their poison is very powerful.

(B) They sting a person many times.

(C) They attack in groups.

**4** What other problems do killer bees cause?

(A) They are not good for honey companies.

(B) They kill animals on farms.

(C) They eat all the plants.

**5** Why are killer bees bad for farmers?

(A) They attack the farmers.

(B) They spread less pollen than normal bees.

(C) They spread into new areas.

Honeybees are very useful insects. They make honey, and they help plants grow by spreading pollen*. However, not all bees are so helpful. In fact, some bees are very dangerous. Killer bees live in South America and in southern parts of the United States. They are a new kind of bee. In the 1950s, scientists were trying to make bees make more honey. They mixed normal honeybees with African honeybees. However, the new bee was very dangerous. It got angry very easily and attacked in groups. These killer bees are no more poisonous than regular* bees, but because they attack in larger groups, they can easily kill a person.

Killer bees cause many problems besides stinging people. The biggest problem is that they are not good for honey companies. Killer bees make much less honey than normal bees, and they are much harder to work with. As killer bees move into new areas, they can destroy the honey business in that area. Also, killer bees do not spread as much pollen as normal bees. So they are bad for farmers as well.

★ **pollen:** a fine powder produced by flowers  ★ **regular:** normal

**Words**  Look at the passage again, and find words with the same meaning.

- To move something to a larger area  _____
- To make two things into one  _____
- To hurt or damage someone  _____

# Negative Fact Questions
잘못된 세부사항 찾기 문제

- 잘못된 세부사항 찾기 문제는 네 개의 보기 중에서 지문의 내용과 일치하지 않거나 관계없는 것을 고르는 문제 유형이다.

- 실제 *i*BT TOEFL에서 출제되는 문제 형식은 다음과 같다.

  > According to the passage, all of the following are true EXCEPT:
  >
  > Ⓐ Jazz was invented by African-American musicians.
  > Ⓑ Jazz is a kind of traditional music in Africa.
  > Ⓒ Jazz started in New Orleans and spread into other regions.
  > Ⓓ Many jazz songs never sound the same way twice.

### 문제풀이 전략

❶ **답이 아닌 것부터 지워 나간다.**
지문의 내용과 일치하는 보기를 하나씩 지워 나가는 것이 답을 찾는 요령이다.

❷ **주어진 문장의 올바른 paraphrase가 아닌 것을 찾는다.**
원래 문장과 다른 표현으로 같은 내용을 전달하는 문장을 paraphrase라고 한다. 세부사항 찾기 문제에서는 주어진 문장의 올바른 paraphrase를 찾아야 했던 것과 반대로, 잘못된 세부사항 찾기 문제에서는 주어진 문장을 잘못 paraphrase한 것을 찾아야 한다. 잘못된 paraphrase는 원래 문장과 의미가 달라졌거나 중요한 정보를 빠뜨린 경우를 가리킨다.

# Basic Drills

Read the following paragraphs and answer the questions. Try to eliminate* any obviously* wrong choices.

**1**

Marcus is going to Florida for vacation this year. It is usually very hot in Florida, so Marcus isn't bringing any pants with him; he is only bringing shorts. Marcus also plans to spend a lot of time at the beach. So he is also bringing sunscreen and a hat. He doesn't want to get sunburned*. He is also bringing his dog, Max. He takes Max everywhere because he loves him very much.

★ **sunburned:** having a red skin after spending too much time in the sun

Marcus is bringing all of the following to Florida EXCEPT

(A) pants          (B) sunscreen          (C) his dog

**2**

Jared had a really busy day today. First, he had a big test in math. He had studied a lot last night, so he got a good grade on it. He also played in a baseball game after school. Although his team didn't win, Jared played well. Then, he met his girlfriend for dinner. They went to the movies too. When Jared came back home, he did his homework. Now he's going to sleep. He had a really long day.

Jared did all of the following today EXCEPT

(A) play baseball
(B) study for his math test
(C) see a movie with his girlfriend

★ **eliminate** [ilímənèit]: v. 제거하다, 삭제하다   ★ **obviously** [ábviəsli/ɔ́b-]: ad. 분명하게, 확실히

---

**Words** Look at the paragraphs again, and find words with the same meaning.

- To think about doing something you want to do    _____
- To use (time or money)                            _____
- A mark students get in school                     _____

**3**

Most people love pets. Did you know that having a pet can actually make you healthier? It sounds strange, but it is true. Scientists found that petting a cat or a dog for 15 minutes a day makes people healthier and happier. In addition, if you have a pet, you are more likely to go outside and get exercise. This is because you will take your pet outside to play. So, if you want to be healthier, get a pet.

All of the following are true EXCEPT:

(A) Petting an animal for a quarter of an hour can make you a healthier person.
(B) People with pets are more likely to exercise than people without pets.
(C) All pet owners are happy and healthy people because they exercise.

**4**

When you look up at the night sky, you can see many stars. In a way, you are actually looking at the past. The light that you see may have left the stars millions of years ago. You see, even the closest stars are very far away. It can take a long time for their light to reach the Earth. The light from the closest star, Alpha Centauri, takes four years to reach the Earth. Some stars are so far away that the Earth didn't even exist when their light left the stars!

All of the following are true EXCEPT:

(A) You could see more stars in the past than you can now.
(B) The light from Alpha Centauri is four years old when it reaches the Earth.
(C) The light from some stars is even older than the Earth.

**WoRds** Look at the paragraphs again, and find words with the same meaning.

- An animal such as a cat or a dog that you keep at home _____
- Strong and not likely to become ill or weak _____
- Unusual _____
- The time that existed before the present _____

**5** Thousands of years ago, there were no countries. But there were cities. The first cities were like countries in some ways. Each city had its own army and its own king. One of the earliest cities was the city of Babylon. Babylon is famous because it was the first city to have laws. The king of Babylon, Hammurabi, wrote the first laws in the world. The penalty for breaking Hammurabi's laws was usually death. Soon, many other cities were copying the laws of Babylon or making their own laws.

All of the following are true EXCEPT:

(A) The king of Babylon made the first laws.
(B) The penalty for breaking most laws in Babylon was death.
(C) Babylon copied the laws of other cities.

**6** Do you like swimming? Do you like cold weather? Then maybe you should join a polar bear club. In polar bear clubs, people go swimming in lakes and rivers during the winter, when the water is very cold, sometimes only a few degrees above freezing. People in polar bear clubs can only swim in such cold water for a few minutes at a time. If they swam longer, they could get sick or even die. People join polar bear clubs because they believe the cold water gives them energy.

All of the following are true of polar bear clubs EXCEPT:

(A) People in polar bear clubs go swimming any time during the year.
(B) Polar bear clubs can be dangerous.
(C) Polar bear clubs believe the cold water gives them energy.

**WoRds** Look at the paragraphs again, and find words with the same meaning.

- Rules of a city or country
- To make something exactly like another thing
- To become a member of a group
- Strength

# Reading Practice  1

## King of the Sky

The biggest passenger plane today is the Airbus A380. The A380 holds over five hundred passengers and can fly almost halfway around the world without stopping. It is 73 meters long, and its wings are 80 meters wide. The makers of the A380 made the plane so big for one reason: more passengers equal more money for the airline. The A380 holds more passengers than any other plane, so it should be able to make more money for the airlines. However, the A380 does have one problem. It cannot land at some airports because of its size. But the makers of the Airbus think that most airports will change to fit the A380.

**1** All of the following are true of the A380 EXCEPT:

(A) It's the largest passenger plane in the world.
(B) It holds exactly five hundred passengers.
(C) The plane is wider than it is long.
(D) It can fly halfway around the world before it must stop.

**2** Why did the makers of the A380 make the plane so big?

(A) Larger planes can travel halfway around the world.
(B) A plane with more passengers can make more money.
(C) People wanted bigger planes.
(D) They needed to change to fit the airports.

**3** What problem does the A380 have?

(A) It does not land well.
(B) It is too large for some airports.
(C) It does not make enough money for airlines.
(D) It is too slow.

# Reading Practice 2

## Loads of Languages

Many countries have more than one language. For example, Spanish is common in the United States in addition to English. Many people in Europe speak several languages, like German and French. Do you know what country has the most languages in the world? The island of Papua New Guinea has over 700 languages! This is more than 25% of all the languages in the world. Why does one country have so many languages? Papua New Guinea has many small tribes, and each tribe has its own language. In addition, the country has very high mountains. For many years, the people of different tribes did not see each other that much because they did not often cross the mountains. As a result, their languages did not have a chance to mix together.

**1** What language other than English is common in the United States?

(A) Spanish
(B) German
(C) Papuan
(D) French

**2** All of the following are true of Papua New Guinea EXCEPT:

(A) It has over one quarter of the world's languages.
(B) It is an island nation.
(C) It has 25% more languages than the rest of the world.
(D) It is very mountainous.

**3** Why does Papua New Guinea have so many languages?

(A) The tribes of the country don't like each other.
(B) The tribes do not meet often because of the high mountains.
(C) Each tribe wants to have its own language.
(D) It is a very large country.

# Reading Practice 3

## A Labor of Love

The Taj Mahal in India is one of the most beautiful buildings in the world. The story behind the making of the Taj Mahal is also beautiful. In 1612, an Indian King, Shah Jahan, married a beautiful young woman. It was his second marriage, but he truly loved his new wife. For the next 18 years, Shah Jahan and his wife, Mumtaz Mahal, traveled everywhere together. Sadly, Mumtaz died after having her 14th child in 1630. Shah Jahan decided to build the most beautiful tomb in the world for his wife. Even with 22,000 workers, the work took over 22 years. Finally, in 1653, Shah Jahan completed his wife's tomb. It was the most beautiful building in the world, and a reminder of the love the Shah had for his wife.

**1** When was the Taj Mahal completed?

(A) In 1612
(B) In 1630
(C) In 1622
(D) In 1653

**2** How did the Shah's wife die?

(A) She died working on the Taj Mahal.
(B) She died after having a child.
(C) Her 14th child murdered her.
(D) She was very old.

**3** All of the following are true of the Taj Mahal EXCEPT:

(A) The Shah built it as a home for his wife.
(B) The Shah built it after his wife died.
(C) The Shah built it because he loved his wife.
(D) It took more than 20 years to build.

# Reading Practice 4

## United in Peace

The United Nations is a group of governments from around the world that work together to solve the world's problems and prevent wars. Sometimes the United Nations is successful, and sometimes it is not. There used to be a group similar to the United Nations called the League of Nations. U.S. President Woodrow Wilson started the League of Nations after World War I because he didn't want the world to have another huge, destructive war. He knew that the world needed a way to solve its problems without fighting. Unfortunately, the League of Nations had little power. Its members often broke its rules, and it did not stop the next big war, World War II. After World War II, the world ended the League of Nations and began the United Nations.

**1** What is one purpose of the United Nations?

(A) To prevent wars
(B) To stop World War II
(C) To give more power to the League of Nations
(D) To make better governments around the world

**2** When did the League of Nations start?

(A) After the United Nations was unsuccessful
(B) After World War I
(C) After World War II
(D) After Woodrow Wilson died

**3** All of the following are true of the League of Nations EXCEPT:

(A) Woodrow Wilson started it.
(B) It didn't have any power.
(C) It was successful in preventing large wars.
(D) Its members didn't follow its rules.

# *i*BT Practice 1

## Coral Reefs

➥ Coral reefs, which you can find on the coasts of most continents and around many islands, are an important part of the ocean environment. A coral reef is actually a living thing. Small animals, polyps, make a hard case around their bodies. When they die, the hard case remains, and new polyps build their cases on top of the old ones. Over thousands of years, these animals build a coral reef.

Coral reefs are important for many reasons. They provide a home for about 25% of all the life in the ocean. Small fish gather around the reefs because they can hide in the reef. They also eat the plants in the coral reef. Coral reefs also serve as hunting areas for larger fish, who eat the smaller fish. **A** Coral reefs are also important because they protect the beaches. **B** The coral reef makes the waves smaller by taking some of the energy out of the waves. **C** Without the reefs, the waves could destroy the beach. **D**

Many reefs around the world are in danger because of people. Pollution, too much fishing, and too many boats can destroy the coral reefs. We should work harder to protect the reefs because they will take thousands of years to replace.

**Glossary**

**polyp:** a small sea animal that has a body like a tube

| REVIEW | HELP | BACK | NEXT | HIDE TIME 00:20:00 |

1. According to paragraph 1, how do coral reefs form?

   A) Waves make them.
   B) They are made from the bodies of dead polyps.
   C) Islands make them.
   D) Small fish make them to hide in.

   Paragraph 1 is marked with an arrow [➡].

2. The word **they** in the passage refers to

   A) coral reefs
   B) polyps
   C) ocean environments
   D) hard cases

3. According to the passage, how much of all sea life lives near coral reefs?

   A) Half
   B) One quarter
   C) One third
   D) One tenth

4. According to the passage, all of the following can destroy reefs EXCEPT

   A) too many people
   B) pollution
   C) too many boats
   D) too much fishing

5. The word **replace** in the passage is closest in meaning to

   A) live
   B) make
   C) form again
   D) die

6. Look at the four squares [■] that indicate where the following sentence could be added to the passage.

   **Without the reefs, these fish would have no food.**

   Where would the sentence best fit? Click on a square [■] to add the sentence to the passage.

46  e-Reading

# *i*BT Practice 2

## Lewis and Clark's Great Trip

➡ In 1803, the French government sold its land in America to the new government of the United States. It was a huge amount of land, and the price was excellent, just over 15 million dollars. There was only one problem for the Americans. They knew almost nothing about the land they had just bought. President Jefferson quickly found two explorers, Meriwether Lewis and William Clark, to explore the new land.

It was a difficult and dangerous trip, but Lewis and Clark were expert explorers. They planned their trip for months before leaving. An important part of their job was to become friends with the Native American tribes who were living in the new territory, so they took many gifts with them. Lewis and Clark left in 1804. **A** They traveled by river for most of the time. However, when they reached the Rocky Mountains in the west, this became impossible. **B**

Lewis and Clark eventually reached the Pacific Ocean. **C** On their long trip, they saw many amazing sights and lived through many dangers. But their trip was only the beginning. **D** Their trip interested many other Americans. Soon, thousands of people were traveling west in search of riches and adventure.

1  According to paragraph 1, why did Jefferson send Lewis and Clark to the West?

   Ⓐ He needed to know about the land.
   Ⓑ He wanted to buy land from the French.
   Ⓒ He wanted to fight the Native Americans.
   Ⓓ He wanted to know about the Rocky Mountains.

   Paragraph 1 is marked with an arrow [➡].

2  The word They in the passage refers to

   Ⓐ Jefferson
   Ⓑ Lewis and Clark
   Ⓒ The Americans
   Ⓓ The French government

3  According to the passage, why did Lewis and Clark bring gifts on their trip?

   Ⓐ They needed to make friends with the French.
   Ⓑ They needed to make friends with the Native American tribes.
   Ⓒ They wanted to buy land from the Native American tribes.
   Ⓓ They wanted to celebrate the end of their trip.

4  The word expert in the passage is closest in meaning to

   Ⓐ brave
   Ⓑ skilled
   Ⓒ exciting
   Ⓓ smart

5  According to the passage, what effect did Lewis and Clark's trip have on American history?

   Ⓐ It made peace with the Native Americans.
   Ⓑ It made other Americans want to go west.
   Ⓒ It taught Jefferson about the new land.
   Ⓓ They saw many amazing sights.

6  Look at the four squares [■] that indicate where the following sentence could be added to the passage.

   **The mountains were huge, much higher than any mountains in the eastern part of the United States.**

   Where would the sentence best fit? Click on a square [■] to add the sentence to the passage.

 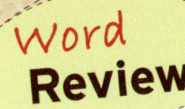

# Word Review

Read the sentences below and choose the correct meaning for each underlined word.

**1** Our city has a <u>law</u> against smoking in buildings.
  (A) movement  (B) rule  (C) idea

**2** The smell of garlic is very <u>powerful</u>.
  (A) big  (B) good  (C) strong

**3** Sometimes, doctors give you medicine to <u>prevent</u> you from getting sick.
  (A) stop  (B) make  (C) cure

**4** Most <u>modern</u> cell phones have cameras.
  (A) good  (B) expensive  (C) new

**5** The accident caused great <u>damage</u>.
  (A) noise  (B) sadness  (C) harm

**6** People in Jeju Island have a unique <u>culture</u>.
  (A) weather  (B) way of life  (C) food

**7** A study shows that loud noise has a <u>negative</u> effect on learning.
  (A) bad  (B) long  (C) great

**8** Caroline <u>spent</u> all her money on clothes.
  (A) used  (B) sent  (C) sold

Chapter 2. Fact and Negative Fact

Read the sentences below and choose one answer choice that best expresses the meaning of the given sentence.

**1** The biggest passenger plane today is the Airbus A380.
(A) The Airbus A380 is the best passenger plane today.
(B) There will be bigger passenger planes than the Airbus A380 in the future.
(C) There are no larger passenger planes today than the Airbus A380.

**2** Spanish is common in the United States in addition to English.
(A) Spanish is more common than English in the United States.
(B) In the United States, Spanish as well as English is commonly used.
(C) In the United States, people use either Spanish or English.

**3** Even with 22,000 workers, the work took over 22 years.
(A) There were too few workers for the work, so it took many years.
(B) Because there were too many workers, the work took many years.
(C) Although there were enough workers, it took many years to finish the work.

**4** Members of the League of Nations often broke its rules, and it did not stop the next big war, World War II.
(A) The Second World War happened because members of the League of Nations followed its rules.
(B) The Second World War happened because there were no rules set by the League of Nations.
(C) The League of Nations could not enforce its rules or prevent World War II.

**5** Younger Inuit and Aborigines no longer want to live in the traditional way.
(A) Younger Inuit and Aborigines don't like to live with their families.
(B) Younger Inuit and Aborigines want to change their way of life and live modern lives.
(C) Most younger Inuit and Aborigines have left for modern cities.

# Chapter 3
# Sentence Simplification

# Chapter 3
## Sentence Simplification

**06** **문장 재구성 문제**
Sentence Simplification Questions
지문의 어떤 문장을 간단히 재구성한 문장을 고르는 문제

# Word Preview

- **adult**
  Children go to school, but **adults** have to work.

- **appear**
  It is dark and cloudy. It **appears** it will rain.

- **aspect**
  I am happy with every **aspect** of my life.

- **control**
  They use a computer to **control** that car. It has no driver.

- **endanger**
  The Florida panther is one of the most **endangered** animals in the world.

- **except**
  No one came **except** Jason. He was the only person at practice.

- **history**
  **History** is my favorite subject. I like to learn about the past.

- **intelligence**
  You should make a decision based on your **intelligence** and experience.

- **seriously**
  A police officer was **seriously** injured while trying to arrest a criminal.

- **temperature**
  The **temperature** will be almost 25 degrees tomorrow.

# Sentence Simplification Questions

문장 재구성 문제

○ 문장 재구성 문제는 지문에 표시된 문장 내의 중요한 정보를 가장 잘 전달하는 문장을 고르는 문제로, Chapter 2에서 학습한 올바른 paraphrase를 고르는 문제 유형이다.

○ 실제 iBT TOEFL에서 에서 출제되는 문제 형식은 다음과 같다.

> Which of the sentences below best expresses the essential information in the highlighted sentence in the passage? *Incorrect* choices change the meaning in important ways or leave out essential information.
>
> Ⓐ Jane couldn't go to school because she was sick.
> Ⓑ Because Jane didn't want to go to school, she stayed home.
> Ⓒ Jane didn't go to school because it was a holiday.
> Ⓓ Jane was late for school because she overslept.

## 문제풀이 전략

❶ **Summary를 이해한다.**

올바른 paraphrase는 길고 복잡한 내용을 간단히 요약한 것일 때가 많다. 예를 들어, 주어진 문장에서 자동차의 engine, tires, doors, windows 등을 이야기할 경우 paraphrase에서는 이것을 "the parts of a car"라고 표현한다.

❷ **중요한 내용에 밑줄을 친다.**

중요한 내용에 밑줄을 치는 것은 paraphrasing을 연습하는 좋은 방법이다. 중요한 내용 중 하나라도 빠진 것이 있다면 그것은 잘못된 paraphrase이다.

(1) If we lose the game, I will be angry, because some members of our team did not practice.
　　　　Idea 1　　　　　　Idea 2　　　　　　　　　　　Idea 3

(2) Since some people skipped practice, I am going to be mad if we don't win.
　　　　　Idea 3　　　　　　　　　Idea 2　　　　　Idea 1

문장 (2)는 문장 (1)과 다른 단어를 사용하고 있고 순서도 다르지만, 문장 (1)의 내용을 모두 전달하고 있다. 따라서 이 문장은 올바른 paraphrase이다.

# Basic Drills 1

**Read the sentences below and choose the answer choice with the same meaning.**

**1** Kyle loves to play baseball, but he isn't very good.

(A) Kyle only likes baseball when he plays well.
(B) Kyle enjoys baseball, but he doesn't practice.
(C) Although Kyle enjoys baseball, he doesn't play well.

**2** Jason didn't go to the movies because he was sick.

(A) Jason was sick of going to the movies.
(B) Jason didn't feel well, so he didn't go to the movies.
(C) Jason was sick because he didn't go to the movies.

**3** Kelly didn't want to go to school because she had a test and she didn't study.

(A) Kelly didn't want to go to school because she didn't want to study for her test.
(B) Kelly didn't want to go to school because she wasn't ready for her test.
(C) Kelly didn't want to go to school because she never studies for her tests.

**4** Today, most people can't imagine a world without computers.

(A) Most people today cannot think without computers.
(B) Computers help people imagine a new world.
(C) Most people today can't imagine not having a computer.

# Basic Drills 2

Read the sentences below and choose the answer choice with the same meaning. Correct answer choices may use different grammar or different vocabulary.

**1** If the sun is really bright, you should wear sunglasses.

(A) You should always wear sunglasses outside.
(B) If you wear sunglasses, the sun should be very bright.
(C) You should wear sunglasses in strong sunlight.

**2** As soon as Kelly gets home, please tell me.

(A) Please tell me that Kelly will get home soon.
(B) When Kelly arrives at home, let me know.
(C) Kelly, please tell me to get home soon.

**3** Jason wanted to buy a new stereo, but it was too expensive.

(A) While Jason wanted to buy a new stereo, it cost too much.
(B) Jason wanted a new stereo, but he didn't have any money.
(C) Jason bought a new stereo, but it was too expensive.

**4** We can't go on vacation for two more weeks because we are very busy.

(A) We can't go on a two-week vacation because we are busy.
(B) We won't take a vacation because we are busy.
(C) We have a lot to do now, so we will take a vacation two weeks later.

**5** Groundhogs look a little bit like squirrels, but they live underground.

(A) Groundhogs are the same as squirrels, except that they live underground.
(B) Squirrels and groundhogs look similar, but groundhogs live underground.
(C) Squirrels like to look at groundhogs underground.

## > Basic Drills 3

Read the sentences below and choose the answer choice with the same meaning.
Correct answer choices will include a summarized* idea from the original sentence.

**1**   Luke plays soccer, baseball, basketball, and tennis, so he is very healthy.

   (A) Luke plays outside, so he is very healthy.
   (B) Luke plays a lot, so he is very healthy.
   (C) Luke plays many sports, so he is very healthy.

**2**   Eating foods like hamburgers, hot dogs, and fried chicken is not really good for you.

   (A) Eating hamburgers is not good for you.
   (B) Eating fast food is not good for you.
   (C) Eating meat is not good for you.

**3**   Lisa went on vacation with her brother, sisters, uncles, aunts, cousins, and grandparents.

   (A) Lisa went on vacation with many people.
   (B) Lisa went on vacation with her relatives.
   (C) Lisa went on vacation with her siblings.

**4**   The farmer grows corn, peas, carrots, lettuce, and beans.

   (A) The farmer grows lots of food.
   (B) The farmer grows many plants.
   (C) The farmer grows vegetables.

**5**   When you play football, you need a helmet, shoulder pads, knee pads, and a mouthpiece.

   (A) When you play football, you need safety equipment.
   (B) When you play football, you need a uniform.
   (C) When you play football, you need to be careful.

---

★ **summarized** [sʌ́məràizd]: a. 요약된

# Basic Drills 4

Read the sentences below and choose the answer choice with the same meaning.
The sentences will have several important ideas, but incorrect* answer choices may not include all of these ideas.

**1**  When you go camping, you shouldn't keep food in your tent because the smell will attract animals.

(A) You shouldn't leave food in your tent, or you will attract insects.
(B) On camping trips, you will attract animals if there is food in your tent.
(C) Never leave food in your tent on a camping trip.

**2**  When we pollute the air, the Earth's temperature rises, and this causes rising sea levels and stronger storms.

(A) Warmer temperatures cause rising sea levels and stronger storms.
(B) Air pollution causes rising sea levels and stronger storms.
(C) Increases in the Earth's temperature, a result of air pollution, cause rising sea levels and stronger storms.

**3**  Students used to go to libraries to study, but now they can study at home because of the Internet.

(A) Students don't go to the library because of the Internet.
(B) Students can now study at home instead of at the library due to the Internet.
(C) Students can now study at home because of the Internet.

**4**  You should always stretch before you play sports, because you can hurt yourself if you don't.

(A) You can hurt yourself if you don't stretch.
(B) You should always stretch before playing sports so you don't hurt yourself.
(C) Before you play sports, you should always stretch.

---

★ incorrect [ìnkərékt]: a. 잘못된, 틀린

# Reading Practice 1

## Roboriders

In many Middle Eastern countries, such as Saudi Arabia and the United Arab Emirates, camel racing is a very popular sport. ❶ The riders, or jockeys, in most camel races are children because a camel can run faster carrying a child than it could carrying an adult. Unfortunately, camel racing is very dangerous as well. Every year, child jockeys are hurt in the camel races, sometimes very seriously. Soon, however, that will no longer be true. Scientists are building robot jockeys to race the camels. ❷ The robots are just as small and light as children, and racers control them by remote control. Over the next few years, most Middle Eastern countries will probably switch to using the robot jockeys. This way they can enjoy their sport without endangering any children.

**1** Which answer choice has the same basic meaning as sentence ❶?

(A) Most camel jockeys are children because camels can run faster carrying a smaller person.
(B) Adults cannot be camel jockeys because the camels cannot run fast carrying them.
(C) Children are better jockeys than adults because they are faster.
(D) Camels can run faster carrying a child than they could carrying an adult.

**2** Which answer choice has the same basic meaning as sentence ❷?

(A) Racers control robots, which are smaller and lighter than children.
(B) Small, light children control the robots by remote control.
(C) Racers use remote control to control the robots, which are as small and light as children.
(D) Remote control robots are as small and light as children.

# Reading Practice

## Bugs, Beware!

Most plants get their food from the ground and from sunlight. They do not "eat" in the same way that we do. But some plants actually do eat like us. Venus flytraps eat insects. This plant has big, open leaves which have tiny hairs on them. ❶ When an insect touches the hairs, the plant knows there is an insect on it, and the leaf closes around the insect. With the insect trapped inside, the plant begins to eat the insect. This takes about a week because the plant has no mouth. Instead, the plant uses an acid* to melt the insect. ❷ Venus flytraps need to eat insects because they usually live in poor soil and do not get enough food from the ground.

★ **acid:** a chemical substance that has a pH of less than 7. Strong acids can burn or melt other substances.

---

**1** Which answer choice has the same basic meaning as sentence ❶?

(A) The plant knows there is an insect on it when the insect touches its hairs.
(B) When a hairy insect touches it, the plant closes its leaf around the insect.
(C) The plant knows there is an insect on it and closes the leaf when the insect touches its hairs.
(D) The plant touches the hairs of the insect and closes its leaf around the insect.

**2** Which answer choice has the same basic meaning as sentence ❷?

(A) Venus flytraps eat insects that live in poor soil, so they do not get enough food.
(B) Venus flytraps cannot get enough food from the ground because they live in poor soil, so they eat insects.
(C) Venus flytraps only eat insects when they live in poor soil and can't get enough food from the ground.
(D) Venus flytraps do not get food from the ground, so they eat insects.

# Reading Practice 3

## Benjamin Franklin

One of the most famous men in early American history is Benjamin Franklin. Franklin was a man with many talents. He started as a printer. ❶ At first, he only had a small print shop, but through his hard work and intelligence it quickly grew. By the time Franklin was 43, he was a rich man. No longer in need of money, he retired from business, but he didn't stop working. He worked for years as a scientist and inventor, and made many important discoveries. ❷ Franklin's most important work, however, came in the 1770s, when the American colonies* were growing tired of British control. Franklin was an important leader for the colonists*. He helped write the Declaration of Independence. During the American Revolution he spent much of his time in France persuading the French to help the colonists in their war.

★ **colony:** a country which is controlled by a more powerful country   ★ **colonist:** someone who settles in a new colony

**1** Which answer choice has the same basic meaning as sentence ❶?

(A) To begin with, he only had a small print shop, but it got bigger because of his intelligence and hard work.
(B) At first, he only had a small print shop, but his hard work and intelligence quickly grew.
(C) At first, he only had a small print shop, but he was intelligent and hard-working.
(D) At first, he was hard-working and intelligent, but he only had a small print shop.

**2** Which answer choice has the same basic meaning as sentence ❷?

(A) Franklin worked in the 1770s, when the American colonies were growing tired of British control.
(B) Franklin's most important work was in the 1770s because the American colonies were growing tired of British control.
(C) Franklin's most important work came at a time when the American colonies were sick of British control.
(D) Franklin's most important work, however, came in the 1770s, when British control was moving toward its end.

# Reading Practice 4

## A Mysterious Monument

The town of Wiltshire in southern England has one of the world's greatest mysteries. It is a huge ring of stones called Stonehenge. We don't know much about Stonehenge except that it was built from 2900 B.C. to 1600 B.C.

Stonehenge has huge stone blocks, some of which weigh as much as 50 tons. How were the builders of Stonehenge able to move such huge blocks? ❶ **To add to the mystery, the stones do not come from anywhere near Stonehenge, but rather from many miles away.** Another amazing aspect of Stonehenge is that the blocks are put in special places. ❷ **On the longest day of summer and the shortest day of winter, the sun hits the stones in a special way.** This makes scientists think that Stonehenge was used as a kind of calendar.

**1** Which answer choice has the same basic meaning as sentence ❶?

(A) The stones at Stonehenge are very mysterious.
(B) The stones come from a great distance, not from around Stonehenge, and this makes it more mysterious.
(C) The mysterious stones of Stonehenge come from very far away.
(D) Mystery adds to the stones because they do not come from around Stonehenge.

**2** Which answer choice has the same basic meaning as sentence ❷?

(A) The sun hits the stones on the longest day of the summer and winter.
(B) In the summer and winter, the sun hits the stones in a special way.
(C) On long summer and winter days, the sun hits the stones in a special way.
(D) On the longest day of summer and shortest day of winter, the sun shines on Stonehenge in a special manner.

# iBT Practice 1

## The 'Curse' of Tutankhamun

The pharaoh Tutankhamun, or King Tut, is probably the most famous of all the Egyptian pharaohs. There are several reasons for this. First, Tutankhamun was pharaoh at a time when Egypt was a very powerful kingdom. Another reason is that his tomb held lots of gold and many jewels, probably more than any other Egyptian pharaoh. But the most interesting reason for King Tut's fame may be his 'curse.'

Like all of their pharaohs, the Egyptians made Tutankhamun into a mummy and filled his tomb with gold and jewels when he died. Then they sealed his tomb. Some stories say that the Egyptians put a curse on his tomb to keep people from stealing the gold and jewels inside. In 1922, an Englishman, Lord Carnarvon, found King Tut's tomb, opened it, and took the gold and jewels out of it. A few weeks later, Lord Carnarvon died suddenly.

Was King Tut's curse to blame? Many people thought it was. Today, however, we know more about King Tut's tomb, and the story of the curse now seems unlikely. King Tut's tomb was thousands of years old, so the air inside was very bad. The dust inside held dangerous germs, and they were probably what made Lord Carnarvon sick. However, many people still believe in the curse of King Tut.

**Glossary**

**mummy:** a dead body that has been preserved by wrapping it in cloth, especially in ancient Egypt

**1** The word **pharaoh** in the passage is closest in meaning to

- Ⓐ Egyptian
- Ⓑ king
- Ⓒ mummy
- Ⓓ curse

**2** According to the passage, all of the following are reasons for Tutankhamun's fame EXCEPT:

- Ⓐ His tomb held many riches.
- Ⓑ He was the ruler of a powerful kingdom.
- Ⓒ He killed Lord Carnarvon.
- Ⓓ People believed his tomb had a curse on it.

**3** The word **their** in the passage refers to

- Ⓐ pharaohs
- Ⓑ mummies
- Ⓒ Egyptians
- Ⓓ King Tut

**4** Which of the sentences below best expresses the essential information in the highlighted sentence in the passage? *Incorrect* choices change the meaning in important ways or leave out essential information.

- Ⓐ According to some stories, the Egyptians cursed the tomb so people would not take the gold inside.
- Ⓑ Some stories say that the Egyptians cursed people if they took gold.
- Ⓒ Some stories say the Egyptians put a curse on the tomb to keep people inside.
- Ⓓ Some stories say that the Egyptians did not want people to steal the gold inside the tomb.

**5** According to the passage, Lord Carnarvon probably died from

- Ⓐ King Tut's curse
- Ⓑ the gold inside the tomb
- Ⓒ the air inside the tomb
- Ⓓ old age

Chapter 3. Sentence Simplification

# iBT Practice 2

## The Running of the Bulls

➡ Each year in the Spanish city of Pampalona, young men do a very strange and dangerous thing. They bring bulls into the streets and then run in front of them. Why do these men do such a dangerous thing? It is the Running of the Bulls, a tradition in Pampalona. The Running of the Bulls is part of a festival, *La Fiesta de San Fermin*. The festival started in 1852, and part of the festival was bullfighting. But the people of Pampalona needed to move the bulls from the stable to the arena, which was more than half a mile away. So each year, brave young men stood in front of the bulls. The bulls chased the young men, who ran to the arena. This is how the bulls were brought to the arena for the fights.

Over time, the Running of the Bulls grew famous. It was a way for men to test their courage. People came from all over Spain to run with the bulls. Soon, people were coming from other parts of Europe and even America to run with the bulls. Running with the bulls is very dangerous, and every year people are injured, and sometimes people even die. Although the running of the bulls is dangerous, it is still very popular. Anyone can run with the bulls, but you need to be very fast!

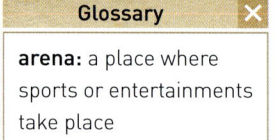

**Glossary**

**arena:** a place where sports or entertainments take place

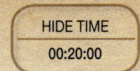

**1** According to paragraph 1, how often is the Running of the Bulls?

    Ⓐ Every year
    Ⓑ Twice a year
    Ⓒ Every week
    Ⓓ Every day

Paragraph 1 is marked with an arrow [➡].

**2** The word festival in the passage is closest in meaning to

    Ⓐ tradition
    Ⓑ bullfight
    Ⓒ holiday
    Ⓓ Pampalona

**3** According to the passage, all of the following are true EXCEPT:

    Ⓐ No one dies in the Running of the Bulls.
    Ⓑ The Running of the Bulls is a way for people to test their courage.
    Ⓒ The Running of the Bulls happens before the bullfights.
    Ⓓ The Running of the Bulls is part of *La Fiesta de San Fermin*.

**4** The word It in the passage refers to

    Ⓐ Time
    Ⓑ Bulls
    Ⓒ The Running of the Bulls
    Ⓓ Test

**5** Which of the sentences below best expresses the essential information in the highlighted sentence in the passage? *Incorrect* choices change the meaning in important ways or leave out essential information.

    Ⓐ Every year, people die in the Running of the Bulls because it is so dangerous.
    Ⓑ There is a lot of danger in running with the bulls, and each year there are injuries and sometimes deaths.
    Ⓒ There are many injuries in the Running of the Bulls, so every year, it is very dangerous.
    Ⓓ Every year, the Running of the Bulls is dangerous, and there are sometimes injuries.

Read the sentences below and choose the correct word for each blank. Use the word bank below.

**Word Bank**

| control | appear | except | aspect |
|---------|--------|--------|--------|
| seriously | temperature | intelligence | endanger |

1. I like most sports _____ baseball.

2. Lately, I have been thinking _____ about life and death.

3. Laurie was drawn to the strength, beauty and _____ of the horse.

4. In the winter, bears _____ to be sleeping, but they are not actually sleeping.

5. A general _____s the army.

6. The water is polluted in the city. It _____s the safety of people.

7. The _____ is much higher in the desert than in other places.

8. Why don't you try to look at it from a different _____?

68  e-Reading

Complete the following sentences by rearranging* the words from the parentheses* to fill in the blanks in the right order*.

**1** The riders, or jockeys, in most camel races are children because a camel can run faster carrying a child _____.

(an, than, it, carrying, adult, could)

**2** _____, the plant begins to eat the insect.

(insect, the, inside, trapped, with)

**3** _____, he retired from business, but he didn't stop working.

(longer, of, in, no, need, money)

**4** Stonehenge has huge stone blocks, _____ 50 tons.

(as, some, weigh, much, as, of, which)

**5** _____ Stonehenge was used as a kind of calendar.

(makes, think, scientists, this, that)

★ **rearrange** [ri:əréindʒ]: v. 다시 배열하다   ★ **parenthesis** [pərénθəsis]: n. 괄호   ★ **order** [ɔ́:rdər]: n. 순서

Chapter 3. Sentence Simplification  **69**

# Chapter 4
# Inference and Purpose

# Chapter 4
## Inference and Purpose

**07** **내용 추론 문제**
Inference Questions
지문의 내용을 토대로 지문에 나와 있지 않은 내용을 추론하는 문제

**08** **수사학적 의도 파악 문제**
Rhetorical Purpose Questions
글쓴이의 수사학적인 의도를 파악하는 문제

# Word Preview

- **accept**
  The boy tried to give his girlfriend some flowers, but she would not **accept** them.

- **cause**
  The floor was very wet, and that **caused** the man to fall.

- **disease**
  **Diseases** like AIDS are a big problem in many parts of the world.

- **infer**
  You should not try to **infer** too much from his success. He was very lucky.

- **location**
  My mom doesn't like the **location** of the picture, so we will move it.

- **mention**
  You will hear my name **mentioned** often on TV because I'm going to be a star!

- **purpose**
  The **purpose** of his visit to New York was not told to the public.

- **rarely**
  Many people are afraid of sharks, but they **rarely** attack people.

- **technology**
  Before the 1900s, people didn't have **technology** like phones and computers.

- **underground**
  Much of the subway in the city is **underground**.

# Inference Questions

내용 추론 문제

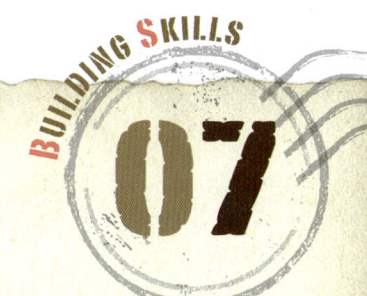

○ 내용 추론 문제는 주어진 지문에 암시되어(implied) 있는 내용을 묻는 문제 유형이다. 예를 들면, 어떤 결과에 해당되는 내용이 지문에 제시되어 있을 경우 그 원인이 무엇인지 묻거나, 몇몇 현상들을 제시하고 그것을 일반화하도록 요구하기도 한다.

○ 실제 *i*BT TOEFL에서 출제되는 문제 형식은 다음과 같다.

> Which of the following can be inferred from the passage?
> Ⓐ Only Greeks run marathons today.
> Ⓑ People only run marathons after wars.
> Ⓒ Marathons are 26 miles long.
> Ⓓ Marathons are most popular in Greece.

### 문제풀이 전략

❶ **주어진 지문에서 실마리를 찾아낸다.**

문제에서 묻는 내용이 비록 지문에 명확히 나와 있지는 않지만, 실마리는 반드시 주어진다. 문장과 문장 사이의 관계에 주목하고, 그 관계를 논리적으로 연결하도록 노력한다. 예를 들어 다음과 같은 두 문장이 주어졌다고 하자.

　(1) 사람들은 오랜 옛날부터 축구를 해 왔다.
　(2) 오늘날과 같이 가죽으로 된 축구공이 공식적으로 쓰이게 된 것은 1872년부터이다.

이 두 문장으로부터 '1872년 이전까지 사람들은 오늘날과 같은 축구공이 아닌 형태의 공으로 축구를 했다'는 사실을 추론해 낼 수 있다.

❷ **넘겨짚지 않는다.**

자신이 갖고 있는 지식에 근거하여 답을 고르지 않도록 한다. 오직 지문에 있는 내용만을 근거로 판단해야 한다.

## Basic Drills 1

Read the short paragraphs below. What inferences can be made?

**1**
> The Yellow River is a huge river in China. Long ago, it used to flood every year. But modern dams can usually keep rivers from flooding. The Yellow River rarely floods anymore.

What can be inferred from this paragraph?

(A) Life on the Yellow River is much better than before.
(B) No one dies on the Yellow River anymore.
(C) The Yellow River now has dams on it.

**2**
> Sports with lots of running are the healthiest sports because they exercise your heart. During a soccer game, a soccer player runs almost eight miles. A basketball player might run five miles during a game. Football players usually only run two or three miles during a game.

What can be inferred from this paragraph?

(A) Soccer is better for your health than basketball or football.
(B) Football is the easiest sport.
(C) Soccer players are taller than football players and basketball players.

---

**WoRds**    Look at the paragraphs again, and find words with the same meaning.

- To cover a place with water, or to become covered with water  _____
- Not often  _____
- To make a part of your body move  _____

**3**

> The United States has one of the highest rates of heart disease in the world. This is largely because of American eating habits. Scientists know that eating too much red meat and fried foods can help cause heart disease.

What can be inferred from this paragraph?

(A) Many Americans die from heart disease.

(B) Americans eat a lot of red meat and fried foods.

(C) Most Americans are very unhealthy.


**4**

> Not all dangerous animals are predators★. Hippos are probably the most dangerous animals in Africa. Every year, hippos kill more people than lions or other big cats. This is because hippos come in contact with humans more often on Africa's rivers.

★ **predator:** an animal that kills and eats other animals

What can be inferred from this paragraph?

(A) Hippos do not like people.

(B) Africans stay away from rivers because they are dangerous.

(C) Hippos are not predators.


**WoRds** Look at the paragraphs again, and find words with the same meaning.

- The number of times that something happens  _____
- An illness  _____
- Something that you do often  _____

Chapter 4. Inference and Purpose  **75**

# Basic Drills 2

Read the passage below and answer the questions. These inferences will come from separate* parts of the passage. You may have to connect information from separate paragraphs to make the correct inference.

In the second century A.D., Claudius Ptolemy, a famous scientist, said that the Earth was at the center of the universe. The Catholic Church liked Ptolemy's idea because it was much like the Church's idea of heaven and hell. For the next 1,200 years, everyone believed Ptolemy's ideas.

In the early 1500s, a young Polish man, Nicolaus Copernicus, began to question Ptolemy's ideas. He made a new map of the universe. But unlike Ptolemy's map, the Sun was at the center of the universe, not the Earth. Copernicus waited almost until his death to tell anyone about his ideas.

Almost a hundred years later, an Italian, Galileo Galilei, used one of the first telescopes to watch the planets. His studies gave the first proof of Copernicus's ideas. The Church was very angry. It would not allow anyone to print Copernicus's book and forced Galileo to say his ideas were wrong. But that did not stop the spread of his ideas. Soon, most of the world believed that the Sun was at the center of the universe.

**1** It can be inferred from the passage that Copernicus waited to tell anyone about his ideas because

(A) he wanted to make sure he was right
(B) people were not interested in his ideas
(C) he was afraid of the Church

**2** It can be inferred from the passage that the Church disliked Copernicus' ideas because

(A) Copernicus was not a Christian
(B) they did not match the Church's idea of heaven and hell
(C) Copernicus' ideas were wrong

★ separate [sépərət]: a. 각기 다른

# Rhetorical Purpose Questions
## 수사학적 의도 파악 문제

○ 수사학적 의도 파악 문제는 지문 내에서 특정 사실이나 예를 언급한 목적을 묻는 문제 유형이다. 또 글쓴이가 어떤 논지 전개 방식을 사용했는지에 대해 묻기도 한다.

○ 실제 *i*BT TOEFL에서 출제되는 문제 형식은 다음과 같다.

> Why does the author mention Hercules?
> Ⓐ To show that Greece had many strong heroes
> Ⓑ To show that Greece has an interesting history
> Ⓒ To give an example of an untrue story from Greek history
> Ⓓ To show that marathons happened before the time of Pheidippides

### 문제풀이 전략

**❶ 나무보다 숲을 본다.**

글쓴이의 수사학적 의도를 파악하려면 글의 전체적인 구조를 이해해야 한다. 글의 중심 내용(main idea)이 무엇인지 파악하고, 문장과 문장, 단락과 단락 간의 관계(예시, 비유, 부연, 원인 등)를 이해할 수 있어야 한다.

**❷ 보기에 나오는 용어를 숙지한다.**

다음은 수사학적 의도 파악 문제의 보기에 자주 사용되는 표현들이다.

- 예시: to give an example of, to show
- 논증: to prove, to argue, to claim
- 설명: to explain, to describe
- 암시: to suggest, to imply
- 강조: to emphasize
- 원인: to give a reason for
- 비교, 대조: to compare, to contrast

#  Basic Drills 1

Read the paragraphs below. Use the main idea in **bold** to help you answer the question about the author's purpose.

**1**
> **Nick is an excellent soccer player.** He is very fast and strong, and he encourages other players as the team leader. Last year, he won his team's most valuable player award. He also led his team to a state championship.

The author mentions the most valuable player award in order to

(A) show that Nick's team really likes him
(B) give an example of Nick's many soccer awards
(C) prove that Nick is a good soccer player

**2**
> When Jack went to school, schools were very safe places. He never worried about going to school, and there was no crime in the school. **But now schools are different.** His old school now has security cameras and guards.

Why does the author mention security cameras and guards?

(A) To illustrate that schools are safer than before
(B) To show that schools want to stop crimes
(C) To show that schools are no longer safe places

---

**WoRds**  Look at the paragraphs again, and find words with the same meaning.

- Useful and helpful  _____
- A prize  _____
- A competition  _____
- Things that are done to keep people safe from danger or crime  _____

**3**

> **Every year, electronics get smaller and faster.** Computers used to be huge machines. The first computers were as large as most cars. They were also very slow. Today, most PDAs are small enough to fit in your pocket and are much more powerful than the first computers.

Why does the author mention PDAs?

(A) To show that the first computers were very bad
(B) To show the progress in electronics
(C) To give an example of a very useful piece of electronics

**4**

> **Tiger Woods is the best golfer the world has ever seen.** In 1996, he first joined the U.S. PGA Tour with the promise of breaking every record. 14 years have passed since then, and we can say that he already has kept his promise. He has won 71 PGA Tour victories and 14 major championship victories. Moreover, he is the highest-paid professional athlete in the world. And he is only in his 30s!

Why does the author give details about the numbers of victories Tiger Woods has won?

(A) To show that it is more difficult to win major championships than to win PGA Tours
(B) To point out that Tiger Woods always keeps his promises
(C) To support the idea that Tiger Woods is the best golfer in history

**Words** Look at the paragraphs again, and find words with the same meaning.

- Equipment like computers and televisions
- Before now; sooner than expected
- The period of time in your life that you spend doing a job
- The money you earn

# Basic Drills 2

Read the paragraphs below and answer the questions.

**1**

Mt. Everest is the highest mountain in the world. It is also the hardest mountain to climb. For thousands of years, no one climbed Everest. This was partly because the local people, Sherpas, believed the mountain was a holy place and people shouldn't climb it. Their beliefs started to change when tourists began to come to Everest to climb it in the 1950s and 60s. As the tourists brought money to the poor Sherpa communities, the Sherpas slowly began to accept the idea of people climbing their sacred mountain. Today, some Sherpas, like Apa Sherpa, even have hotels for climbers.

The author mentions Apa Sherpa in order to

(A) show that some Sherpas are very rich
(B) show that Sherpas now accept people climbing their holy mountain
(C) show that more and more tourists are coming to climb Everest

**2**

Twenty thousand years ago, the world was a much colder place. Ice covered much of the Earth, and huge rivers of ice, glaciers, stretched down from the mountains. They moved very slowly, but they were very heavy. As they moved, they changed the shape of the land, digging huge holes in the ground. Later, when the Earth got warmer, the glaciers melted, and the melting ice filled the holes with water. This made huge new bodies of water. You can see this in the Great Lakes in the United States, which are as large as some seas.

Why does the author mention the Great Lakes?

(A) To show that there were large glaciers in the United States
(B) To give an example of new bodies of water made by the glaciers
(C) To show that glaciers were very important in shaping the land

# Reading Practice 1

## The Nuclear Age

World War II ended in the summer of 1945, when the United States dropped atomic bombs* on the cities of Nagasaki and Hiroshima. But the end of the war did not make the Earth a safer place. It began the nuclear age. The nuclear age was a frightening time because any new war could include atomic bombs. Both of the two superpowers*, the United States and Russia, had enough atomic bombs to destroy the Earth. People in the 1950s and 60s were well aware of this and lived in fear of nuclear war.

Many Americans at that time built bomb shelters. Bomb shelters were rooms under the ground which people built to save themselves in a nuclear war. They kept months of food and water in their bomb shelters because it would not be safe to eat plants after a nuclear war. Most of the bomb shelters were too small to actually save people in a nuclear war, but they made people feel a little bit safer.

★ **atomic bomb:** a very powerful bomb that kills a lot of people and destroys large areas   ★ **superpower:** a very powerful country

**1** The author mentions bomb shelters in order to

(A) show that people were very afraid of a nuclear war
(B) show that many Americans could save themselves
(C) show that most Americans would be safe in a nuclear war
(D) show that you must go underground in a nuclear war

**2** What can be inferred about the effects of nuclear weapons?

(A) Nuclear weapons are not as dangerous as people thought.
(B) Nuclear weapons cause earthquakes.
(C) Nuclear weapons poison plants.
(D) Nuclear weapons cannot destroy bomb shelters.

# Reading Practice 2

## Tornadoes

Tornadoes are perhaps the strongest storms on Earth. With winds of up to 300 miles per hour, tornadoes can cause a lot of damage. In the United States, there is an average of 800 tornadoes each year. Most of them are in "tornado alley*," the area of low, flat land between Texas and Nebraska. The United States, because of its location, has more tornadoes than any other country. As warm, moist air comes up from Mexico and cold air comes down from Canada, they meet above tornado alley.

Tornadoes are very dangerous because there is little warning, and people do not have much time to find a safe place. TV stations often give tornado warnings, but even with modern technology, the warning time is usually only about 12 minutes.

★ alley: a narrow way

**1** What can be inferred from the passage about tornadoes?

(A) Tornadoes only happen in the United States.
(B) Tornadoes kill many people in the United States.
(C) Tornadoes form when cold air and warm air meet.
(D) No one lives in tornado alley.

**2** The author mentions tornado warnings in order to

(A) explain how technology can save lives
(B) show that the TV stations save many people
(C) show that people have very little time in a tornado
(D) explain why tornadoes are no longer very dangerous

# Reading Practice 3

## The Last Great Zeppelin

Did you know that the biggest flying vehicle in history was not an airplane? It was an airship. Airships, or zeppelins as they were commonly known, were like blimps★, but they were much bigger. The biggest airship in history was the *Hindenburg*. The *Hindenburg* was huge, only a little bit smaller than the *Titanic*. Like the *Titanic*, it has a sad story.

When Germans built the *Hindenburg* in the 1930s, they wanted to fill the *Hindenburg* with helium, because helium does not catch fire. However, the United States is the only significant source of helium in the world, and would not sell any to the Germans. Americans feared the Germans would use the *Hindenburg* as a weapon of war, as they had done with other zeppelins in World War I. So the Germans had to use hydrogen instead. The Germans knew that they had to be much more careful with hydrogen than helium. They took all matches and lighters from the passengers before the beginning of the trip. Although they were careful, the *Hindenburg* caught fire on its first flight, and thirty-six people died. After that, no one wanted to fly in airships anymore.

★ **blimp:** a type of aircraft similar to a large balloon

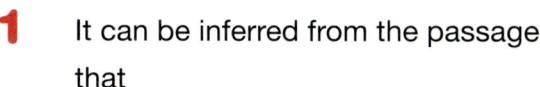

**1** It can be inferred from the passage that

(A) hydrogen catches fire
(B) helium is poisonous
(C) helium is very expensive
(D) the Americans needed all of their helium

**2** The author mentions matches and lighters in order to

(A) show that hydrogen is very dangerous
(B) show that the Germans were careful
(C) show that people couldn't smoke on the *Hindenburg*
(D) explain how the fire started on the *Hindenburg*

# Reading Practice 4

## The Origin of the Marathon

The marathon, the longest and most famous running race, has a long and interesting history. In the 4th century B.C., the Persians* decided to attack Athens, a famous Greek city. Athens needed help, so they sent their best runner, Pheidippides, to Sparta, another Greek city. It was 140 miles away, but Pheidippides ran this distance in 36 hours. Unfortunately, the Spartans could not help Athens, so Pheidippides ran back to Athens, another 140 miles, to give them the bad news. With no help and little hope of success, the Athenians fought the Persians at Marathon, 26 miles away from Athens. Amazingly, Athens won the battle. Pheidippides ran back to Athens to give the king the good news. After that, the Greeks held a race from Marathon to Athens each year to honor Pheidippides's amazing run. Today, we still do the same.

However, not everyone believes the story of Pheidippides. Not all stories from history are true. The story of Hercules was also a popular story of the Greeks. We may never know if the story of Pheidippides is true, but the marathon will always be a famous and popular race.

★ Persia: an ancient kingdom in the Middle East

**1** It can be inferred from the passage that

(A) only Greeks run marathons today
(B) people only run marathons after wars
(C) marathons are 26 miles long
(D) marathons are most popular in Greece

**2** Why does the author mention Hercules?

(A) To show that Greece had many strong heroes
(B) To show that Greece has an interesting history
(C) To give an example of an untrue story from Greek history
(D) To show that marathons happened before the time of Pheidippides

# Early European Explorers

In the late 1400s and early 1500s, much of the Europeans' information about North and South America was either extremely inaccurate or just plain wrong. Wild stories about cities of gold spread across Europe after Columbus returned from his first trip. These stories made many people want to travel to the New World.

➡ One such man was Juan Ponce de León from Spain. He heard a story about the fountain of youth. According to the story, washing in this fountain would make a person young forever. The story said the fountain was on the island of Bimini, but no one could find the island. Juan left Spain and traveled to the New World to find the fountain of youth. Juan spent the rest of his life looking for Bimini and the fountain of youth. He discovered many new islands in the Caribbean. He was the first European to land in Florida. He took all of these lands for Spain, and his king was very happy with him, but the fountain of youth was just a legend.

Another wild story brought the great explorer Sir Walter Raleigh to the New World. This was the story of *El Dorado*, a legendary Native American king. According to the legend, he washed in gold dust every day and lived in a golden city. Raleigh traveled through much of South America looking for *El Dorado* and his golden city, but he never found it. *El Dorado* was just another fountain of youth.

**Glossary**

just plain wrong: completely wrong

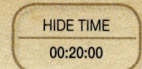

**1** According to paragraph 2, all of the following are true of Juan Ponce de León are true EXCEPT:

   Ⓐ He took many new lands for Spain.
   Ⓑ His search for the fountain of youth was successful.
   Ⓒ He thought the fountain of youth was on the island of Bimini.
   Ⓓ He was the first European in Florida.

   Paragraph 2 is marked with an arrow [➡].

**2** It can be inferred from paragraph 2 that

   Ⓐ Juan Ponce de León was not a good explorer
   Ⓑ Juan Ponce de León was very old
   Ⓒ Spain gained many colonies in the Caribbean
   Ⓓ the Spanish believed many wild stories

   Paragraph 2 is marked with an arrow [➡].

**3** According to the passage, *El Dorado* was

   Ⓐ a great explorer
   Ⓑ a city of gold
   Ⓒ a Native American king
   Ⓓ a legendary island

**4** The word legend in the passage is closest in meaning to

   Ⓐ information
   Ⓑ story
   Ⓒ explorer
   Ⓓ king

**5** Why does the author mention the fountain of youth?

   Ⓐ To show that Raleigh wanted to be young forever
   Ⓑ To suggest that *El Dorado* was on the island of Bimini
   Ⓒ To suggest that *El Dorado* was not real
   Ⓓ To show that Raleigh was successful

**6** **Directions:** An introductory sentence for a brief summary of the passage is provided below. Choose THREE answers to complete the summary. Wrong answer choices use minor ideas from the passage or use information that is not in the passage. **This question is worth 2 points.**

*Many European explorers came to the New World because of legends in Europe.*

- 
- 
- 

**Answer Choices**

(A) Europeans did not know much about the New World.

(B) Juan Ponce de León came looking for the fountain of youth.

(C) Juan Ponce de León took Florida for Spain.

(D) Sir Walter Raleigh came to find a city of gold.

(E) Most explorers were unsuccessful in their searches.

(F) *El Dorado* was a legendary Native American king.

Drag your answer choices to the spaces where they belong. To remove an answer choice, click on it. To review the passage, click **View Text**.

# iBT Practice 2

## The Human Heart

The strongest part of every human body is the heart. The heart is an amazing muscle. Unlike other muscles, the heart never gets tired, and it never stops during your lifetime. How strong is the human heart? Well, get a tennis ball and squeeze it. Your heart squeezes this hard to push blood through your body. How many times can you squeeze that tennis ball? Your heart does this 100,000 times each day!

➥ The heart has four "rooms," or chambers. Each "room" has a "door," or valve. The upper rooms are atria, and the bottom rooms are ventricles. The basic job of the heart is to move blood through the body. Blood first moves into the heart from the right atrium. Then, it moves down into the right ventricle and out into the lungs. Blood comes back into the heart by the left atrium and then moves down into the left ventricle. Finally, the heart pumps the blood back out into the body.

➥ When you exercise, your heart beats faster. **A** This is because your muscles are using more oxygen. **B** You can find your fastest healthy heartbeat by subtracting your age from 220. **C** For example, the maximum heartbeat for a 20-year-old is about 200 beats per minute. **D** Your heart can beat faster than this, but it is not healthy.

1. The author mentions a tennis ball in order to
   - Ⓐ show that tennis players have healthy hearts
   - Ⓑ show how many times your heart beats each day
   - Ⓒ give an example of the heart's strength
   - Ⓓ show your heart is stronger than your hand

2. According to the passage, all of the following are true EXCEPT:
   - Ⓐ The human heart is a muscle.
   - Ⓑ The human heart has five chambers.
   - Ⓒ The human heart never gets tired.
   - Ⓓ The human heart beats 100,000 times a day.

3. According to paragraph 2, where does blood go after it leaves the right ventricle?
   - Ⓐ To the lungs
   - Ⓑ To the body
   - Ⓒ To the left atrium
   - Ⓓ To the left ventricle

   Paragraph 2 is marked with an arrow [➡].

4. Look at the four squares [■] that indicate where the following sentence could be added to the passage.

   **The average heartbeat is about 70 beats per minute.**

   Where would the sentence best fit? Click on a square [■] to add the sentence to the passage.

5. The word maximum in the passage is closest in meaning to
   - Ⓐ best
   - Ⓑ hardest
   - Ⓒ highest
   - Ⓓ most dangerous

6. It can be inferred from paragraph 3 that
   - Ⓐ blood brings oxygen to the body
   - Ⓑ you lose blood when you exercise
   - Ⓒ blood moves quickly through the body
   - Ⓓ sport players need more blood

   Paragraph 3 is marked with an arrow [➡].

**7** **Directions:** An introductory sentence for a brief summary of the passage is provided below. Choose THREE answers to complete the summary. Wrong answer choices use minor ideas from the passage or use information that is not in the passage. **This question is worth 2 points.**

*The human heart is an important part of our body.*

- 
- 
- 

**Answer Choices**

(A) The heart is the strongest part of our body.

(B) The heart squeezes 100,000 times each day to push blood through your body.

(C) The heart moves blood through the body, using its four chambers.

(D) The four chambers of the heart are called atria and ventricles.

(E) People have different heartbeats according to their age.

(F) Your heart beats faster when you exercise, but it is not healthy.

Drag your answer choices to the spaces where they belong. To remove an answer choice, click on it. To review the passage, click **View Text**.

# Word Review

Read the sentences below and choose the correct word for each blank. Use the word bank below.

**Word Bank**

| accept | purpose | order | technology |
| infer | location | mention | underground |

1. The teacher _____ed her students to be quiet.

2. Rabbits build their homes _____.

3. Maps can help you find any _____ on Earth.

4. What can you _____ from the story you've just read?

5. This store won't take credit cards. They only _____ cash.

6. Which country did you _____? Was it Ukraine?

7. _____ changes so fast. I think I should get a new cell phone like yours.

8. The presidents will meet next week for the _____ of making peace between the two countries.

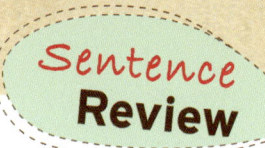

Complete the following sentences by rearranging the words from the parentheses to fill in the blanks in the right order.

**1** However, the end of the war did not _____.

(Earth, place, a, make, safer, the)

**2** The nuclear age was a frightening time because _____ atomic bombs.

(new, could, include, any, war)

**3** TV stations often give tornado warnings, _____, the warning time is usually only about 12 minutes.

(with, but, technology, even, modern)

**4** The United States is the only significant source of helium in the world, and _____ the Germans.

(sell, any, not, would, to, they)

**5** The marathon, _____, has a long and interesting history.

(most, and, longest, race, running, famous, the)

Memo

# Chapter 5
# Insert Text

# Chapter 5
## Insert Text

**09 문장 삽입 문제**
Insert Text Questions

글의 흐름이 자연스럽게 이어지도록
주어진 문장이 들어갈 부분을 찾는 문제

# Word Preview

- **attention**
  Gail likes it when people listen to her sing. She likes the **attention**.

- **bury**
  Our dog loves to **bury** bones under the tree in the backyard.

- **creature**
  There are many **creatures** living under the sea.

- **deadly**
  A wrong-way driver caused a **deadly** crash.

- **especially**
  Work out and keep in shape, **especially** if you want to lose weight.

- **fear**
  My brother **fears** bees. He is afraid of them.

- **insert**
  Do not **insert** your card into the machine! It's out of order.

- **poison**
  Some snakes have deadly **poison** which can kill a person immediately.

- **produce**
  The company **produces** CD players, TVs and video games.

- **religion**
  You need to be careful when asking about other people's **religion** because it is personal.

# Insert Text Questions

## 문장 삽입 문제

- 문장 삽입 문제는 주어진 문장이 지문 내의 어느 부분에 들어가야 적절한지를 묻는 문제 유형이다. 문장 삽입 문제는 보통 지문당 한 문제가 출제된다.

- 실제 *i*BT TOEFL에서 출제되는 문제 형식은 다음과 같다.

> Look at the four squares [■] that indicate where the following sentence could be added to the passage.
>
> Dog owners should remember this fact.
>
> Where would the sentence best fit?

> ... Once the pack chooses an alpha male, they will follow him without question. **A** Pet dogs are the same as wild dogs in some ways. **B** They need an alpha male to follow. **C** Dog owners must be strong and strict with their dogs. Speaking in a strong voice and looking into the dog's eyes shows that the owner is the alpha male. **D** If your dog thinks it is the alpha male, it will be very hard to control.

### 문제풀이 전략

**❶ 지시어와 연결어에서 실마리를 찾는다.**

It, they, this와 같은 대명사나 such, following과 같은 어구에 주목하고, 그것이 무엇을 가리키는지 찾아본다. 또한 however, therefore, for example과 같은 연결어에서도 힌트를 얻을 수 있다. 예를 들어 주어진 문장이 However로 시작한다면, 그 앞에는 이 문장과 반대되는 내용이 나온다.

**❷ 흐름이 어색한 곳을 찾아본다.**

지문을 읽을 때 문장 사이의 흐름이 어색한 곳을 찾아보도록 한다. 그런 부분이 발견되면 주어진 문장을 넣어보고, 자연스럽게 연결되는지 점검해 본다.

**❸ 논리적으로 따져 본다.**

문장 삽입 문제에서 가장 중요한 것은 논리적인 사고이다. 만약 주어진 문장이 예를 들고 있다면, 그것이 지문의 어떤 내용을 뒷받침하는지 논리적으로 따져 본다.

# Basic Drills 1

**Read the sentences below and put them into the correct order.**

**1**
(A) You need to practice a lot.
(B) Then, you will be ready to play with the pros.
(C) Many people want to play professional sports.
(D) But becoming a professional sports player is not easy.

_____ → _____ → _____ → _____

**2**
(A) They put them in holes near trees.
(B) Squirrels work hard to prepare for winter.
(C) Later, they dig them up and eat them.
(D) For example, squirrels spend the fall gathering nuts.

_____ → _____ → _____ → _____

**3**
(A) Most Americans decorate their homes for Christmas.
(B) They decorate the tree with lights and ornaments.
(C) Christmas is a popular holiday in America.
(D) The Christmas tree is the most important decoration.

_____ → _____ → _____ → _____

**4**
(A) We need gasoline for our cars.
(B) Countries like Saudi Arabia produce oil.
(C) Then oil companies change the oil into gasoline.
(D) The gasoline for our cars comes from oil.

_____ → _____ → _____ → _____

**5**
(A) Now we know much more about space.
(B) Telescopes help us to see into space.
(C) People use telescopes to see faraway things.
(D) For example, we know that Jupiter has many moons.

_____ → _____ → _____ → _____

# Basic Drills 2

Read the paragraphs below. One sentence is out of order. Write the number of the sentence in the space below. Then write the correct order for the sentences.

**1**

❶ Jaguars are large cats. ❷ They live mostly in the jungles of South America. ❸ However, jaguars are losing their homes because people are cutting down the jungles. ❹ Soon, there might not be any jaguars left. ❺ They look like leopards, but they have black fur.

(1) What sentence is out of order? _____
(2) What is the correct order for the sentences?

_____ → _____ → _____ → _____ → _____

**2**

❶ MP3 players are very popular these days. ❷ However, CD players had several problems. ❸ They were too big for most people's pockets. ❹ They also broke very easily. ❺ People also didn't like carrying all of their CDs with them. ❻ MP3 players are better because you don't have to carry your CDs. ❼ Before MP3 players, people used CD players.

(1) What sentence is out of order? _____
(2) What is the correct order for the sentences?

_____ → _____ → _____ → _____ → _____ → _____ → _____

---

**Words** Look at the paragraphs again, and find words with the same meaning.
- A thick forest with many large plants growing very close together _____
- The thick, soft hair that covers the bodies of some animals _____
- More than a few, but not a lot _____
- (machines) To stop working well _____

Chapter 5. Insert Text  99

# Basic Drills 3

Read the paragraphs below and insert the sentence in the correct place. Use the pronoun in **bold** to help you.

**1**

Water sports are very popular in the United States. **A** Water skiing is probably the most famous water sport, but there are many others. **B** For example, sailboarding is a very popular sport. A sailboard is like a surfboard with a sail on the top of it. **C** People ride sailboards in windy areas. **D** With a strong wind, sailboards can go very fast and are very exciting.

Where should the sentence below go? Choose the correct square [ ].

**That** is because many people live near lakes or rivers.

**2**

Blue whales are the biggest animals on Earth. **A** They are even bigger than the largest dinosaurs* were. **B** An average blue whale is 80 feet long. **C** Blue whales are also the loudest animals on Earth. Their voices are louder than a jet engine! Although blue whales are very big, they eat some of the smallest animals on Earth. Blue whales eat plankton*. **D** These animals are no bigger than a bit of dust. Blue whales eat millions of them each day.

★ **dinosaur:** one of a group of animals that lived millions of years ago
★ **plankton:** very small plants and animals that live in the sea and are eaten by fish

Where should the sentence below go? Choose the correct square [ ].

**Its** heart is as big as a small car.

**WoRds**   Look at the paragraphs again, and find words with the same meaning.

- Likely
- A large piece of cloth fixed onto a boat, so that the wind will push the boat along
- Not unusually big or small

# Basic Drills 4

Read the paragraphs below and insert the sentence in the correct place. Use the signal word in **bold** to help you.

**1**
> Space is a dangerous place to work. There is no air, and temperatures change a lot. They can be as high as 250°F, or as low as -250°F! To work in these dangerous conditions, astronauts* need spacesuits. **A** Spacesuits give the astronaut air and protect him or her from very high or very low temperatures. **B** NASA spent years making its spacesuits. **C** The spacesuits work very well. **D**

★ **astronaut:** someone who travels and works in a spacecraft

Where should the sentence below go? Choose the correct square [■].

**However,** at over 12 million dollars each, the spacesuits are not cheap.

**2**
> Walt Disney is famous for his wonderful cartoons. People around the world know and love his characters, especially Mickey Mouse. **A** Walt Disney started making cartoons in the 1920s. **B** He added many new things to cartoons. **C** Walt Disney also did many things to help people. **D** In addition to his cartoons, he made films for school. These films taught children about safety and other important things.

Where should the sentence below go? Choose the correct square [■].

**For example,** he was the first person to make a full-color cartoon.

---

**WoRds** Look at the paragraphs again, and find words with the same meaning.

- A measure of how hot or cold a place or thing is  _____
- To keep someone or something safe from harm, damage, or illness  _____
- A short film that is made by photographing a series of drawings  _____
- A person in a book, play, film, etc.  _____

# Reading Practice 1

## Brazil's Deadly Sport

The young people of Rio de Janeiro, Brazil, sometimes play a deadly sport. They call it train surfing. In train surfing, young people stand on the tops of moving trains. **A** It is very dangerous. Train surfers, or *surfistas*, can fall off the trains. **B** They can also hit the trains' electrical wires. **C** Many *surfistas* die each year doing their deadly sport. **D**

*Surfistas* know that their sport is dangerous. **A** However, the *surfistas* often come from very poor parts of the city, and they don't see much hope in their lives. **B** The police and the train companies try to stop the *surfistas*, but it is very difficult. Brazil is not a rich country and does not have enough police to guard the trains. **C** Instead, Brazil tries to teach its young people about the dangers of train surfing. **D** Sadly, the *surfistas* probably won't stop until their lives get better.

**1** Where should the sentence below go? Choose the correct square [ ■ ].

**Both of these accidents can easily kill a *surfista*.**

**2** Where should the sentence below go? Choose the correct circle [ ● ].

**Because of this, they say they do not fear death.**

# Reading Practice 2

## The Heroes of the Rodeo

The rodeo is a popular sport in the American Southwest. In a rodeo, cowboys ride bulls, large male cows. **A** The bulls are very strong and very angry. **B** Cowboys get points for the number of seconds they can stay on the bull, but they usually fall off after just a few seconds. At this point, their sport becomes really dangerous. Horses try very hard not to step on a person after they fall off the horse. **C** Bulls actually try to step on people, or stab them with their horns. **D** After they fall, cowboys are in great danger.

However, the cowboys are not alone. When they fall, clowns save them. **A** Rodeo clowns are very different from normal clowns at the circus. **B** Rodeo clowns get the attention of the bull. When the bull chases the rodeo clown, the cowboy can get to safety. **C** Of course, being a rodeo clown is very dangerous. Still, most clowns love their jobs. **D**

**1** Where should the sentence below go? Choose the correct square [■].

**Bulls are not as kind as this.**

**2** Where should the sentence below go? Choose the correct circle [●].

**They wear the same funny clothes, but they have a much more important job.**

# Reading Practice 3

## Zombies: More than Movie Monsters

Zombies, the walking dead, are very popular in horror movies. However, there were stories of zombies long before there were movies. **A** The first stories of zombies came from the Caribbean in the 1500s and 1600s. **B** The slaves from Africa made a new religion, voodoo. Their religion had magicians called bokors. The bokors claimed they could bring dead people back to life. These zombies would then be the slaves of the bokors. Scientists didn't believe the bokors could raise the dead. **C** But many bokors had zombie slaves. **D** How was this possible?

Today, scientists think they know more about these "zombies." The zombies are not dead. They are normal people. **A** The bokors learned to make a special poison which didn't kill people, but it made them look like they were dead. After a bokor poisoned them, the families of "dead" persons would bury them, thinking  they were actually dead. Later, the bokors would dig them out of the ground. **B** The poison would stop working, and the person would wake up. **C** This was so frightening, most of the "zombies" actually thought they were dead, and became the bokor's slaves! **D**

**1** Where should the sentence below go? Choose the correct square [ ■ ].

**For a long time, this confused scientists.**

**2** Where should the sentence below go? Choose the correct circle [ ● ].

**The bokors would tell them that they had died and they were now zombies.**

# Reading Practice 4

## Water Webs

Spiders are very interesting creatures, but the water spider is especially interesting. **A** The water spider lives underwater, but it breathes air. **B** The water spider builds a special web that holds air inside of it, like a balloon. **C** The water spider has special hairs on it, which hold air. **D** When the water spider finishes its web, it can live underwater.

Water spiders are excellent swimmers. **A** Most spiders use their webs to catch their food, but water spiders can't do this. **B** They already use their webs to hold their air. **C** When small insects swim near the web, the water spider quickly swims out and bites them. Its poison quickly kills the insect. **D** Then, the water spider can take it back to its web to eat it.

---

**1** Where should the sentence below go? Choose the correct square [■].

**The water spider uses these to take air from the surface to its underwater web.**

**2** Where should the sentence below go? Choose the correct circle [●].

**They have to be.**

# iBT Practice 1

## The Birth of the Steamboat

By the early 1800s, steam engines were not a new idea. James Watt, from Scotland, made the first steam engines in 1769. Most of Watt's steam engines powered machines in factories. This was very useful, but the steam engine became
5  really useful in 1807. In that year, Robert Fulton, an American, made his first steamboat. **A** His boat, the *North River*, used a steam engine to push it up the river. Before that, traveling up a river was very difficult, because people had to row their boat or use horses and ropes to pull the boat. This was very slow,
10  but the *North River* was much faster. **B** By 1860, there were thousands of steamboats traveling up America's rivers.

Steamboats changed America. **C** They made travel much easier, and they were good for business. Businessmen could now sell their goods in faraway cities. **D** However, steamboats
15  also had a problem. Steam engines were very dangerous. Sometimes the steam engines would explode. Although people made better, safer steam engines over the years, they were always dangerous. Still, the steam engine was an important part of life in the 1800s.

1. According to the passage, who made the first steam engine?

   A Robert Fulton
   B Factory workers
   C James Watt
   D Steamboat owners

2. According to the passage, all of the following are true of Fulton's steamboats EXCEPT:

   A They were faster than other ways of traveling up rivers.
   B They were dangerous.
   C They were not very popular.
   D They were good for business.

3. It can be inferred from the passage that

   A Fulton was a very rich man
   B many people died in steamboats
   C people living up rivers benefited from steamboats
   D people didn't need horses after Fulton made his steamboat

4. The word goods in the passage is closest in meaning to

   A products
   B stores
   C nice
   D businesses

5. The word they in the passage refers to

   A people
   B steamboats
   C steam engines
   D years

6. Look at the four squares [■] that indicate where the following sentence could be added to the passage.

   **Soon, many people were building steamboats.**

   Where would the sentence best fit? Click on a square [■] to add the sentence to the passage.

**7** **Directions:** An introductory sentence for a brief summary of the passage is provided below. Choose THREE answers to complete the summary. Wrong answer choices use minor ideas from the passage or use information that is not in the passage. **This question is worth 2 points.**

*In 1807, Robert Fulton invented the steamboat, which became an important part of American life in the 1800s.*

- 
- 
- 

### Answer Choices

(A) The *North River*, Fulton's first steamboat, could travel up a river fast.

(B) Steamboats soon became popular because they could travel up rivers fast.

(C) Steamboats changed America's travel and business.

(D) Businessmen could sell their products in faraway cities using steamboats.

(E) Although steamboats had an advantage in terms of speed, they were very dangerous.

(F) People made better and safer steam engines afterwards.

Drag your answer choices to the spaces where they belong. To remove an answer choice, click on it. To review the passage, click **View Text**.

# iBT Practice 2

## The Siberian Mystery

➡ In 1908, there was a huge explosion in Siberia, the cold eastern part of Russia. It destroyed trees for miles around. People could hear the explosion hundreds of miles away. Scientists can now guess the power of this explosion. It was as powerful as the largest nuclear bombs today, but there were no nuclear bombs in 1908. What caused the explosion?

For many years, that was a mystery. Now, scientists think they know the answer: an asteroid caused the explosion. **A** Each year, hundreds of small asteroids hit the Earth. **B** But most of **them** don't actually reach the ground. **C** Asteroids travel at over 12 km per second. At this speed, they create a lot of heat. As a result, most asteroids burn up before they reach the ground. **D** A large asteroid would not burn up. It would hit the ground and make a huge **crater**. But there is no crater in Siberia. Scientists think this asteroid was medium-sized. It was too big to burn up, and it was too small to hit the ground. Instead, it exploded about 6 km above the ground, so it didn't make a crater.

Scientists think similar asteroids hit the Earth once every two or three hundred years. This could explain many mysteries in history. Many early societies told stories of fire coming from the sky. Early people thought the fire came from angry gods, but now we think not.

| | | | | |
|---|---|---|---|---|
| REVIEW | HELP | BACK | NEXT | HIDE TIME 00:20:00 |

**1** According to paragraph 1, all of the following are true of the Siberian explosion EXCEPT:

  Ⓐ It happened in the early 1900s.
  Ⓑ It was very destructive.
  Ⓒ A nuclear bomb caused the explosion.
  Ⓓ It was very loud.

  Paragraph 1 is marked with an arrow [➡].

**2** According to the passage, why don't most asteroids reach the Earth?

  Ⓐ They only come every 200 years.
  Ⓑ They burn up in the air.
  Ⓒ They are too large.
  Ⓓ They explode.

**3** The word them in the passage refers to

  Ⓐ Earth
  Ⓑ small asteroids
  Ⓒ rocks from space
  Ⓓ explosions

**4** The word crater in the passage is closest in meaning to

  Ⓐ hole
  Ⓑ explosion
  Ⓒ asteroid
  Ⓓ fire

**5** Look at the four squares [■] that indicate where the following sentence could be added to the passage.

  **Asteroids are rocks from space.**

  Where would the sentence best fit? Click on a square [■] to add the sentence to the passage.

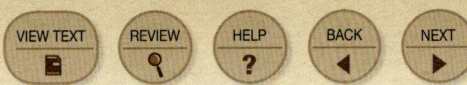

**6** **Directions:** An introductory sentence for a brief summary of the passage is provided below. Choose THREE answers to complete the summary. Wrong answer choices use minor ideas from the passage or use information that is not in the passage.
**This question is worth 2 points.**

*In 1908, there was a huge explosion over Siberia.*

- 
- 
- 

**Answer Choices**

(A) Siberia is in eastern Russia.

(B) Scientists know that an asteroid caused the explosion.

(C) Asteroids move very fast and create a lot of heat.

(D) Most asteroids burn up in the air, but a medium-sized asteroid would explode.

(E) The asteroid did not leave a crater.

(F) Medium-sized asteroids could explain some of the mysterious disasters of early societies.

Drag your answer choices to the spaces where they belong. To remove an answer choice, click on it. To review the passage, click **View Text**.

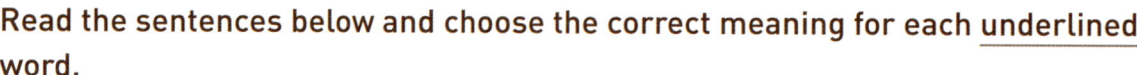

Read the sentences below and choose the correct meaning for each underlined word.

**1** Insert more coins to continue the game.
(A) Put in
(B) Draw out
(C) Throw away

**2** Sometimes little children are bad to get attention.
(A) help
(B) notice
(C) kindness

**3** The southern part of the country was hit by deadly floods.
(A) very dangerous
(B) huge
(C) unusual

**4** Do cats have poison in their claws?
(A) dangerous liquid
(B) a substance that can catch fire
(C) a substance that can cause illness or death

**5** The pirates buried their treasure on the island.
(A) burned
(B) carried to another place
(C) put under the ground

**6** You can see all kinds of wild creatures out here.
(A) life
(B) people
(C) mountains

**7** Sally thinks her dog is smarter than the average dog.
(A) normal
(B) big
(C) next

**8** You need to learn how to protect yourself.
(A) train
(B) cheer
(C) keep safe

## Sentence Review

Read the sentences below and choose one answer choice that best expresses the meaning of the given sentence.

**1** Water skiing is probably the most famous water sport, but there are many others.

(A) People think that water skiing is the most famous water sport, but it is not.
(B) Although water skiing is very well-known, there are also many other water sports.
(C) Water skiing is the most famous and exciting water sport.

**2** The *surfistas* probably won't stop train surfing until their lives get better.

(A) The *surfistas* are likely to continue train surfing unless they see more hope in their lives.
(B) The *surfistas* promised that they will stop train surfing if their lives get better.
(C) The *surfistas* do train surfing in order to make their lives better.

**3** When the bull chases the rodeo clown, the cowboy can get to safety.

(A) The cowboy is no longer in danger, because the rodeo clown chases the bull.
(B) When the bull sees the rodeo clown, it begins to chase him.
(C) While the rodeo clown gets the attention of the bull, the cowboy can get to a safe area.

**4** There were stories of zombies long before there were movies.

(A) People didn't believe in zombies until they saw them in movies.
(B) After seeing zombies in horror movies, people made many stories about zombies.
(C) Even before zombie movies were made, people talked about zombies.

**5** Spiders are very interesting creatures, but the water spider is especially interesting.

(A) The water spider is even more interesting than other spiders.
(B) Unlike other spiders, the water spider is very interesting.
(C) The water spider is very different from other spiders.

Chapter 5. Insert Text

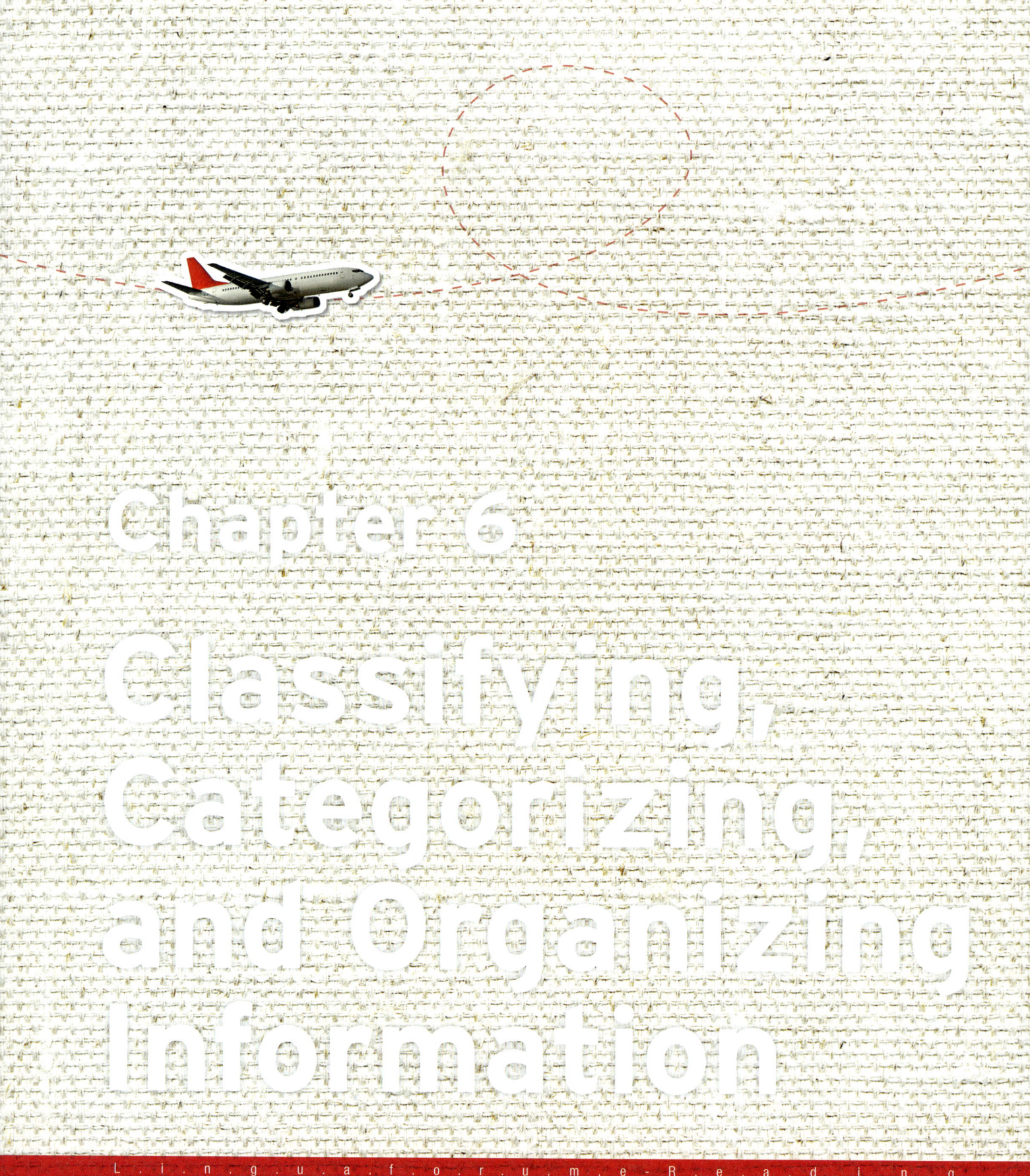

# Chapter 6
# Classifying, Categorizing, and Organizing Information

# Chapter 6
Classifying, Categorizing, and Organizing Information

**10** 정보 분류 문제
Classifying, Categorizing, and Organizing Information Questions

지문에 열거된 정보를 분류하여 정리하는 문제

# Word Preview

- **ability**
  Penguins can't fly. They don't have that **ability**.

- **century**
  A new **century** started in the year 2001.

- **college**
  After he finishes high school, Mark will go to **college**.

- **contrast**
  The final match will present a **contrast** in play style between the two players.

- **distance**
  The **distance** between the door and the window is 10 meters.

- **equal**
  The prices of the two books are **equal**. They are the same price.

- **lift**
  Greg is very strong, so he can **lift** that box.

- **signal**
  Are frequent El Niños a **signal** of global warming?

- **society**
  Egyptian **society** is thousands of years old.

- **trust**
  I don't tell secrets to Hank because I don't **trust** him.

# Classifying, Categorizing, and Organizing Information Questions

정보 분류 문제

○ 정보 분류 문제는 주어진 정보를 분류할 수 있는 능력을 평가하는 문제 유형이다. 두 대상을 비교·대조하는 글을 읽고, 각 대상에 해당되는 보기들을 골라야 한다. 7개의 보기 중 5개를 선택하는 문제(3점)와 9개의 보기 중 7개를 선택하는 문제(4점)가 있다.

○ 실제 *i*BT TOEFL에서 출제되는 문제 형식은 다음과 같다.

> **Directions:** Select the appropriate phrases from the answer choices and match them to the type of camera to which they relate. TWO of the answer choices will NOT be used. **This question is worth 3 points.**
>
> **Answer choices**
> Ⓐ Cheap and convenient
> Ⓑ For professional photographers
> Ⓒ Various choices for film type
> Ⓓ Don't need batteries
> Ⓔ Don't need film
> Ⓕ Better color quality
> Ⓖ Better resolution
>
> **Digital Cameras**
> •
> •
> •
>
> **Film Cameras**
> •
> •

### 문제풀이 전략

**❶ 연결어에 항상 주의한다.**

두 대상을 비교 · 대조하는 글에서는 내용이 자주 전환되므로 연결어가 많이 사용된다.
① 역접을 나타내는 연결어: but, however, though, although, in contrast, unlike, on the other hand
② 부연 설명을 나타내는 연결어: in addition, moreover, for example, furthermore, also

**❷ 관계없는 내용을 찾을 수 있어야 한다.**

보기 중 두 개는 어느 쪽에도 속하지 않으므로 무관한 정보를 가려낼 수 있어야 한다. 보기와 비슷한 표현이 지문에 있다고 해서 섣불리 선택해서는 안된다.

**❸ Note taking을 연습한다.**

평소에 note taking 연습을 하여 두 가지 대상에 해당되는 내용에 서로 다른 표시를 하며 글을 읽는다.

# Basic Drills 1

The paragraph below is about the differences between whales and fish. Five signal words in the paragraph show changes between these two subjects, or show additional* information about the same subject. Underline the five signal words.

> Not all animals in the sea are fish. Whales may look like fish, but they are very different. Fish do not breathe like land animals. They do not have lungs. They have gills*. Their gills let them breathe water. Whales, on the other hand, do have lungs. They breathe air just like land animals. Furthermore, they are warm-blooded, while fish are cold-blooded. Finally, whales have live babies as opposed to laying eggs like fish.

★ gill: one of the organs on the sides of a fish through which it breathes

Which signal words show contrast or a change in topic? Which show more information about the same topic? Write the signal words in the correct spaces below.

Contrast/Change Subject  ............................................  Same Subject
............................................  ............................................
............................................  ............................................
............................................

Now use the signal words to help you complete the table below.

|  | Whales | Fish |
|---|---|---|
| Breathe water |  |  |
| Eggs |  |  |
| Live babies |  |  |
| Warm-blooded |  |  |
| Cold-blooded |  |  |

★ additional [ədíʃənəl]: a. 추가적인

# Basic Drills 2

The paragraph below is about the differences between the Northern States and the Southern States before the start of the American Civil War. Three signal words in the paragraph show changes between these two subjects, or show additional information about the same subject. <u>Underline</u> the three signal words.

> The American Civil War was the worst war in U.S. history. Most people think that slavery* was the cause of the war, but this is only partly true. There were many important differences between the Northern States and the Southern States, and all of these differences led to the start of the war. Slavery was of course one important difference. The Southern States wanted slavery because they needed slaves to work on their farms. The Northern States, however, did not want slavery. Another important difference between the North and the South was money. The Southern States were farming states. The Northern States, on the other hand, were factory states. The factories made more money than the farms, and the Northern States were richer. Furthermore, they had more people than the Southern States. Over two-thirds of all Americans lived in the Northern States. This gave the Northern States much more power in government.

★ **slavery:** the system of having slaves (= someone who is owned by another person)

Which signal words show contrast or a change in topic? Which show more information about the same topic? Write the signal words in the correct spaces below.

Contrast / Change Subject                     Same Subject

_____                       _____

_____

Now use the signal words to help you complete the table below.

|  | Southern States | Northern States |
|---|---|---|
| More money |  |  |
| More people |  |  |
| Farm states |  |  |
| Wanted slavery |  |  |
| Factory states |  |  |

Chapter 6. Classifying, Categorizing, and Organizing Information

# Basic Drills 3

The passage below is about sailboats and speedboats. <u>Underline</u> any information about sailboats and <u>double underline</u> any information about speedboats.

Many people love boats. Going out on the water on a warm summer day is a lot of fun. However, different people like different kinds of boats. Two of the most popular kinds of boats are sailboats and speedboats. Sailboats use the wind to give them power. They only have small engines. In contrast, speedboats have large engines and go very fast. Furthermore, speedboats are usually not as big as sailboats. Speedboats are small so that they can go fast. Sailboats, on the other hand, are big so that they are more comfortable. In addition, sailboats can travel into the ocean, but this would be very dangerous in a speedboat. You can only use most speedboats on rivers and lakes.

Now use the signal words to help you complete the table below.

|  | Sailboats | Speedboats |
|---|---|---|
| Wind power |  |  |
| Large engines |  |  |
| Small and fast |  |  |
| Large and comfortable |  |  |
| For lakes and rivers |  |  |

# Basic Drills 4

The passage below is about sprinters and distance runners. <u>Underline</u> any information about sprinters and <u>double underline</u> any information about distance runners.

Running is a big sport in the summer Olympics. Running was one of the first Olympic sports. There are two kinds of runners in the Olympics. Sprinters run for short distances, usually less than 400 meters. Distance runners run for long distances, sometimes up to 10,000 meters! Distance runners and sprinters have very different training programs. Sprinters need very strong legs. This is because they must go very fast, but only for a short time. They usually lift a lot of weights with their legs to make their muscles bigger. Distance runners, on the other hand, do not need to run as fast, but they must run for much longer. They do not need very large leg muscles and usually do not lift many weights. Furthermore, distance runners must have very strong hearts because their hearts must work hard for a long time.

Now use the signal words to help you complete the table below.

|  | Sprinters | Distance Runners |
|---|---|---|
| Large leg muscles |  |  |
| Strong hearts |  |  |
| Run short distances |  |  |
| Do not lift weights |  |  |
| Run for a long time |  |  |

# Reading Practice 1

## The Tribes* of North and South America

When the Europeans came to North and South America, they found people already living there. However, the Native Americans of North and South America were very different from each other. The Native Americans of South America, such as the Aztecs and the Incas, lived in large kingdoms which were much like the kingdoms of Europe in some ways. They had kings or emperors*, large governments, and powerful armies. The tribes of North America, however, were generally much smaller. They did not have kingdoms. Instead, each tribe had a chief, or a group of chiefs. The chiefs did not have as much power as the kings of South American tribes.

In addition, their homes were very different. The South American tribes built large cities, sometimes as large as the biggest European cities. Furthermore, they built large palaces and temples. In contrast, the North American tribes lived in smaller communities. They did not build large buildings, because they moved more often than South American tribes.

★ **tribe:** a group of people of the same race, language, and customs   ★ **emperor:** the ruler of a group of countries

**Directions:** Select the appropriate* phrases from the answer choices and match them to the tribes to which they relate*. TWO of the answer choices will NOT be used.

### South American Tribes

- _____
- _____
- _____

### North American Tribes

- _____
- _____

**Answer Choices**

- (A) Large temples
- (B) Chiefs
- (C) Fought against Europeans
- (D) Large armies
- (E) Powerful kings
- (F) Excellent hunters
- (G) Small communities

★ **appropriate** [əpróupriət]: a. 적절한
★ **relate** [riléit]: v. ~와 관련되다 (to)

# Reading Practice 2

## The Great Cities of Sparta and Athens

Greece was an important place in the 4$^{th}$ and 5$^{th}$ centuries. Unlike Egypt or ancient Persia, Greece was not a single kingdom. Greece was a group of independent cities. Sometimes these cities worked together. Sometimes they fought each other. Two of the most important and powerful cities were Athens and Sparta.

The cities of Sparta and Athens were quite different. Athens was famous for its culture and art. Many great thinkers, such as Socrates and Plato, came from Athens. Sparta, on the other hand, was famous mostly for its army. The Spartan army controlled the city and was the best army in Greece. All Spartan men had to serve in the army. Boys started training for the army at age seven and remained in the army until they were thirty. Sparta had many rules, and people did not have much freedom. Life was quite different in Athens, where men served in the army but for a much shorter time. In addition, the people of Athens chose their leaders, rather than having a military government.

**Directions:** Select the appropriate phrases from the answer choices and match them to the city to which they relate. TWO of the answer choices will NOT be used.

**Answer Choices**

- (A) Great thinkers
- (B) Powerful army
- (C) First Greek city
- (D) Many rules
- (E) People chose leaders
- (F) Fought many wars
- (G) Long time in army

**Athens**

- _____
- _____

**Sparta**

- _____
- _____
- _____

# Reading Practice 3

## Dubois and Washington: Two Great African-American Leaders

At the beginning of the 20th century, African-Americans were not equal members of American society. For example, they could not go to the same schools as white people, and they could not vote*. Many African-American leaders at the time wanted more freedom and a better life for African-Americans. Two of the most important African-American leaders of the time were W.E.B. Dubois and Booker T. Washington.

Dubois and Washington both wanted to help African-Americans, but they had very different plans and ideas. Washington wanted to teach job skills to large numbers of African-Americans. For example, he wanted to train African-Americans for jobs as carpenters and mechanics. Dubois, on the other hand, wanted to send the most intelligent African-Americans to college to become doctors and lawyers. Dubois called his plan "the talented tenth." He believed that African-Americans needed powerful jobs (like those of doctors and lawyers) to change America. Washington, on the other hand, thought that America would slowly change on its own, and whites and African-Americans would learn to live together naturally.

★ **vote:** to officially show your choice by raising your hand or marking a paper

**Directions:** Select the appropriate phrases from the answer choices and match them to the person to which they relate. TWO of the answer choices will NOT be used.

**Booker T. Washington**

- _____
- _____

**W.E.B Dubois**

- _____
- _____
- _____

**Answer Choices**

- (A) Wanted to teach many people job skills
- (B) Did not trust whites
- (C) Wanted to send most intelligent African-Americans to college
- (D) Thought African-Americans must change America
- (E) Thought African-Americans could not change America
- (F) Thought America would change naturally
- (G) Thought African-Americans needed powerful jobs

# Reading Practice 4

## How the Colonists Won the War

At the start of the American Revolution, the British thought the colonists had no chance of winning the war. After all, Britain had a much larger army and was far richer than the colonies. Although the British didn't know it at the time, the colonists actually had many advantages.

The British army was very good at fighting European-style wars in which large armies met on a field of battle and attacked each other in the open. The colonists, however, did not fight this way. They attacked in small groups and then hid from the British. Furthermore, the colonists had much better guns than the British. They could shoot the British before the British got close enough to shoot back. Moreover, the British had to get all of their supplies, guns, food, etc. from Britain. The colonists, on the other hand, were fighting on their own land and could get supplies more easily. Finally, while British soldiers had better training, they did not know the land. The colonists knew the land well, and this helped them greatly.

**Directions:** Select the appropriate phrases from the answer choices and match them to the group to which they relate. TWO of the answer choices will NOT be used.

**Answer Choices**

A) Help from Native Americans
B) Better guns
C) Fought far from home
D) Larger army
E) Attacked in small groups
F) Smarter leaders
G) Fought in European style

**Colonists**
- _____
- _____

**British**
- _____
- _____
- _____

# iBT Practice 1

## Space Capsules vs. Space Shuttles

Space travel started in the 1960s. At the time, only the U.S. and Russia sent people into space. Although the two countries did not work together, their spaceships were very similar. Both countries used space capsules, which are like large metal balls launched into space by a rocket. When they return to Earth, they use parachutes to slow their speed and fall back to Earth. While the Russians still use space capsules, the U.S. stopped using space capsules in the early 1980s. Instead, they built space shuttles, which are more like planes. They have wings and fly back to Earth. Both space capsules and space shuttles have good points and bad points.

➡ The best thing about space shuttles is that they can travel into space many times. Space capsules, however, can only travel in space one time. Then, you must make a new space capsule. Space shuttles are more expensive to build, but over time, space shuttles save money because you don't build a new one for each trip into space. While space shuttles have many **advantages**, they are harder to build. This makes them more dangerous. The U.S. showed this in the 1986 and 2003 disasters when two of its space shuttles were lost. In contrast, the Russian space capsules have a better safety record.

---

**Glossary**

**launch:** send a rocket, missile, etc. into space

**parachute:** a large piece of thin cloth attached to the capsule by strings, which makes the capsule fall slowly and safely to the ground

1. According to the passage, all of the following are true of the American space program EXCEPT:

   Ⓐ It originally used space capsules.
   Ⓑ It has a perfect safety record.
   Ⓒ It now uses space shuttles.
   Ⓓ It saves more money than the Russian program over time.

2. According to the passage, when did the U.S. start using space shuttles?

   Ⓐ In the 1960s
   Ⓑ In the early 1980s
   Ⓒ In 1986
   Ⓓ In 2003

3. According to paragraph 2, how do space shuttles save money?

   Ⓐ They are cheaper to build.
   Ⓑ You can use them many times.
   Ⓒ They can travel into space faster.
   Ⓓ They are easier to make.

   Paragraph 2 is marked with an arrow [➡].

4. The word advantages in the passage is closest in meaning to

   Ⓐ trips
   Ⓑ dangers
   Ⓒ savings
   Ⓓ good points

5. The author mentions the 1986 and 2003 disasters in order to

   Ⓐ show that the Russians are better at space travel than the Americans
   Ⓑ show that space travel is very dangerous
   Ⓒ show the dangers of space shuttles
   Ⓓ show that the U.S. needs more space shuttles

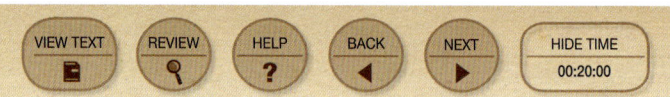

**6** **Directions:** Select the appropriate phrases from the answer choices and match them to the type of spaceship to which they relate. TWO of the answer choices will NOT be used. **This question is worth 3 points.**

Drag your answer choices to the spaces where they belong. To remove an answer choice, click on it. To review the passage, click **View Text**.

**Answer Choices**

(A) Most trips into space

(B) Large metal ball

(C) Fly back to Earth

(D) Very easy to build

(E) Cheaper to build

(F) Perfect safety record

(G) Still used by Russians

**Space Capsules**

●

●

●

●

**Space Shuttles**

●

# iBT Practice 2

## Hunter-gatherers vs. Farming Groups

➡ Thousands of years ago, early humans lived in two kinds of societies: hunter-gatherer groups, and farming groups. Hunter-gatherer groups traveled around a lot because they lived by hunting animals and gathering wild plants. Farming
5 groups usually stayed in one place and built permanent homes. Although farming groups did hunt animals, they spent most of their time farming and growing food. **A**

Over time, farming groups grew more powerful and took the land from hunter-gatherer groups. There are several
10 reasons for this. **B** First, hunter-gatherer groups were small in size. Large groups of hunter-gatherers could not find enough food for everyone in the group, so hunter-gatherer groups were usually smaller than 100 people. Farming groups, on the other hand, could grow lots of food and feed more people.
15 **C** Because they could feed more people, not everyone in a farming group had to grow food. Some people could have different jobs, such as being a soldier. **D** In hunter-gatherer groups, everyone had to look for food, so they did not have any professional soldiers. This made it easy for the farming groups
20 to take the land from the hunter-gatherers.

1. According to paragraph 1, all of the following are true of farming groups EXCEPT:

   Ⓐ They built permanent homes.
   Ⓑ They did not hunt.
   Ⓒ They grew most of their food.
   Ⓓ They stayed in one place.

   Paragraph 1 is marked with an arrow [➡].

2. The word they in the passage refers to

   Ⓐ animals
   Ⓑ hunter-gatherer groups
   Ⓒ farming groups
   Ⓓ early humans

3. Look at the four squares [■] that indicate where the following sentence could be added to the passage.

   **Having more people gave them many advantages.**

   Where would the sentence best fit? Click on a square [■] to add the sentence to the passage.

4. Which of the sentences below best expresses the essential information in the highlighted sentence in the passage? *Incorrect* choices change the meaning in important ways or leave out essential information.

   Ⓐ Hunter-gatherer groups were small because they could not feed large groups of people.
   Ⓑ Small hunter-gatherer groups did not want to feed large groups of people.
   Ⓒ Large hunter-gatherer groups could not find enough food, so they only fed 100 people.
   Ⓓ Small hunter-gatherer groups did not have enough people to find food.

5. The word soldier in the passage is closest in meaning to

   Ⓐ hunter
   Ⓑ farmer
   Ⓒ warrior
   Ⓓ guard

**6** **Directions:** Select the appropriate phrases from the answer choices and match them to the groups to which they relate. TWO of the answer choices will NOT be used.
**This question is worth 3 points.**

> Drag your answer choices to the spaces where they belong. To remove an answer choice, click on it. To review the passage, click **View Text**.

**Answer Choices**

- (A) Small groups
- (B) Often hungry
- (C) Had soldiers
- (D) Took land
- (E) Lived in tents
- (F) More people
- (G) Built permanent homes

**Hunter-gatherer Groups**
- •

**Farming Groups**
- •
- •
- •
- •

 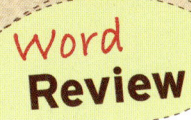

# Word Review

Read the sentences below and choose the correct meaning for each underlined word.

**1** Almost every <u>society</u> has a government.
(A) group of people in a country
(B) ancient country
(C) organization

**2** The dark blue color of the water creates a strong <u>contrast</u> with the bright yellow sand.
(A) difference
(B) harmony
(C) effect

**3** The cake has <u>equal</u> amounts of sugar and chocolate.
(A) average
(B) exact
(C) the same

**4** Many <u>centuries</u> ago, people didn't live very long.
(A) ten years
(B) hundred years
(C) thousand years

**5** The strong wind <u>lifted</u> the kite off the ground.
(A) moved upwards
(B) moved downwards
(C) shook

**6** This year, many Asian countries showed <u>signals</u> of adopting democracy.
(A) signs
(B) results
(C) agreements

**7** We have to take care of disabled children in our <u>community</u>.
(A) club
(B) home
(C) society

**8** Many American women <u>served</u> in the army during World War II.
(A) gave up
(B) worked
(C) died

## Sentence Review

Read the sentences below and choose one answer choice that best expresses the meaning of the given sentence.

**1** Whales have live babies as opposed to laying eggs like fish.

(A) Unlike fish, which lay eggs, whales have live babies.
(B) Whales have live babies as fish do.
(C) Whales can lay eggs like fish, but they usually have live babies.

**2** When the Europeans came to North and South America, they found people already living there.

(A) When the Europeans came to North and South America, they tried to find people living there.
(B) When the Europeans came to North and South America, there were no people living there.
(C) People were living in North and South America before the Europeans came.

**3** African-Americans were not equal members of American society.

(A) African-Americans didn't make as much money as white people.
(B) African-Americans were not treated equally with white people.
(C) African-Americans were separated from white people.

**4** The people of Athens chose their leaders, rather than having a military government.

(A) The people of Athens didn't have a military government, and they voted for their leaders.
(B) The people of Athens chose their leader of the military government.
(C) The people of Athens hated the idea of a military government.

**5** The British thought the colonists had no chance of winning the war.

(A) The British never thought that they could win the war over the colonists.
(B) The British had more chance of winning the war than the colonists.
(C) The British thought that they would win the war very easily.

Chapter 6. Classifying, Categorizing, and Organizing Information

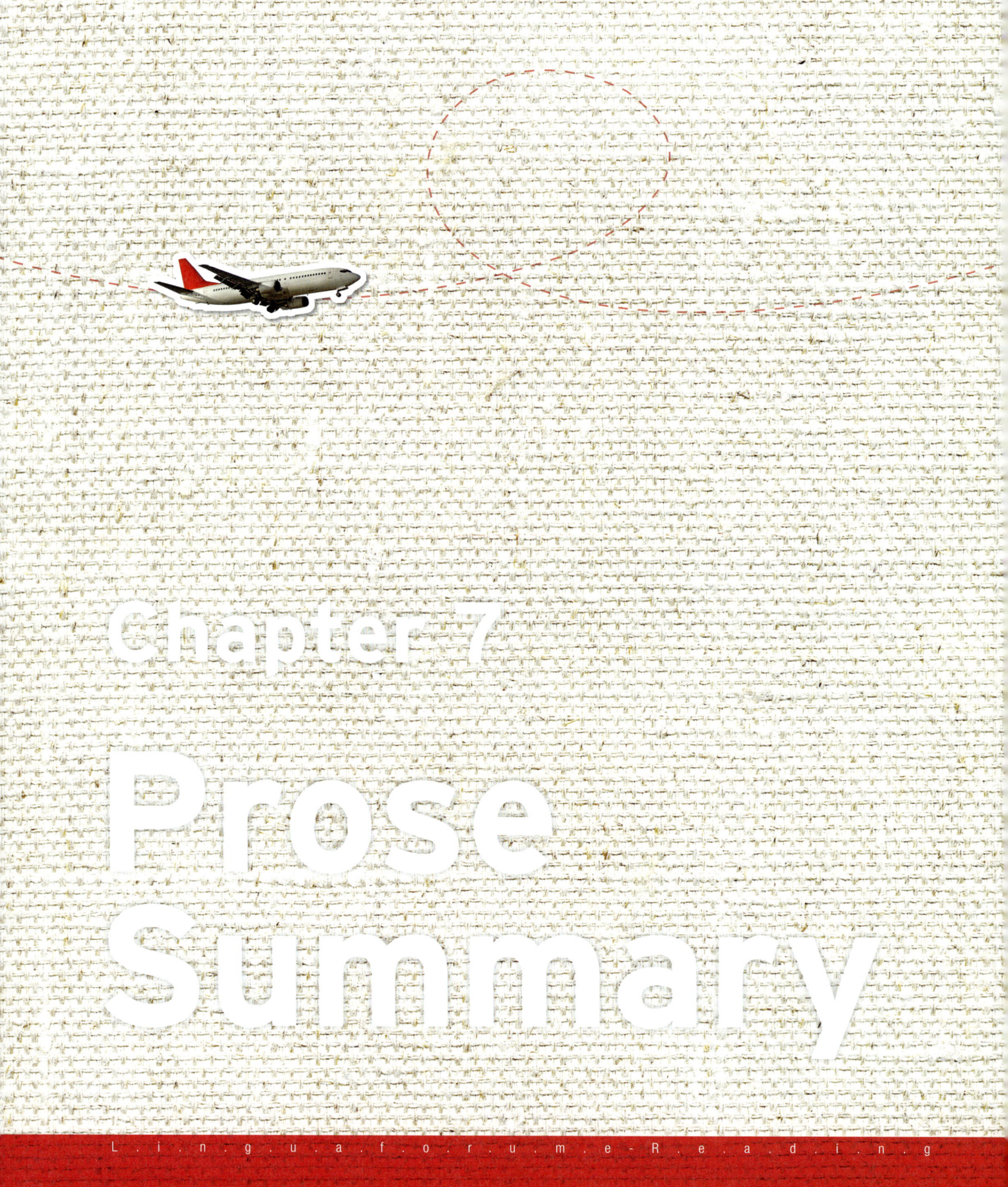

Chapter 7
Prose Summary

# Chapter 7
## Prose Summary

**11** **지문 요약 문제**
Prose Summary Questions
지문 전체의 내용을 몇 개의 문장으로 요약하는 문제

# Word Preview

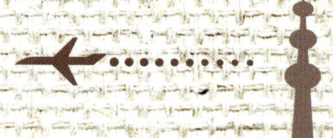

- **average**
  My **average** score in bowling is 140. I usually get about 140 points each game.

- **colony**
  Korea was a Japanese **colony** from 1910 to 1945.

- **electric**
  Michelle has an **electric** car, so she doesn't buy gas.

- **evil**
  The latest *Star Wars* film has the traditional theme of good against **evil**.

- **invention**
  The electric light was Thomas Edison's greatest **invention**.

- **minor**
  Scott's brother is an actor. He played a **minor** role in a TV series.

- **notice**
  Did you **notice** the player got slightly injured yesterday?

- **spread**
  My brother likes to **spread** jam on his toast.

- **summary**
  This report will give a **summary** of the meeting.

- **valuable**
  It will be a **valuable** lesson for Kevin. He needs to grow up!

# Prose Summary Questions

## 지문 요약 문제

○ 지문 요약 문제는 지문의 내용을 몇 개의 문장으로 요약하는 문제 유형이다. 요약문의 첫 문장을 제시해 주고, 그 뒤에 이어질 세 개의 문장을 여섯 개의 보기 중에서 선택할 것을 요구한다.

○ 지문 요약 문제는 마지막 문제로 출제되며, 각 지문마다 정보 분류 문제나 지문 요약 문제 중 하나가 반드시 포함된다. 지문 요약 문제의 배점은 2점이다.

○ 실제 *i*BT TOEFL에서 출제되는 문제 형식은 다음과 같다.

> **Directions:** An introductory sentence for a brief summary of the passage is provided below. Complete the summary by selecting the THREE answer choices that express important ideas in the passage. Some sentences do not belong in the summary because they express ideas that are not presented in the passage or are minor ideas in the passage. **This question is worth 2 points.**
>
> *The Sun is the primary source of energy for life on Earth.*
>
> - 
> - 
> - 
>
> **Answer Choices**
>
> (A) There are other stars that also produce energy, but they are too far away.
>
> (B) The Sun is a star of average temperature, but it has a greater influence on the Earth because it is closer to the Earth.
>
> (C) The Sun enables living things to grow.
>
> (D) The Sun governs the weather and the climate on Earth.
>
> (E) Most living things require food, air and water in order to survive.
>
> (F) Plants transform sunlight into chemicals, which are absorbed by animals and human beings.

### 문제풀이 전략

**❶ 각 단락의 중심 내용을 찾는다.**

일반적으로 중심 내용(main idea)은 글의 첫 단락에서 제시되는 경우가 많고, 나머지 단락들은 이를 뒷받침한다. 지문 요약 문제에서는 요약문의 첫 문장을 제시해 주는데, 대개의 경우 이것은 글의 주제와 일치한다. 이때 우리가 선택해야 하는 세 문장은 나머지 단락들의 중심 내용이 된다.

**❷ 중요한 내용(major idea)과 중요하지 않은 내용(minor idea)을 구별한다.**

요약문에 포함되는 문장은 중요한 내용을 담고 있어야 한다. 중요한 내용이란 글의 중심 내용을 직접적으로 뒷받침하는 것을 의미한다. 중심 내용과 직접적인 관련이 없는 내용은 중요하지 않은 내용이다. 다음 예문을 살펴보자.

(1) Jessica is very healthy. (main idea)
(2) She runs 10 km every day. (major idea)
(3) It takes her 40 minutes to run 10 km. (minor idea)

여기서 두 번째 문장은 주제를 직접적으로 뒷받침하지만, 세 번째 문장은 두 번째 문장에 대한 구체적인 설명이지, 주제와 직접적인 관계가 없다.

이처럼, 하나의 글을 구성하는 여러 내용은 같은 레벨에 있는 것이 아니다. 내용 간의 수평적인 관계와 수직적인 관계를 이해하면 글의 구조를 한눈에 파악할 수 있게 된다.

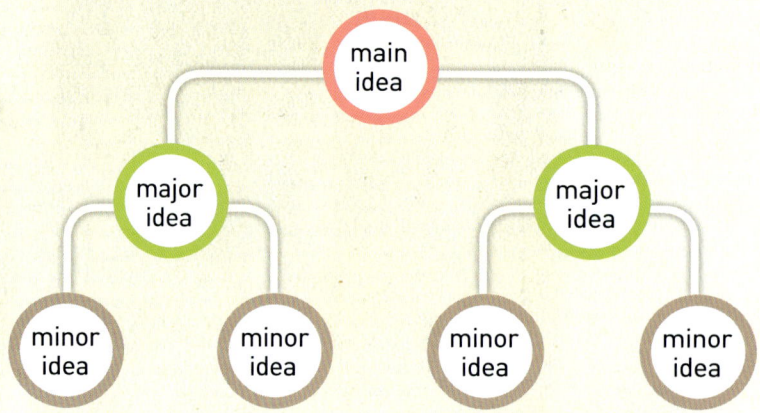

# Basic Drills 1

Read the paragraphs below and underline the main idea in each paragraph.

**1**   Hornets* are the natural enemies of honeybees. When a hornet attacks a honeybee nest, the honeybees have an interesting way of fighting. Honeybees cannot kill a hornet with their sting because they are too small. Instead, many honeybees land on the hornet and cover it with their bodies. Then, they rub their bodies together. This makes heat. The group of honeybees gets hotter and hotter, and so does the hornet. Honeybees can live at higher temperatures than hornets. After a few minutes, the hornet dies, and the honeybees are safe again.

★ hornet: a large black and yellow flying insect that can sting

**2**   Britain started many colonies around the world. They started the colonies in America for religious freedom, but they started other colonies for different reasons. For example, Australia was once a colony for British criminals. Instead of building more jails, Britain simply sent its criminals to Australia. On the other hand, India became a British colony for business reasons. The British wanted tea and valuable spices from India.

**3**   As an instrument, the guitar is about 500 years old. But in the 1930s, people started making electric guitars. The invention of the electric guitar greatly changed music. Before, guitars were only a small part of music, but the electric guitar quickly became the most important instrument in a band. In addition, electric guitars could make many different sounds, and this changed music as well. Blues and Rock and Roll both grew as a result of electric guitars.

---

**Words**   Look at the paragraphs again, and find words with the same meaning.

- A powder made from plants that you put into food to give it flavor   _____
- Needing electricity to work   _____
- The making, designing, or thinking of a new type of thing   _____

# Basic Drills 2

Read the three paragraphs below.

**1** The world's forests are getting smaller and smaller. Large forests, such as the Amazon rainforest, are up to 20% smaller than they were 50 years ago. For a long time, no one noticed this. Since the forests were huge and very hard to measure, no one knew their true size. But now we have pictures from airplanes and satellites. These pictures clearly show that the forests are getting smaller every year.

**2** Many things are causing the world's forests to get smaller. Logging companies cut down many trees. Sometimes these companies plant new trees, but the new trees take a long time to grow, and the companies cut down more trees during that time. Farmers also cut down trees to get more land for farming. This is especially true in poor countries.

**3** The world's forests are getting smaller, and this is causing many problems. The large forests of the world make most of our fresh air. As these forests get smaller, the air gets worse. Bad air causes many health problems for people. In addition, the forests are home to many animals. Many of these animals are dying as the forests get smaller. This is bad for humans because many of these animals are useful to humans.

Now match the number of each paragraph with the correct summary sentence below. There is one extra sentence.

_____ Humans are the main cause of shrinking forests.
_____ Shrinking forests cause problems for the Earth and for people.
_____ Shrinking forests are causing pollution.
_____ Modern technology brought attention to shrinking forests.

# Basic Drills 3

Read the paragraphs below. Each paragraph has TWO important ideas. Underline the important ideas. DO NOT underline minor details. Use the main idea in **bold** to help you.

**1**

> **Early humans used dead animals for many things.** They used animal skins as clothing. The animal skins were tough and strong. They were also warm and were very important during the cold winters. Early humans also used animal bones to make tools and weapons. Early humans made some of the first knives from animal bones. They also made arrows and other weapons from animal bones.

**2**

> Female black widow spiders are very poisonous, but male black widow spiders are not. **You can tell a male black widow from a female black widow in many ways.** Female black widows look different from male black widows. A female black widow is about twice the size of a male. In addition, female black widows have a red spot on their bellies. Males are completely black and have no spots. Moreover, females usually build larger webs than males. A female's web may be several feet across. Males usually do not build webs as large as this.

**3**

> Tattoos are very popular these days. Most parents don't like tattoos because they are permanent. Once a child gets a tattoo, the child can never take it off. **Some kinds of tattoos, however, are not permanent.** Henna tattoos use a special ink to color the skin. The ink stays on the skin for about a month and then washes off. Henna tattoos originally come from India. Young people can also get temporary tattoos. Temporary tattoos are like stickers for your skin. They usually come off in about two weeks.

---

**Words**   Look at the paragraphs again, and find words with the same meaning.

- Things that people wear          _____
- Totally                          _____
- Lasting forever; not temporary   _____

# Reading Practice 1

## The Water of Life

Blood is the water of life. Without blood, you could not live. The average person has about 5 liters of blood. Although you can't see them, blood actually has three different parts. Red blood cells* are small cells. They carry oxygen and food to different parts of the body. Red blood cells look a little like round pillows. You can't actually see red blood cells because they are too small to see, but you have a lot of them. There are over 250 million red blood cells in a single drop of blood. White blood cells are larger than red blood cells. White blood cells fight germs*, so they are very important when you get sick. You don't have as many white blood cells as red blood cells. There are only about one million white blood cells in every drop of blood. Actually, there are five different kinds of white blood cells, each of which fights a different kind of germ. Finally, 55% of your blood is plasma. Plasma is a little like water. Its job is to move the red and white blood cells around the body.

★ **cell:** the smallest part of an animal or plant   ★ **germ:** a very small living thing that can make you ill

**Directions:** Look at the sentence in bold. It is the introductory* sentence of a short summary for the passage. Choose THREE answers to complete the summary. Wrong answer choices use minor ideas from the passage or use information that is not in the passage.

**Blood is very important to life and is made of three different parts.**

(A) Without blood, you could not live.
(B) Red blood cells are the smallest blood cells, and carry oxygen and food to the body.
(C) Red blood cells are too small to see, but they look like round pillows.
(D) There are five different kinds of white blood cells.
(E) White blood cells are less common than red blood cells, and fight germs.
(F) Plasma is like water and moves blood cells around the body.

★ **introductory** [ìntrədʌ́ktəri]: a. 서두의, 첫머리의

# Reading Practice 2

## The Black Death

In 1347, a terrible disease began to spread across Europe. People called it the Black Death, because it turned the skin black. In just five years, the Black Death killed over 25 million people. That was almost one third of all the people in Europe. The Europeans tried to stop the Black Death, but many of their actions actually helped the disease spread faster.

The disease scared the Europeans very badly. Once a person in a village had the disease, the other people would run away to other villages. This helped the disease spread, because many of these people already had the disease. They just didn't know it yet. By running away, they took the disease into new areas. In addition, the Europeans thought cats spread the disease. At the time, Europeans thought cats were evil, so the Europeans killed millions of cats. Unfortunately, rats actually spread the Black Death, so by killing cats, the Europeans only helped the disease spread more.

**Directions:** Look at the sentence in bold. It is the introductory sentence of a short summary for the passage. Choose THREE answers to complete the summary. Wrong answer choices use minor ideas from the passage or use information that is not in the passage.

**The Black Death killed millions of people in Europe.**

Ⓐ The disease was called the Black Death because it turned the skin black.
Ⓑ Many of the Europeans' actions actually made the disease worse.
Ⓒ The Europeans were very scared of the disease.
Ⓓ By running away once a person had the disease, the Europeans took the disease into new areas.
Ⓔ Rats actually spread the Black Death.
Ⓕ Europeans killed cats to stop the disease, but this was a mistake.

# Reading Practice 3

## The Leaning Tower

Most famous buildings are famous because of their excellent construction. One building, however, is famous because its builders did a really bad job. The Leaning Tower of Pisa is a famous tower in Pisa, Italy. Most buildings stand straight up, but the Tower of Pisa doesn't. It leans! The tower leans 10 degrees to the south. How did this happen?

The Tower of Pisa was begun in 1173, and almost immediately there were problems. The ground under the tower was very soft, and one side of the tower started to sink into the ground. The problem could not be fixed with the technology at that time, but the people of Pisa did not give up. They simply continued to build the tower even though it was leaning.

Amazingly, the tower did not fall down, and over the years, it became a famous landmark. People came from all over Europe to see Pisa's leaning tower. Over the years, the tower had a great deal of work done to it. Early repairs focused on trying to straighten the tower. However, as the people of Pisa began to realize that the leaning tower was more popular than a straight tower would be, they stopped trying to straighten the tower.

---

**Directions:** Look at the sentence in bold. It is the introductory sentence of a short summary for the passage. Choose THREE answers to complete the summary. Wrong answer choices use minor ideas from the passage or use information that is not in the passage.

**The Leaning Tower of Pisa is famous because it is not straight.**

Ⓐ The tower leans 10 degrees to the south.
Ⓑ The tower started leaning during construction, but the builders did not stop working.
Ⓒ The ground under the tower is very soft.
Ⓓ The people of Pisa didn't have the technology to solve the problem.
Ⓔ Over the years, the Leaning Tower became a very famous landmark.
Ⓕ At first, the people of Pisa tried to fix the tower, but stopped when they saw it was a tourist attraction.

# Reading Practice 4

## The Emperor's Army

In the city of Xian in China, you can find the oldest army in the world. Each warrior is over 2,000 years old, and they are still ready for battle! This is possible because the warriors are statues, and the army is one of the largest works of art in history.

In the 2nd century B.C., a great king, Qin Shihuang, became the first king to control all of China. He is also the king who started the Great Wall of China. Emperor Qin also had a large and powerful army which he wanted to bring with him when he died, so he told his artists to build him a copy of his army. It was a huge job. They had to make over 6,000 stone warriors. They even had to make horses for the army! It took thousands of workers over thirty-six years to build the emperor's army. When the emperor died, his artists buried the army next to his tomb to guard him forever.

**Directions:** Look at the sentence in bold. It is the introductory sentence of a short summary for the passage. Choose THREE answers to complete the summary. Wrong answer choices use minor ideas from the passage or use information that is not in the passage.

**In the 2nd century B.C., Emperor Qin Shihuang had a huge stone army built for him.**

Ⓐ The Emperor's army is one of the oldest and largest works of art in the world.

Ⓑ Emperor Qin started the Great Wall of China.

Ⓒ Emperor Qin built the stone army because he wanted his army to follow him when he died.

Ⓓ The Emperor's army has thousands of warriors and took years to build.

Ⓔ The army even has horses made of stone.

Ⓕ The Emperor's army will guard him forever.

# The Panama Canal

➡ For hundreds of years, ships had to travel around the bottom of South America to travel from the Atlantic to the Pacific Ocean. This took a lot of time, and it was also very dangerous. The southern tip of South America is famous for
5 its terrible storms. Then, in the late 1800s, the French decided to build a canal in Panama. A canal is like an artificial river that connects two other bodies of water. In this case, the canal would connect the Atlantic and Pacific Oceans.

➡ The French project had problems from the start.
10 Although the French had good plans, their equipment was too small, and they had over 50 miles of canal to dig. They needed huge digging machines, but only America had machines large enough for the job. In addition, Panama is a jungle. There were millions of bugs, many of which carried diseases that the
15 French were not used to. As a result, the French work force was constantly sick, and the work went very slowly.

In 1888, the French stopped work on the canal. In 1904, the U.S. took over the building of the canal. First, the Americans killed the bugs to prevent disease. Then, they
20 brought in their huge digging machines. Even with their better machines, it took over 39,000 men ten years to finish the canal.

**Glossary**

artificial: made by people; not natural

1. According to the information in paragraph 1, the term canal can best be explained as

   (A) a fast way to travel
   (B) a water road that connects two bodies of water
   (C) a large river in Panama
   (D) a construction project

   Paragraph 1 is marked with an arrow [➡].

2. According to paragraph 2, all of the following were problems with the French canal project EXCEPT:

   (A) They did not have the right equipment.
   (B) The French workers did not like the heat.
   (C) Bugs spread disease among the workers.
   (D) They had a very long canal to build.

   Paragraph 2 is marked with an arrow [➡].

3. According to the passage, how did the Americans improve on the French project?

   (A) They built a shorter canal.
   (B) They used more men.
   (C) They killed the bugs.
   (D) They worked harder.

4. The word constantly in the passage is closest in meaning to

   (A) very
   (B) always
   (C) deadly
   (D) seriously

5. It can be inferred from the passage that the Panama Canal made sea travel

   (A) cheaper
   (B) safer
   (C) more common
   (D) more important

**6** **Directions:** An introductory sentence for a brief summary of the passage is provided below. Choose THREE answers to complete the summary. Wrong answer choices use minor ideas from the passage or use information that is not in the passage. **This question is worth 2 points.**

*The Panama Canal connects the Atlantic and Pacific Oceans.*

- 
- 
- 

### Answer Choices

A) Before the canal, crossing from the Atlantic to the Pacific required a long and dangerous journey.

B) The tip of South America is famous for terrible storms.

C) The French started the canal, but poor equipment and disease stopped their work.

D) The bugs of the jungle carried many diseases.

E) The U.S. succeeded in building the canal because they had larger equipment and prevented disease.

F) Even with bigger machines, it took thousands of men many years to complete the canal.

Drag your answer choices to the spaces where they belong. To remove an answer choice, click on it. To review the passage, click **View Text**.

# iBT Practice 2

**TOEFL** Reading

## The La Brea Tar Pits

➥ For some scientists, there is no better place than La Brea, California. If you want to study animals from thousands of years ago, La Brea may be the best place in the world. **A** That is because La Brea is home to the La Brea tar pits. **B** Tar comes from oil. Today, we have large tar factories because it is used to build roads, but you can also find it in nature. **C**

From 40,000 years ago to 8,000 years ago, La Brea had huge tar pits. **D** Animals would walk into the tar pits, but they couldn't get out. They would sink into the tar and die. The tar, however, would preserve their bodies in one piece. Later, as they were mining the tar, people discovered the animal bodies. Scientists have found over 59 kinds of land animals and 135 kinds of birds in the tar pits.

These bodies are very useful to scientists because most of these animals disappeared thousands of years ago. For example, scientists have found the bodies of huge cats, saber-tooth tigers, in the tar pits. These animals disappeared over ten thousand years ago. Scientists have learned a lot from the tar pits. They know much more about North America than before they found the tar pits. We now know that America had many large and dangerous animals such as the saber-tooth tiger. However, most of these animals disappeared before humans arrived 15,000 years ago.

**Glossary**

**pit:** a mine; a deep hole in the ground that people dig so that they can remove coal, gold, tin, etc.

1. According to paragraph 1, why is La Brea a good place for scientists?

   A) They can study tar pits there.
   B) There are many animals in La Brea.
   C) They can study the bodies of ancient animals there.
   D) La Brea is the best place in the world.

   Paragraph 1 is marked with an arrow [➡].

2. Look at the four squares [■] that indicate where the following sentence could be added to the passage.

   **Tar is a thick, black, sticky material.**

   Where would the sentence best fit? Click on a square [■] to add the sentence to the passage.

3. According to the passage, all of the following are true EXCEPT:

   A) Tar trapped the animals in La Brea.
   B) La Brea is very useful to scientists.
   C) You can also see most of the animals in La Brea in zoos.
   D) The tar in La Brea kept the animals' bodies in one piece.

4. The word discovered in the passage is closest in meaning to

   A) found
   B) saw
   C) caught
   D) learned

5. It can be inferred from the passage that

   A) North American animals are very different than 40,000 years ago
   B) La Brea is a dangerous place for scientists
   C) saber-tooth tigers disappeared because of the La Brea tar pits
   D) many humans died in tar pits as well

**6** **Directions:** An introductory sentence for a brief summary of the passage is provided below. Choose THREE answers to complete the summary. Wrong answer choices use minor ideas from the passage or use information that is not in the passage. **This question is worth 2 points.**

*The La Brea tar pits are an important place for scientists.*

- 
- 
- 

**Answer Choices**

(A) Scientists discovered many ancient animals in the tar pits.

(B) Tar is a black, sticky material and comes from oil.

(C) The animals got trapped in the tar pits, and the tar kept their bodies in one piece.

(D) There are many saber-tooth tigers in the tar pits.

(E) Scientists learned a great deal about early North America from the tar pits.

(F) Most large animals disappeared thousands of years ago.

Drag your answer choices to the spaces where they belong. To remove an answer choice, click on it. To review the passage, click **View Text**.

# Word Review

Read the sentences below and choose the correct word for each blank. Use the word bank below.

**Word Bank**

| average | electric | summary | minor |
| invention | spread | colony | notice |

1. The web site provides a brief _____ of the new transportation system.

2. In summer, the _____ temperature is 28°C.

3. At first, I didn't _____ anything wrong. Everything seemed to be all right.

4. The fire quickly _____ to other houses.

5. Hong Kong, a former British _____, is one of the largest cities in Asia.

6. When there is no more gas, we will have to use _____ cars.

7. There are many new _____s today, such as MP3 players, PDP TVs, etc.

8. Sometimes, famous baseball players are sent to the _____ league camp due to injuries.

152  e-Reading

Complete the following sentences by rearranging the words from the parentheses to fill in the blanks in the right order.

**1** Actually, there are five different kinds of white blood cells, _____ fights a different kind of germ.

(which, of, kind, each)

**2** People called it the Black Death, because _____.

(turned, skin, the, black, it)

**3** The Europeans tried to stop the Black Death, but many of their actions actually _____.

(faster, disease, helped, the, spread)

**4** Over the years, the tower _____.

(great, to, done, it, a, had, work, deal, of)

**5** _____ to build the emperor's army.

(took, workers, thirty-six, years, thousands, it, of, over)

Chapter 7. Prose Summary  **153**

# Mini Test 1

# Passage 1

## Hoover and the FBI

The Federal Bureau of Investigation, or FBI, is the most famous police force in America. FBI agents are very different from normal police officers. Normal police officers only have jurisdiction in their state, meaning that they can only work and arrest people in their state. In contrast, FBI agents have jurisdiction all across the United States. The most famous FBI agent was J. Edgar Hoover.

➡ Hoover started his career as a lawyer for the government. He worked on many important cases, but his most famous case was the Palmer Raids. In the Palmer Raids, the government arrested thousands of people because Hoover thought they were working against the government. **A** Actually, most of the people were innocent, but Hoover thought they were the enemies of the United States. **B**

➡ In 1924, Hoover became the director of the Federal Bureau of Investigation. At the time, the Bureau was a small agency and had little power. **C** Over the years, he made the FBI into a large and powerful agency. In the 1930s, the FBI became famous for arresting gangsters like Al Capone and Baby Face Nelson. Hoover also brought science into police work. **D** For example, he started the first fingerprint laboratories.

However, not all of Hoover's actions were so good. He thought many people were the enemies of the United States. During the 1940s and 1950s, Hoover arrested many people. He thought they were communists, but this was really just like the Palmer Raids.

**Glossary**

**jurisdiction:** the right to use an official power that a court of law or an official has

**laboratory:** a building or a room where scientific experiments are carried out

# Passage 1

Question 1 of 25

**1** According to the passage, all of the following are true EXCEPT:

- A) FBI agents only have power in one state.
- B) The FBI started as a small police force.
- C) The FBI is the most famous police force in America.
- D) FBI agents are not the same as other police officers.

**2** According to paragraph 2, how did Hoover start his career?

- A) He became the director of the FBI.
- B) He planned the Palmer Raids.
- C) He worked as a government lawyer.
- D) He arrested gangsters.

Paragraph 2 is marked with an arrow [➡].

**3** The word *innocent* in the passage is closest in meaning to

- A) good
- B) not guilty
- C) good criminals
- D) friends

**4** The word *they* in the passage refers to

- A) enemies
- B) Hoover
- C) government
- D) people

**5** Look at the four squares [■] that indicate where the following sentence could be added to the passage.

**Hoover changed all of that.**

Where would the sentence best fit? Click on a square [■] to add the sentence to the passage.

**6** The word *gangsters* in the passage is closest in meaning to

- A) enemies
- B) criminals
- C) people
- D) communists

**7** According to paragraph 3, how did the FBI become famous?

- A) By starting the first fingerprint labs
- B) By becoming a large and powerful agency
- C) By arresting gangsters
- D) By using science in police work

Paragraph 3 is marked with an arrow [➡].

**8** The author mentions the Palmer Raids in order to

- A) show that the United States had many enemies in the 1940s
- B) suggest that Hoover arrested many innocent people
- C) show that Hoover hated communists
- D) show that Hoover was a good FBI agent

# Passage 1

**9  Directions:** An introductory sentence for a brief summary of the passage is provided below. Choose THREE answers to complete the summary. Wrong answer choices use minor ideas from the passage or use information that is not in the passage. **This question is worth 2 points.**

*J. Edgar Hoover was the first director of the FBI and a famous FBI agent.*

- 
- 
- 

### Answer Choices

(A) Hoover began working for the government as a lawyer.

(B) Most people in the Palmer Raids were innocent.

(C) Hoover changed the FBI into a large and powerful police force.

(D) Hoover started the first fingerprint labs.

(E) While Hoover did many good things, he also arrested many innocent people.

(F) Hoover arrested many gangsters like Al Capone.

Drag your answer choices to the spaces where they belong. To remove an answer choice, click on it. To review the passage, click **View Text**.

# The Two Poles

The North and South Poles are the two coldest places on Earth. At the top and bottom of the world, the temperature never rises above 0°C, and it is usually much colder. Huge sheets of ice cover the land, and the seas are full of icebergs. However, **extreme** cold and lots of ice are just about the only similarities between the North and South Poles. They are actually very different from each other.

➡ Although most of the North Pole is actually a huge sea of ice, there is still lots of life at the North Pole. Many plants can live in the cold weather. The snow actually helps these plants. Temperatures under the snow can be up to 25°C warmer than above the snow. The snow covers the plants and keeps them warm. There are also lots of animals at the North Pole. Some animals leave during the cold winters, but some animals, like Arctic foxes, live in the cold all year.

➡ **A** The South Pole is actually a huge continent, but the land is under thousands of feet of ice. **B** Because the South Pole is much higher than the North Pole, **it** is also colder. Life is also much different at the South Pole. **C** There is very little plant life, and there is no life at all in the center of the South Pole. **D** There is only life at the **coasts**, near the sea. Here, there are many birds and fish, but there are no large animals like the polar bears of the north.

**Glossary**
pole: the most northern or most southern point on Earth

## Passage 2

**10** The word **extreme** in the passage is closest in meaning to

- A  big
- B  terrible
- C  many
- D  winter

**11** According to paragraph 2, plants are able to live at the North Pole because

- A  the North Pole is mostly ice
- B  the snow keeps them warm
- C  the North Pole is warm in the summer
- D  plants at the North Pole are very strong

Paragraph 2 is marked with an arrow [➡].

**12** It can be inferred from the passage that

- A  the North Pole is a dangerous place to live
- B  Arctic foxes only live at the North Pole
- C  the North Pole has very little land
- D  it snows all year at the North Pole

**13** According to paragraph 3, the South Pole is colder than the North Pole because

- A  it is a huge continent
- B  it has more ice
- C  it is higher
- D  it gets less sunlight

Paragraph 3 is marked with an arrow [➡].

**14** The word **it** in the passage refers to

- A  the North Pole
- B  ice
- C  the South Pole
- D  continent

**15** Look at the four squares [■] that indicate where the following sentence could be added to the passage.

**Huge mountains cover much of the South Pole.**

Where would the sentence best fit? Click on a square [■] to add the sentence to the passage.

**16** The word **coasts** in the passage is closest in meaning to

- A  land
- B  beaches
- C  water
- D  parts

## Passage 2

**17** **Directions:** Select the appropriate phrases from the answer choices and match them to the area to which they relate. TWO of the answer choices will NOT be used. **This question is worth 3 points.**

Drag your answer choices to the spaces where they belong. To remove an answer choice, click on it. To review the passage, click *View Text*.

**Answer Choices**

- (A) Huge continent
- (B) No animals
- (C) Sea of ice
- (D) Almost no plants
- (E) Large animals
- (F) Not as cold
- (G) Snow all year

**North Pole**
- •
- •
- •

**South Pole**
- •
- •

# Eating Right

What are you going to have for lunch today? This is a very important question. Food "builds" your body. You wouldn't want to build a house from paper, right? Of course not! It wouldn't be strong. If you want your body to be strong, you need to choose your foods carefully.

Your most basic food should be grains, like rice and bread. These foods are high in carbohydrates, the basic fuel of the body. Carbohydrates give you energy. If you do not get enough bread and rice, you will feel tired easily.

Your next largest group of foods should be fruits and vegetables. Your body needs about four or five fruits and vegetables a day. Fruits and vegetables give your body important vitamins. For example, the vitamin C in oranges and other fruits helps fight sickness.

Take one step forward. You just used 54 different muscles. If you want your muscles to be strong and healthy, you need protein. Most of our protein comes from meat, but you can also get protein from beans and nuts.

When you took that step forward, you moved 16 different bones. But that is only a small number, because you have 206 bones in your body. Each of them needs calcium to remain strong. Calcium comes mostly from milk products like cheese, yogurt, and of course milk. If you eat the right foods, you will be much healthier.

**Glossary**

**carbohydrate:** a substance that is in foods such as sugar, bread, potatoes, which provides your body with heat and energy

## Passage 3

**18** Why does the author mention a house?

- Ⓐ To show that the body is very strong
- Ⓑ To show that food affects the strength of your body
- Ⓒ To show that a weak body is not good
- Ⓓ To show that you should eat in your house

**19** The word basic in the passage is closest in meaning to

- Ⓐ delicious
- Ⓑ simple
- Ⓒ essential
- Ⓓ big

**20** According to the passage, what food should you eat the most of?

- Ⓐ Bread and rice
- Ⓑ Meat
- Ⓒ Milk and cheese
- Ⓓ Salt and sugar

**21** According to the passage, what foods contain most of your vitamins?

- Ⓐ Meat
- Ⓑ Bread and rice
- Ⓒ Vegetables and fruits
- Ⓓ Milk and cheese

**22** The word them in the passage refers to

- Ⓐ body
- Ⓑ bones
- Ⓒ number
- Ⓓ calcium

**23** The word remain in the passage is closest in meaning to

- Ⓐ come
- Ⓑ stay
- Ⓒ grow
- Ⓓ break

**24** According to the passage, if people's bones are weak, what should they eat?

- Ⓐ They should have more salt.
- Ⓑ They should have more cheese.
- Ⓒ They should eat beans and nuts.
- Ⓓ They need more rice.

# Passage 3

Question 25 of 25

**25 Directions:** An introductory sentence for a brief summary of the passage is provided below. Choose THREE answers to complete the summary. Wrong answer choices use minor ideas from the passage or use information that is not in the passage. **This question is worth 2 points.**

*Eating the right foods is very important if you want a healthy body.*

- 
- 
- 

### Answer Choices

(A) Building your body is like building a house.

(B) The carbohydrates in grains will give you energy.

(C) You should eat a lot of rice.

(D) Vitamin C helps you fight sickness.

(E) You get vitamins from fruits and vegetables.

(F) Meat and milk products will keep your bones and muscles strong.

Drag your answer choices to the spaces where they belong. To remove an answer choice, click on it. To review the passage, click **View Text**.

# Hurricane Mitch

➡ Hurricanes are very powerful storms. One of the worst hurricanes in history was hurricane Mitch. In late October and early November 1998, hurricane Mitch killed over 11,000 people, destroyed the homes of hundreds of thousands of people, and caused billions of dollars in damage. Mitch hit the hardest in two countries, Honduras and Nicaragua, where it caused the most destruction and the highest number of fatalities. Why did Mitch kill so many people in these two countries but not in other countries? There are several reasons.

➡ First, hurricanes usually move quickly, but due to unusual weather conditions, hurricane Mitch moved very slowly over Honduras and Nicaragua. So, Honduras and Nicaragua got much more rain than other countries. **A** Honduras and Nicaragua got almost three feet of rain in three days. There were terrible floods in both countries, and the high waters killed many people.

Second, both Nicaragua and Honduras are poor countries. **B** Many of their houses are of low quality and not very strong. **C** These houses were easily destroyed by the strong winds of the hurricane. **D**

Finally, both countries are small countries. In larger countries, people went to safe places during the hurricane. For example, Americans left Florida and went to Georgia during the hurricane. The hurricane did not hit Georgia, so the people were safe. In Honduras and Nicaragua, hurricane Mitch hit the whole country, so there was no safe place for people to go.

---

**Glossary**

**fatality:** a death in an accident

## Passage 1

**1** According to paragraph 1, how many people died in hurricane Mitch?

- (A) 1998
- (B) Less than 11,000
- (C) More than 11,000
- (D) 11,000

Paragraph 1 is marked with an arrow [➡].

**2** According to paragraph 2, why did Honduras and Nicaragua get more rain than other countries?

- (A) Hurricane Mitch was stronger in these two countries.
- (B) These countries always get more rain.
- (C) It was the rainy season in Honduras and Nicaragua.
- (D) Hurricane Mitch moved more slowly over these two countries.

Paragraph 2 is marked with an arrow [➡].

**3** Look at the four squares [■] that indicate where the following sentence could be added to the passage.

**Many people died in their houses when the walls fell down in the strong winds.**

Where would the sentence best fit? Click on a square [■] to add the sentence to the passage.

**4** The word their in the passage refers to

- (A) hurricane Mitch
- (B) poor countries
- (C) Honduras and Nicaragua
- (D) poor people

**5** According to the passage, why couldn't the people of Honduras and Nicaragua go to a safe place?

- (A) They were too poor.
- (B) They couldn't go to Georgia.
- (C) The hurricane hit the whole country.
- (D) They loved their homes.

**6** The author mentions Georgia in order to

- (A) show that Americans were more prepared for the hurricane
- (B) help explain why more people died in Honduras and Nicaragua than in other countries
- (C) show that Georgia is a safe place to go during a hurricane
- (D) show that hurricane Mitch was weaker when it reached the United States

# Passage 1

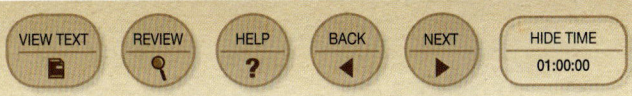

**7** **Directions:** An introductory sentence for a brief summary of the passage is provided below. Choose THREE answers to complete the summary. Wrong answer choices use minor ideas from the passage or use information that is not in the passage. **This question is worth 2 points.**

*There are several reasons why hurricane Mitch caused such great damage in Honduras and Nicaragua.*

- 
- 
- 

### Answer Choices

(A) Hurricane Mitch killed over 11,000 people and caused a great deal of damage.

(B) Honduras and Nicaragua had unusual weather conditions.

(C) Hurricane Mitch dropped almost three feet of rain on Honduras and Nicaragua and caused terrible floods.

(D) Strong winds destroyed the low-quality houses in Honduras and Nicaragua.

(E) Honduras and Nicaragua are very poor countries.

(F) Hurricane Mitch covered the entire countries of Nicaragua and Honduras, so there was no safe place to go.

Drag your answer choices to the spaces where they belong. To remove an answer choice, click on it. To review the passage, click **View Text**.

## Passage 2

### Brazil's Soccer Star

➥ Soccer is full of heroes and superstars. Today, Ronaldo from Brazil and David Beckham from England are known and loved by fans all over the world. However, one soccer player is far more famous than either one of these players. His name
5 is Edson Arantes do Nascimento, but he is more commonly known as Pelé.

Pelé was born in 1940 in Brazil, where soccer is a national passion, and Pelé grew up playing the game. His father was a talented soccer player until he broke his leg. After that, he
10 could not play soccer, so he spent his time teaching his son about the game. In 1956, Pelé joined his first professional soccer club, the Santos Football Club. With Pelé on their team, Santos became one of the top soccer teams in South America, and Pelé quickly became famous in South America.

15 Then came the magical year of 1958. This was perhaps the greatest year of Pelé's career, in which he scored 158 goals and led Brazil to the World Cup Championship. Under Pelé's leadership, Brazil won the World Cup again in 1962 and in 1970.

20 In addition to helping his team to great victories, Pelé achieved amazing things for himself. In 1969, he scored his 1,000th goal. By the time he stopped playing soccer, he had scored 1,282 goals in 1,363 games. This is almost one goal for every game. No other player in soccer has even come close to
25 challenging this record.

**Passage 2**

Question 8 of 23

8. According to paragraph 1, who is the most famous soccer player?

   A. Ronaldo
   B. Pelé
   C. David Beckham
   D. Maradona

   Paragraph 1 is marked with an arrow [➡].

9. The word His in the passage refers to

   A. Pelé
   B. One soccer player
   C. Ronaldo
   D. David Beckham

10. According to the passage, Pelé grew up playing soccer because

    A. he wanted to be like Ronaldo
    B. he was very poor and wanted to be famous
    C. he lived in a country that loved soccer
    D. he was fast

11. According to the passage, why did Pelé's father spend so much time teaching him to play soccer?

    A. He did not have a job.
    B. He wanted Pelé to be famous.
    C. He was Brazilian.
    D. He broke his leg and could not play soccer himself.

12. According to the passage, what was Pelé's best year as a soccer player?

    A. 1958
    B. 1962
    C. 1969
    D. 1978

13. The word victories in the passage is closest in meaning to

    A. games
    B. championships
    C. wins
    D. goals

14. According to the passage, all of the following are true EXCEPT:

    A. Pelé won three World Cups.
    B. Pelé scored a goal in every game he played.
    C. Pelé scored 158 goals in one year.
    D. Pelé was 16 when he started playing professional soccer.

## Passage 2

Question 15 of 23

**15 Directions:** An introductory sentence for a brief summary of the passage is provided below. Choose THREE answers to complete the summary. Wrong answer choices use minor ideas from the passage or use information that is not in the passage. **This question is worth 2 points.**

*Pelé is probably the greatest soccer player of all time.*

- 
- 
- 

**Answer Choices**

(A) Soccer is a national passion in Brazil.

(B) Pelé grew up playing soccer.

(C) His father was a soccer player until he broke his leg.

(D) Pelé led Brazil to three World Cup Championships.

(E) He scored 158 goals in 1958.

(F) He holds the record for the highest number of career goals.

Drag your answer choices to the spaces where they belong. To remove an answer choice, click on it. To review the passage, click **View Text**.

# The Space Race

→ In 1957, Russia launched a small metal ball, Sputnik, into space. As it circled the Earth, it did nothing but send a simple radio message back to Earth. That message, however, was enough to frighten the Americans badly. The Russians were winning the space race. But what was the space race? Very simply, it was a race to see which country could get into space first. Both Russia and the United States wanted to win very much. With Sputnik, Russia won the first part of the race, but the next stage, putting a man into space, was far more important to both countries.

→ The American program to put a man into space was the Mercury program. The Americans chose Alan Shepard, a Navy test pilot, to be their first astronaut. They called his mission Mercury Freedom 7. Shepard went through months of training for his mission. Meanwhile, the engineers and scientists tested every part of his spaceship to make sure it was safe. Finally, in 1961, after the Americans safely sent a monkey into space, they were ready to send Shephard. In the last week of February, Shepard's Redstone rocket was on the launch pad, but a last-minute problem meant that they could not launch. They rescheduled the launch for May 5. Then on April 12, the Americans received terrible news. Yuri Gagarin, a Russian, was in space. The Russians had beaten the Americans again.

## Passage 3

**16** According to the passage, which of the following was the first to go into space?

Ⓐ Mercury Freedom 7
Ⓑ A monkey
Ⓒ Yuri Gagarin
Ⓓ Sputnik

**17** According to paragraph 1, the term space race is best explained as

Ⓐ the race to build the fastest rocket
Ⓑ the race to get into space first
Ⓒ the race to reach the moon first
Ⓓ the race to launch Sputnik

Paragraph 1 is marked with an arrow [➡].

**18** The word They in the passage refers to

Ⓐ The Russians
Ⓑ The Americans
Ⓒ The Navy
Ⓓ The Mercury program

**19** According to paragraph 2, why did the Americans lose the second part of the space race?

Ⓐ They could not build a rocket as fast as the Russians.
Ⓑ A problem forced them to reschedule their launch.
Ⓒ Their program was unsafe.
Ⓓ Their monkey died.

Paragraph 2 is marked with an arrow [➡].

**20** It can be inferred from the passage that the Americans sent a monkey into space in order to

Ⓐ test their rocket's safety
Ⓑ get into space faster than the Russians
Ⓒ help train Shepard
Ⓓ fix a problem with their rocket

**21** According to the passage, when did the first human go into space?

Ⓐ In 1957
Ⓑ In February 1961
Ⓒ On April 12, 1961
Ⓓ On May 5, 1961

**22** The word rescheduled in the passage is closest in meaning to

Ⓐ planned
Ⓑ launched
Ⓒ did
Ⓓ reset

# Passage 3

**23 Directions:** Select the appropriate phrases from the answer choices and match them to the country to which they relate. **TWO of the answer choices will NOT be used. This question is worth 3 points.**

> Drag your answer choices to the spaces where they belong. To remove an answer choice, click on it. To review the passage, click **View Text**.

**Answer Choices**

- (A) Mercury program
- (B) First man in space
- (C) Changed launch plan
- (D) Used monkeys in space program
- (E) Better scientists
- (F) Sputnik
- (G) First man on moon

**United States**
- ●
- ●
- ●

**Russia**
- ●
- ●

## Passage 1

# Presidential Killers

John Wilkes Booth and Lee Harvey Oswald are two of the most famous killers in American history. John Wilkes Booth killed President Lincoln in 1865, and Oswald killed President Kennedy almost 100 years later. There are interesting similarities and differences between these two killers.

➥ Both Booth and Oswald were enemies not only of the president, but of the United States as well. For much of the Civil War, Booth worked to secretly bring food and medicine to the Southern Army. Oswald, on the other hand, was an open enemy of the United States. In 1959, he left the U.S. to live in the Soviet Union. Later, he returned to the U.S. and worked to support Cuba, another enemy of the U.S.

While both men hated the United States government, their lives were very different. Booth came from a good family. **A** He became an actor and was very successful. Oswald's life was not so happy. **B** His father died before he was born. **C** He also had mental problems throughout his life, and he never had a very good job. **D**

Finally, while both men died before their trials, they died in very different ways. Oswald was caught by the police just hours after he shot President Kennedy. He died when Jack Ruby shot him on his way from the jail to the courthouse. In contrast, it took over 12 days to catch Booth because he had help from friends who also hated the government. When he was caught, he would not give up. He died in a gunfight with Union soldiers.

# Passage 1

1. According to the passage, all of the following are true EXCEPT:
   - A) Booth and Oswald went to jail for their crimes.
   - B) Booth and Oswald were enemies of the United States.
   - C) Booth and Oswald had very different families.
   - D) Booth and Oswald both killed presidents.

2. The word **he** in the passage refers to
   - A) John Wilkes Booth
   - B) the president
   - C) Lee Harvey Oswald
   - D) enemy

3. It can be inferred from paragraph 2 that
   - A) Booth was very clever
   - B) the Soviet Union was an enemy of the United States
   - C) Oswald was a spy for the Soviet Union
   - D) Oswald was Cuban

   Paragraph 2 is marked with an arrow [➡].

4. The word **support** in the passage is closest in meaning to
   - A) help
   - B) free
   - C) fight
   - D) secret

5. According to the passage, Booth was an enemy of the United States because
   - A) he gave supplies to enemy soldiers
   - B) he traveled to the Soviet Union
   - C) he was a criminal
   - D) he had mental problems

6. Look at the four squares [■] that indicate where the following sentence could be added to the passage.

   **So, his life as a child was very difficult.**

   Where would the sentence best fit? Click on a square [■] to add the sentence to the passage.

7. The word **trials** in the passage is closest in meaning to
   - A) crimes
   - B) caught
   - C) cases
   - D) jails

# Passage 1

Question 8 of 25

8  **Directions:** Select the appropriate phrases from the answer choices and match them to the person to which they relate. TWO of the answer choices will NOT be used. **This question is worth 3 points.**

> Drag your answer choices to the spaces where they belong. To remove an answer choice, click on it. To review the passage, click *View Text*.

**Answer Choices**

(A) Killed President Kennedy

(B) Good childhood

(C) Helped U.S. enemies secretly

(D) Killed president for money

(E) Took a long time to catch

(F) Never had a good job

(G) Was never caught

**John Wilkes Booth**

●

●

●

**Lee Harvey Oswald**

●

●

## Scientists Escape to America

➥ Albert Einstein was one of the greatest scientists in history. **A** At first, Einstein was not a professional scientist. **B** He worked for the Swiss government and did his scientific work in his free time. **C** In 1905, Einstein wrote one of his most important scientific papers, his *Special Theory of Relativity*. Instantly, Einstein became one of the most important scientists in the world. He returned to Germany and started working as a professor there. **D** In 1916, Einstein wrote his *General Theory of Relativity*. Together, these two theories explained much of the universe.

In the 1930s, the Nazis took power in Germany. The Nazi government was very cruel. Einstein did not like the Nazis and left Germany for America. This was a huge loss for Germany and a huge gain for America. Einstein began teaching in American universities and training a new generation of scientists, many of whom would later work in the NASA space program.

Einstein was not the only great scientist to leave his country and come to the United States. Enrico Fermi was a famous Italian scientist. Like the Nazis, the Italian government of the 1930s was very cruel, so Fermi left Italy in 1939. In the United States, Fermi helped to build the first atomic bombs. Both Fermi and Einstein helped the United States greatly. Not only did they train new scientists, but their work also allowed the United States to become the most powerful nation in the world.

**Passage 2**

9. According to paragraph 1, all of the following are true of Einstein EXCEPT:

   Ⓐ He worked for the Swiss government.
   Ⓑ He became a famous scientist in 1905.
   Ⓒ He left Switzerland to work in Germany.
   Ⓓ He worked for the German space program.

   Paragraph 1 is marked with an arrow [➡].

10. It can be inferred from the passage that

    Ⓐ Einstein was German
    Ⓑ Einstein made a lot of money from his theories
    Ⓒ Einstein was smarter than Fermi
    Ⓓ Einstein was very happy in America

11. Look at the four squares [■] that indicate where the following sentence could be added to the passage.

    **That quickly changed, however.**

    Where would the sentence best fit? Click on a square [■] to add the sentence to the passage.

12. The word cruel in the passage is closest in meaning to

    Ⓐ powerful
    Ⓑ unkind
    Ⓒ wrong
    Ⓓ hurt

13. According to the passage, why did Einstein leave Germany?

    Ⓐ To work for a better university in America
    Ⓑ To become a professional scientist
    Ⓒ To escape the Nazis
    Ⓓ To work on the space program

14. The word whom in the passage refers to

    Ⓐ universities
    Ⓑ Einstein
    Ⓒ scientists
    Ⓓ Nazis

15. According to the passage, how did Fermi help the United States?

    Ⓐ He worked on the space program.
    Ⓑ He made the first nuclear weapons.
    Ⓒ He trained scientists.
    Ⓓ He was a famous scientist.

16. The word allowed in the passage is closest in meaning to

    Ⓐ let
    Ⓑ made
    Ⓒ used
    Ⓓ had

## Passage 2

Question 17 of 25

**17** **Directions:** An introductory sentence for a brief summary of the passage is provided below. Choose THREE answers to complete the summary. Wrong answer choices use minor ideas from the passage or use information that is not in the passage. **This question is worth 2 points.**

*The U.S. gained many great scientists in the years before World War II.*

- 
- 
- 

**Answer Choices**

(A) At first, Einstein was not a professional scientist, and worked for the Swiss government.

(B) Einstein wrote his first scientific paper in 1905, which made him famous.

(C) Einstein came to America in order to escape the Nazi government in Germany.

(D) Einstein helped the U.S. by training young scientists.

(E) Other famous scientists, such as Enrico Fermi, came to the U.S. in order to escape their governments.

(F) Fermi created the first nuclear bombs.

Drag your answer choices to the spaces where they belong. To remove an answer choice, click on it. To review the passage, click **View Text**.

# Passage 3

## The Brain

The brain is probably the most complicated part of our body. We don't know much about the brain. For example, the average person only uses 15% of their brain. What is the other 85% for? Scientists have no idea. **A** Most of our knowledge about the brain comes from studying people with brain injuries. **B** When people damage their brain, they often lose an ability. By matching the damaged part of the brain with the lost ability, we can guess the purpose of different parts of the brain. **C**

➡ Today we know that there are three basic parts of the brain: the cerebrum, the cerebellum, and the brain stem. **D** The cerebrum is the largest part of the brain and is located in the frontal part of the skull. The cerebrum is the most advanced part of the brain. It controls all of our higher thoughts, such as language ability and the ability to solve problems. It has two halves. The right half controls artistic and creative abilities, and the left half controls language and math abilities.

The cerebellum is located in the lower, rear part of the skull and mostly controls body movement. The brain stem is located in the center of our brain, beneath the cerebrum and the cerebellum. It acts as a messenger, passing signals from different parts of the body to the brain. It also controls all of our important life functions like breathing and our heartbeat.

**Glossary**
complicated: difficult to understand

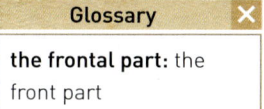
the frontal part: the front part

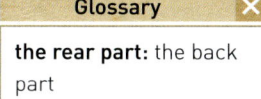
the rear part: the back part

# Passage 3

**18** According to the passage, how much of our brain do we use?

- Ⓐ 15%
- Ⓑ 85%
- Ⓒ 100%
- Ⓓ Only the left side

**19** According to paragraph 2, what part of the brain is the largest?

- Ⓐ The cerebellum
- Ⓑ The cerebrum
- Ⓒ The brain stem
- Ⓓ The skull

Paragraph 2 is marked with an arrow [➡].

**20** The word advanced in the passage is closest in meaning to

- Ⓐ big
- Ⓑ new
- Ⓒ complicated
- Ⓓ good

**21** According to the passage, the cerebrum controls all of the following EXCEPT

- Ⓐ your heartbeat
- Ⓑ artistic abilities
- Ⓒ math abilities
- Ⓓ problem-solving abilities

**22** It can be inferred from the passage that if you damage the left side of your cerebrum,

- Ⓐ you'll probably die
- Ⓑ you might not be able to walk
- Ⓒ you might lose your sight
- Ⓓ you might not be able to talk

**23** The word skull in the passage is closest in meaning to

- Ⓐ head
- Ⓑ brain
- Ⓒ bone
- Ⓓ hair

**24** Look at the four squares [■] that indicate where the following sentence could be added to the passage.

**Still, we are slowly learning more and more about the brain.**

Where would the sentence best fit? Click on a square [■] to add the sentence to the passage.

**25 Directions:** An introductory sentence for a brief summary of the passage is provided below. Choose THREE answers to complete the summary. Wrong answer choices use minor ideas from the passage or use information that is not in the passage. **This question is worth 2 points.**

*The brain is the most complicated part of our bodies and has three basic parts.*

- 
- 
- 

**Answer Choices**

(A) Scientists learn about the brain by studying people with brain damage.

(B) The cerebrum is the largest part of the brain and controls higher thought processes.

(C) The cerebrum has two halves: the right half and the left half.

(D) The cerebellum controls body movement.

(E) The brain stem passes signals from the body to the brain.

(F) Most people only use 15% of their brains.

Drag your answer choices to the spaces where they belong. To remove an answer choice, click on it. To review the passage, click **View Text**.

Memo

# Final iBT

http://www.finalibt.co.kr

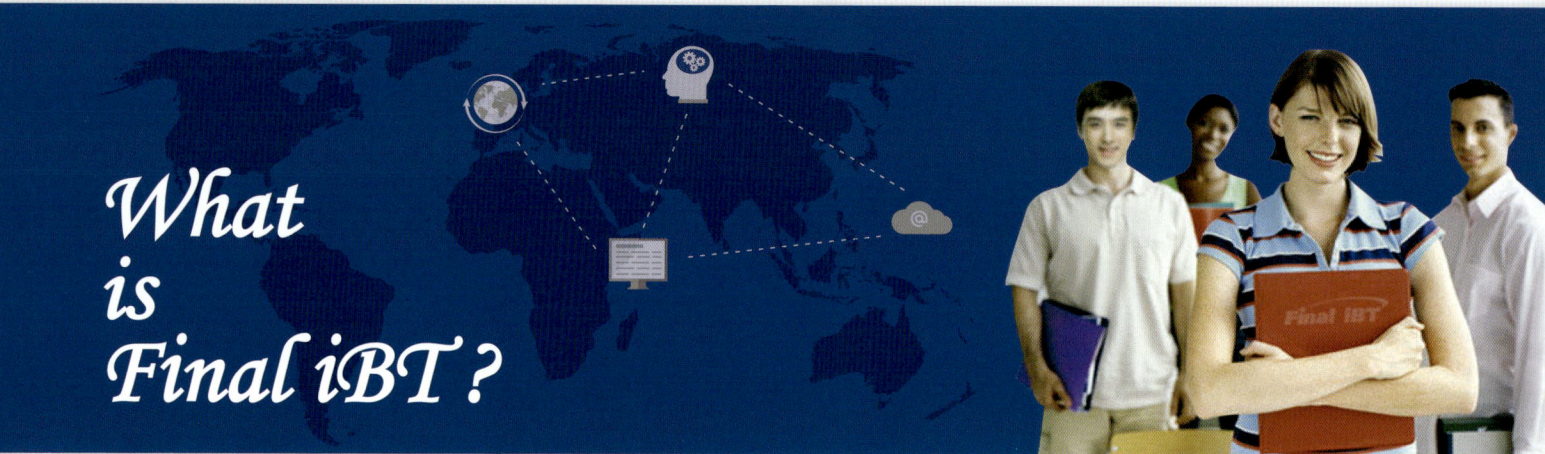

## What is Final iBT?

Final iBT는 TOEFL 시험을 준비하는 학습자를 위한 완벽한 준비 도구로서 실제 IBT시험을 치르는 것과 같은 full-length의 연습테스트를 제공합니다. 지난 시험들을 통해 철저히 분석된 문제들을 연습하게 되며 48시간 이내에 점수를 받아볼 수 있습니다.

시험을 마친 후 상세한 그래프와 함께 자신의 점수를 분석할 수 있습니다. 또한 자신이 풀었던 문제와 답뿐만 아니라 Reading, Listening, Speaking, Writing의 스크립트를 제공받아 철저한 복습이 가능합니다.
Final iBT는 토플 모의 시험으로써 토플 준비를 위한 완벽한 학습 자료가 될 것입니다.

## 시험 구성

: 시험 구성은 다음과 같습니다.

| Level | Test Version | Questions (문항) | | | |
|---|---|---|---|---|---|
| | | Reading | Listening | Speaking | Writing |
| 고급 | Full | 39~42 | 34 | 6 | 2 |
| | Short | 14~28 | 17 | 3 | 1 |
| | Half (R/L) | 39~42 | 34 | X | X |
| | Half (S/W) | X | X | 6 | 2 |
| 초급 | Short | 21~24 | 13 | 2 | 1 |

* 총 40회분의 시험이 제공됩니다.

http://www.finalibt.co.kr

PERFECT SOLUTION for **TOEFL Junior**

# iBT e TOEFL READING

**NEW EDITION**

## Answer Key

LinguaForum

# Answer Key

LinguaForum

# Chapter 1
# Reference and Words

## 01 _ Reference Questions

### Basic Drills    p.12

1. (B)   2. (D)   3. (A)   4. (D)   5. (C)
6. (B)

WORDS   p.12   vacation, nervous
        p.13   athlete, serious, forest

1. 호주에는 아름다운 해변들이 있다. 많은 사람들이 여름 휴가로 호주에 간다. 그 중 많은 사람들이 서퍼들이다. 호주의 해변에는 서핑하기에 매우 좋은 파도가 있다.

2. 빙벽 등반은 매우 위험한 운동이다. 빙벽 등반을 하는 사람들은 산의 경사면에 있는 거대한 얼음 벽을 타고 올라간다. 빙벽을 올라가려면 얼음도끼나 특수장화 등 특별한 장비가 필요하다. 하지만 날씨가 너무 따뜻해지면 얼음이 부서져 등산객들이 다칠 수도 있고 심지어 죽을 수도 있다.

3. 켈리는 내일 스페인어 수업에서 중요한 시험이 있다. 스페인어는 학교에서 그녀가 가장 어려워하는 과목이다. 그녀는 어젯밤에 세 시간 동안 공부를 했다. 그녀는 준비가 됐다고 생각하지만 여전히 초조하다.

4. 대부분의 프로 스포츠팀에는 전속 의사가 있다. 운동선수들은 시즌 중에 종종 가벼운 부상을 입는다. 이것이 심각한 부상이 되지 않도록 하는 것이 전속 의사의 임무이다.

5. 대부분의 공원에서 캠프파이어가 금지되어 있다. 캠프파이어로 인해 산불이 발생할 수 있기 때문이다. 캠프파이어를 할 때 아주 조심한다고 하더라도 바람에 의해서 작은 불씨가 숲으로 날아갈 수 있다. 이것이 산불을 일으킬 수 있다.

6. 잭이 가장 좋아하는 계절은 여름이다. 여름에는 항상 태양이 빛나고 날씨가 덥다. 잭은 여름이 일년 중 최고의 시기라고 생각한다.

## 02 _ Vocabulary Questions

### Basic Drills    p.15

1. (C)   2. (B)   3. (C)

WORDS   lift, sign, fault

1. 역도는 어려운 경기이다. 선수들에게는 역기를 들 수 있는 세 번의 시도가 주어진다. 세 번째까지 역기를 들지 못하면 경기에서 탈락하게 된다.

2. 스카이다이빙은 박진감이 넘친다. 몇 분 동안 새처럼 자유로운 기분을 느낄 수 있다. 그러나 스카이다이빙은 위험하기도 하다. 스카이다이빙을 하고 싶으면 우선 강의를 들어야 한다. 또한 스카이다이빙 회사는 당신에게 어떤 서류에 서명을 하도록 요구할 것이다. 그 서류에는 당신이 다치더라도 회사에는 책임이 없다는 내용이 들어있다. 이는 필수 조건이다. 이 서류에 서명을 하지 않으면 스카이다이빙을 할 수 없다.

3. 인터넷은 여러 면에서 매우 유용하다. 인터넷을 이용하여 정보를 검색하거나 친구와 채팅을 할 수 있다. 그 밖에도 인터넷을 통해 할 수 있는 일들은 많이 있다. 예를 들면, 인터넷으로 휴대폰 요금을 결제할 수 있다. 이것은 직접 지불하는 것보다 빠르고 쉽다.

## 03 _ Essential Term Questions

### Basic Drills    p.17

1. (C)   2. (C)

WORDS   popular, equipment, goal

1. 암벽등반은 여러 나라에서 크게 유행하고 있다. 암벽등반에는 여러 종류가 있다. 어떤 것은 초보자들도 할 수 있지만, 프리클라이밍은 전문가들만이 할 수 있다. 프리클라이밍은 암벽등반 중 가장 위험한 종목이다. 왜냐하면 프리클라이밍에는 두 번째 기회가 존재하지 않기 때문이다. 보통은 등반을 하다 떨어지면 밧줄이 당신을 지탱해 줄 것이다. 그러나 프리클라이밍에는 밧줄이나 안전장치가 없다.

2. 대부분의 국가에서 나이가 어린 범죄자들은 감옥에 가지

않는다. 대신 그들은 소년원에 간다. 소년원의 목적은 어린 범죄자들이 더 나은 사람이 되도록 가르치고 그들이 공동체의 규범을 따르도록 하는 것이다. 감독관과 담장이 있기는 하지만 소년원의 생활환경은 실제 감옥보다 훨씬 양호하다.

## Reading Practice ❶  p.18

1. (C)   2. (B)   3. (B)

### 황야의 전투

하이에나는 사자의 천적이다. 하이에나와 사자는 먹이를 얻기 위해 서로 경쟁해야 한다. 사자의 몸집이 더 크고 힘이 세다는 것을 고려하면 사자가 하이에나를 쉽게 이기리라고 생각할지 모르지만, 사실은 그렇게 간단하지 않다. 숫사자는 혼자서 다니지만 하이에나는 무리동물이다. 그들은 떼를 지어 사냥을 하고 싸우기 때문에 수적인 우위를 지닌다. 또한 하이에나는 매우 영리하다. 그들은 사자가 어떤 짐승을 죽일 때까지 기다렸다가 그것을 훔친다. 사자가 몇 마리의 하이에나와 싸우는 동안 다른 하이에나들은 먹이를 훔친다.

/ 해 / 설 /

1. "Male lions live alone"과 "hyenas are pack animals"가 "but"으로 연결되어 있는 것을 통해 "pack animals"라는 것이 "live alone"과 반대되는 개념임을 알 수 있다. 또한 이어지는 "They hunt and fight in teams"에서도 힌트를 얻을 수 있다.

2. "They"는 "lions"와 "hyenas"를 둘 다 받을 수 있지만 일반적으로 대명사는 바로 앞에 나온 명사를 받으며, 또 내용상으로 "hyenas"임을 알 수 있다.

3. "clever"의 뒷부분을 읽어보면 그 의미를 알 수 있다. 사자가 잡은 먹이를 교묘히 훔치는 하이에나의 모습에서 "clever"의 의미를 유추할 수 있다.

## Reading Practice ❷  p.19

1. (B)   2. (D)   3. (A)

### 스타를 찾아서

음반회사들은 항상 새로운 수퍼스타를 찾고 있지만, 제 2의 브리트니 스피어스나 저스틴 팀버레이크를 찾는 것은 쉬운 일이 아니다. 음반회사들은 헤드헌터를 고용하여 신인을 발굴한다. 헤드헌터들은 전 세계로 신인가수들을 찾아 다닌다 그들은 콘테스트에도 가고 소규모의 지방 콘서트에도 간다. 인재를 발견하면 그들은 그 사람을 음반회사로 데려간다. 음반회사는 그들에게 노래와 춤을 가르쳐서 수퍼스타가 되도록 준비시킨다. 물론 이러한 젊은 가수들이 모두 수퍼스타가 되는 것은 아니다. 하지만 그렇게 될 수 있는 단 한 명의 가수를 찾는 것이 헤드헌터의 몫이다.

/ 해 / 설 /

1. "Record companies hire head-hunters to find new musicians for them."이라는 문장을 올바로 해석하면 쉽게 답을 찾을 수 있다.

2. "record companies", "head-hunters", "new musicians" 모두 "them"으로 받을 수 있으므로 혼란스럽다. 문장을 정확히 해석하여 내용상 셋 중 어느 것을 가리키는지 판단한다.

3. 역시 문장을 해석하면 풀 수 있는 문제이다. 헤드헌터들이 어떤 사람을 찾아야 음반회사로 데려올 것인지 생각해 본다.

## Reading Practice ❸  p.20

1. (B)   2. (B)   3. (C)

### 꿈을 이루어주는 사람들

세상에는 불치병을 앓고 있는 어린이들이 많이 있다. 그런 아이들에게 주어진 시간은 많지 않다. 그들은 불과 몇 년 또는 몇 개월 동안만 살 수 있을지 모른다. Make-A-Wish 재단은 이런 아이들의 마지막 소원을 이루어줌으로써 그들을 돕고자 한다. 어떤 아이들은 특별한 장소에 가고 싶어하기도 하고, 유명한 사람을 만나고 싶어하기도 한다.

Make-A-Wish 재단은 크리스 그레시어스라는 어린 소년과 함께 시작되었다. 크리스는 경찰관이 되고 싶어했지만 많이 아팠다. 크리스가 죽기 전에 애리조나 경찰국 외에 여러 사람들이 그의 소원을 이루어 주기 위하여 열심히 노력했다. 그들은 크리스를 명예 경찰관으로 임명하고 그를 위한 특별한 제복을 만들어 주었다. 크리스는 그 후 얼마 안되어서 죽었지만, 죽기 전에 가장 큰 소원을 이룰 수 있었다.

/ 해 / 설 /

1. (C), (D)도 어느 정도 답에 근접하지만, 이 아이들이 몇 달 내지 몇 년밖에 살지 못한다는 것에서 "terminal illness"가 치료될 수 없는 병이라는 것을 짐작할 수 있다.

2. "They"는 앞에 나온 복수 명사를 받으므로 "children"과 "terminal illnesses"가 답이 될 수 있으나 내용상 사람을 가리키고 있으므로 "children"이 답이 된다.

3. 네 개의 보기를 "grant"의 자리에 넣어보고 가장 적절한 것을 찾는다.

## Reading Practice ❹ p.21

1. (C)  2. (B)  3. (C)

### 푸르고 깨끗한 도시를 위하여

당신이 사는 곳에는 나무가 얼마나 많이 있는가? 어떤 도시에는 나무가 거의 없다. 이것은 심각한 문제이다. 이렇게 되면 도시의 미관뿐 아니라 공기도 나빠진다. 나무는 산소를 배출하기 때문에 우리에게 필요하다. 나무가 거의 없는 도시는 공기가 매우 좋지 않다.

이 문제를 해결하기 위해 이제 많은 도시들은 녹지대를 만들고 있다. 녹지대는 거대한 공원 같은 것이다. 이 안에는 새로운 길이나 건물을 만들 수 없다. 보통 녹지대는 도시의 바로 외곽에 있다. 이로 인해 또 다른 문제가 발생한다. 도시는 확장할 공간이 필요한데 녹지대로는 뻗어나갈 수 없다. 도시가 성장하도록 하는 것과 충분한 수목을 확보하는 것 사이에 적절한 균형점을 찾는 것은 매우 어려운 일이다.

/ 해 / 설 /

1. "produce"의 자리에 보기들을 대입해 보고 가장 적절한 것을 선택한다.

2. 글을 끝까지 읽어본 후 답을 고르도록 한다. "The green zones are like giant parks."라는 문장만 보면 (A)를 답으로 고를 수 있다. 그러나 뒤를 보면 "green zones"는 도시 외곽(just outside of the city)에 위치한다. "No new roads or buildings can be built in them."을 읽어 보면 (B)가 "green zones"의 의미를 정확히 설명하고 있음을 알 수 있다.

3. 일반적으로 대명사는 바로 앞에 나온 주어를 가리키는 경우가 가장 많다. 앞 문장의 주어인 "The green zones"를 "them"의 자리에 넣어 보고 뜻이 통하는지 확인한다.

## iBT Practice ① p.22

1. (B)  2. (B)  3. (B)  4. (B)  5. (A)
6. C

### 우두머리 수컷(Alpha Males)

개를 기르는 사람들 중 대부분은 한 마리만 기르지만 본래 개는 집단생활을 하는 동물이다. 개는 야생에서 단체로 생활하며 사냥을 한다. 모든 무리동물처럼, 집단에 속한 어떤 개들(가장 몸집이 크고 힘이 센 개들)은 다른 개들보다 영향력이 있다. 다른 개들은 모두 이 개들을 따른다. 그들은 항상 수컷이고 우두머리 수컷(alpha male)이라 불린다. 모든 무리동물에는 싸움을 거쳐 선발된 우두머리 수컷이 있다. 보통 이 싸움은 다른 동물들에게 겁을 주는 정도이며 별로 폭력적이지 않다. 일단 우두머리 수컷이 선정되면 무리들은 그 수컷에게 무조건 복종한다.

어떤 면에서는 애완견도 야생 개들과 같다. 그들에게는 복종해야 할 우두머리 수컷이 필요하다. 개 주인은 개에게 강하고 엄격하게 대해야 한다. 강한 어조로 말하고 개의 눈을 똑바로 들여다보면 개에게 주인이 우두머리 수컷임을 보여주는 것이 된다. 그러나 만약 개가 자신을 우두머리 수컷이라고 생각한다면 통제하기가 매우 어려울 것이다.

/ 해 / 설 /

1. 문장에서 "alpha males"는 "they"이며, "they"는 앞 문장의 "these dogs"를, "these dogs"는 그 앞 문장의 "some dogs(the biggest and the strongest in the group)"을 가리키고 있다.

2. 6째 줄의 "All pack animals have alpha males, whom they choose through fights."에 나와 있다.

3. 문맥상으로는 (A), (B), (C) 모두 가능하나, "force"가 "violence"의 의미에 가장 가깝다.

4. 일반적으로 대명사는 바로 앞에 나온 주어를 가리키는 경우가 가장 많다. 앞 문장의 주어인 "pet dogs"를 넣어 뜻이 통하는지 확인한다.

5. 글의 마지막 문장을 통해, 개 주인이 강하고 엄격한 태도로 개를 대하지 않으면, 개가 자기 자신을 "alpha male"이라고 생각하게 됨을 알 수 있다.

6. "this fact"가 가리키는 것이 무엇인지 생각해 보고, 글의 흐름이 자연스럽게 되는 위치를 찾는다.

# *i*BT Practice ②  p.24

1. (A)　2. (C)　3. (B)　4. (D)　5. (B)
6. (C)

### 현대 의학의 아버지

기원전 430년경에 살았던 그리스인 의사 히포크라테스는 현대 의학의 아버지이다. 히포크라테스 이전에도 의사들이 있었지만 치료제와 인체에 대한 그의 견해는 그 시대 다른 의사들과 달랐다. 그 당시 사람들은 질병이 분노한 신이나 죽은 사람의 혼에 의해 발생하는 것이라고 생각했다. 그러나 히포크라테스는 모든 질병에는 자연적인 원인이 있다고 생각했다. 그는 또한 인체를 세부적으로 연구한 최초의 의사였다. 그는 연구를 통해 많은 질병을 규명했고, 인간의 생각이 뇌에서 나온다는 것을 최초로 주장한 의사이기도 하다. 그 전까지 사람들은 인간의 생각이나 느낌이 심장에서 나온다고 믿었다.

히포크라테스가 남긴 가장 큰 업적은 히포크라테스 선서이다. 히포크라테스는 환자에 대한 의사의 힘이 막강하다는 것을 알았다. 그는 일부 의사들이 자신의 권력을 부당하게 사용할 것을 염려했다. 그래서 그는 선서를 만들었다. 그 선서의 내용은 의사는 오로지 환자들을 돕는 일만을 하고 환자를 다치게 해서는 안 된다는 것이었다. 그는 모든 제자들이 이 선서를 하도록 했다. 오늘날에도 처음 의사가 되는 사람들은 히포크라테스 선서를 한다.

/ 해 / 설 /

1. 글의 내용에서 히포크라테스가 의사라는 것을 알 수 있다. 특히 3-4째 줄의 그가 동시대의 다른 의사들과는 달랐다는 말에서 확실히 드러난다.

2. 5째 줄의 "At the time, it was believed that diseases were caused by angry gods or spirits. Hippocrates, however,..." 부분에서 알 수 있다.

3. 히포크라테스가 많은 병을 규명(identify)했다는 것은 언급되어 있지만 그에 대한 치료법을 찾아냈다는 설명은 없다. '히포크라테스는 훌륭한 의사였으니까 치료법도 많이 발명했을 것이다'라는 식으로 넘겨짚지 않도록 한다. 지문에 그런 내용이 나와 있는지를 반드시 확인해야 한다.

4. 16째 줄의 "It said that doctors would only work to help their patients, never to hurt them."에서 알 수 있다.

5. 14-15째 줄의 "He worried that some doctors would not use this power properly."라는 문장에서 알 수 있다.

6. "only work to help their patients, never to hurt them"은 병렬구조로 되어 있으므로, "their patients"와 "them"은 같은 것이어야 한다.

## *Word* Review  p.26

1. (C)　2. (B)　3. (B)　4. (C)　5. (A)
6. (C)　7. (A)　8. (B)

## *Sentence* Review  p.27

1. (B)　2. (C)　3. (B)　4. (A)　5. (C)

# Chapter 2
# Fact and Negative Fact

## 04 _ Factual Information Questions

### Basic Drills 1   p.32

1. (B)   2. (C)

**WORDS**  damage, destroy, environment, celebrate

1. 지진은 항상 위험하지만 해저에서 발생하는 지진은 매우 위험할 수 있다. 해저에서 지진이 발생하면 거대한 파도, 즉 쓰나미가 생성될 수 있다. 쓰나미의 파도는 매우 높아서 때로는 30미터 높이에까지 이를 수 있다. 쓰나미가 육지를 강타하면 많은 피해가 발생한다. 바닷물이 나무와 건물 등, 진행 방향에 있는 모든 것을 파괴한다.

2. 3월 21일이 무슨 날인지 알고 있는가? 바로 지구의 날이다. 지구의 날은 사람들이 환경 문제에 관심을 갖도록 하기 위해 존 맥코넬이 1970년에 시작한 것이다. 지구의 날은 샌프란시스코에서 시작되었지만 오늘날에는 전 세계의 나라에서 그날을 기념한다.

### Basic Drills 2   p.33

1. (C)   2. (B)   3. (C)   4. (B)   5. (B)

**WORDS**  modern, ancestor(s), culture, traditional, pollution

이 세상의 대부분의 사람들이 현대적인 생활을 한다. 그들은 자동차를 운전하고, 사무실에서 일을 한다. 그들의 생활은 조상들의 생활과 전혀 다르다. 그러나 현대적인 삶을 살지 않는 사람들도 있다. 그들은 고유의 문화와 생활 양식을 보존하기 위해 그들의 조상들처럼 살아간다.

이뉴잇은 그 좋은 예이다. 이뉴잇은 캐나다 가장 북부 지역과 그린란드 일부 지역에서 생활한다. 대부분의 이뉴잇은 작은 공동체를 이루어 살아가며 사냥과 어업을 통해 생활을 꾸려나간다. 또 다른 예로 호주의 애보리진을 들 수 있다. 애보리진은 수천 년 전에 살던 조상들과 흡사한 생활을 한다. 그들은 조상들이 살던 것과 같은 종류의 집에서 살고, 또 같은 방식으로 사냥을 한다.

하지만 이뉴잇과 애보리진의 생활 방식은 위험에 처해 있다. 여기에는 여러 가지 원인이 있다. 가장 큰 이유는 젊은 이뉴잇과 애보리진이 더 이상 전통적인 생활 방식대로 살고 싶어 하지 않기 때문일 것이다. 젊은 사람들이 현대적인 도시로 떠나면 전통적 생활방식을 이어나갈 사람이 없어진다. 공해 역시 이들의 생활방식을 위협하는 요소이다. 대부분의 전통적인 원주민들은 사냥으로 생계를 꾸려나가는데, 공해로 인해 충분한 동물을 사냥하기가 어렵다. 매우 안타까운 일이지만 몇 년 후에는 세계 어느 곳에도 전통문화가 남아있지 않을지도 모른다.

### Basic Drills 3   p.35

1. (B)   2. (B)   3. (C)   4. (A)   5. (B)

**WORDS**  spread, mix, attack (destroy도 가능)

꿀벌은 매우 유용한 곤충이다. 그들은 꿀을 만들고 꽃가루를 퍼뜨림으로써 식물의 성장을 돕는다. 하지만 모든 벌이 그렇게 유용한 것은 아니다. 사실 어떤 벌들은 매우 위험하다. 살인벌은 남미와 미국 남부에 서식한다. 그들은 새로운 종류의 벌이다. 1950년대에 과학자들은 벌이 더 많은 꿀을 생산하도록 만들고자 했다. 그들은 일반 꿀벌과 아프리카 꿀벌을 교배하였다. 그렇지만 새로운 벌은 매우 위험했다. 그들은 쉽게 흥분했고 집단으로 공격했다. 이러한 살인벌들은 일반 벌들보다 독성이 강하지는 않지만 대규모 공격을 하기 때문에 쉽게 사람을 죽일 수 있다.

살인벌은 사람들을 쏘는 것 외에도 많은 문제를 일으킨다. 가장 큰 문제는 그들이 양봉 회사들에게 손해를 끼친다는 것이다. 살인벌은 일반 벌보다 훨씬 적은 양의 꿀을 만들고 길들이기도 훨씬 어렵다. 살인벌이 새로운 지역으로 이동하면 그 지역의 양봉 산업을 파괴시킬 수 있다. 또한 살인벌들은 일반 벌보다 꽃가루를 많이 옮기지 못하기 때문에 농부들에게도 좋지 않다.

## 05 _ Negative Fact Questions

### Basic Drills    p.38

> 1. (A)　2. (B)　3. (C)　4. (A)　5. (C)
> 6. (A)
> ---
> WORDS　p.38　plan, spend, grade
> 　　　　　p.39　pet, healthy, strange, past
> 　　　　　p.40　law, copy, join, energy

1. 마커스는 올해 플로리다로 휴가를 간다. 플로리다는 매우 덥다. 그래서 마커스는 긴 바지는 가져가지 않고 짧은 바지만 가져갈 것이다. 마커스는 또 해변에서 많은 시간을 보낼 계획이다. 그래서 그는 자외선 차단제와 모자를 가지고 갈 것이다. 햇볕에 타고 싶지 않기 때문이다. 그는 또 애완견 맥스도 데리고 갈 것이다. 그는 맥스를 굉장히 사랑하기 때문에 어디든지 데리고 다닌다.

2. 자레드는 오늘 정말 바빴다. 먼저 중요한 수학 시험이 있었다. 그는 전날 밤 많이 공부했기 때문에 좋은 점수를 얻었다. 또 방과 후에는 야구경기를 했다. 비록 그의 팀이 이기지는 못했지만 자레드는 좋은 플레이를 했다. 그리고 나서 그는 여자친구를 만나 저녁을 먹었다. 그들은 영화도 보러 갔다. 자레드는 집에 돌아와서 숙제를 했다. 이제 그는 잠을 잘 것이다. 정말로 긴 하루였다.

3. 대부분의 사람들은 애완동물을 좋아한다. 애완동물이 실제로 사람을 건강하게 한다는 사실을 알고 있는가? 이상하게 들리겠지만 사실이다. 과학자들은 고양이나 개를 하루에 15분씩 돌보면 더 건강해지고 행복해진다는 것을 알아냈다. 게다가 애완동물이 있으면 밖에 나가 운동할 일이 더 많아진다. 애완동물을 데리고 나가 놀아주기 때문이다. 그러니 건강해지고 싶다면 애완동물을 키워보자.

4. 밤하늘을 올려다보면 많은 별들을 볼 수 있다. 사실 어떤 의미에서 당신은 과거를 보는 것이다. 당신이 보고 있는 빛은 수백만 년 전에 그 별을 떠났을지도 모른다. 가장 가까운 별들조차도 사실은 굉장히 멀리 떨어져 있다. 그 별들의 빛이 지구에 도달하려면 많은 시간이 걸린다. 가장 가까운 별인 켄타우루스 자리의 알파 별의 빛이 지구에 도달하는 데에만 4년이 걸린다. 어떤 별은 너무 멀어서 빛이 그 별을 떠났을 때 지구는 존재하지도 않았다.

5. 수천 년 전에는 국가가 없었다. 하지만 도시는 있었다. 최초의 도시는 어떤 면에서 국가와 비슷했다. 각각의 도시에는 고유의 군대와 왕이 있었다. 바빌론은 이러한 초기 도시들 중 하나였다. 바빌론은 법률이 있었던 최초의 도시로 유명하다. 바빌론의 왕 함무라비는 세계 최초로 법을 제정했다. 함무라비의 법을 어긴 것에 대한 벌은 대체로 사형이었다. 곧 다른 도시들은 바빌론의 법을 모방하거나 자기들만의 법을 만들었다.

6. 당신은 수영을 좋아하는가? 추운 날씨를 좋아하는가? 그렇다면 아마 당신은 '북극곰 클럽'에 가입해야 할 것이다. 북극곰 클럽에서 사람들은 겨울에 호수나 강으로 수영을 가는데 이때 물은 매우 차가워서 때때로 빙점보다 겨우 몇 도 높은 정도이다. 북극곰 클럽의 사람들은 차가운 물 속에서 한 번에 몇 분 동안만 수영을 할 수 있다. 더 오래 수영하면 아프거나 죽을 수도 있다. 사람들은 차가운 물이 그들에게 에너지를 준다고 믿기 때문에 북극곰 클럽에 가입한다.

### Reading Practice ❶    p.41

> 1. (B)　2. (B)　3. (B)
> ---
> **창공의 왕**
>
> 　오늘날 가장 큰 여객기는 에어버스 A380이다. A380은 5백 명 이상의 승객을 수용할 수 있으며 멈추지 않고 전 세계의 절반 가량을 여행할 수 있다. A380의 길이는 73미터이고 날개의 폭은 80미터이다. A380의 제작자가 이렇게 큰 비행기를 만든 이유는 한 가지이다. 항공사에게 있어서 더 많은 승객은 곧 더 많은 수입을 뜻한다. A380은 다른 어떤 비행기보다도 많은 승객을 태울 수 있기 때문에 더 많은 수입을 창출할 수 있는 것이다. 그러나 A380에는 한 가지 문제점이 있다. A380의 크기 때문에 몇몇 공항에는 착륙할 수가 없다는 것이다. 하지만 에어버스 제작자들은 대부분의 공항이 A380에 맞추어 개조될 것이라고 생각한다.

/ 해 / 설 /

1. 1-2째 줄의 "The A380 holds over five hundred passengers"에서 A380은 500명이 넘는 인원을 수용한다고 나와 있으므로, (B)의 "exactly five hundred passengers"는 잘못된 것이다.

2. "more passengers equal more money for the airline"의 뜻을 이해하면 답을 찾을 수 있다.

3. "However, the A380 does have one problem." 문장 이하에 설명되어 있다.

## Reading Practice ❷    p.42

1. (A)    2. (C)    3. (B)

### 수많은 언어들

많은 나라에서 하나 이상의 언어가 사용된다. 예를 들어 스페인어는 영어와 함께 미국에서 일반적으로 쓰이는 말이다. 많은 유럽 사람들은 독일어와 프랑스어 등 몇 가지 언어를 구사한다. 어떤 나라가 세계에서 가장 많은 언어를 사용하는지 알고 있는가? 파푸아뉴기니 섬에서는 700가지 이상의 언어가 사용된다! 이는 전 세계 언어의 25%를 넘는 수치이다. 왜 한 나라에서 이렇게 많은 언어를 쓰는 것일까? 파푸아뉴기니는 수많은 작은 부족들로 구성되어 있는데 각각의 부족은 고유의 언어를 갖고 있다. 게다가 그 나라에는 높은 산들이 많이 있다. 사람들은 산을 자주 넘어 다니지 않았기 때문에 여러 해 동안 다른 부족 사람들끼리 서로 자주 보지 못했다. 그 결과 그들의 언어가 섞일 기회가 없었다.

/ 해 / 설 /

1. 1-2째 줄의 "For example, Spanish is common in the United States in addition to English."에 나와 있다.

2. 올바른 paraphrase를 고를 수 있는가를 평가하는 문제이다. 지문에서 파푸아 뉴기니의 언어 수에 대해 "This is more than 25% of all the languages in the world."라고 말한 문장의 올바른 paraphrase는 (A)이다. (C)는 파푸아 뉴기니가 세계의 나머지 지역보다 25% 더 많은 언어를 갖고 있다는 뜻이므로 의미가 다르다.

3. 글의 마지막 부분에 그 이유가 설명되어 있다.

## Reading Practice ❸    p.43

1. (D)    2. (B)    3. (A)

### 사랑의 노작

인도의 타지마할은 세계에서 가장 아름다운 건축물 중 하나이다. 타지마할의 탄생 이면에 있는 이야기 또한 아름답다. 1612년, 인도의 왕 샤 자한은 아름다운 젊은 여인과 결혼을 했다. 두 번째 결혼이었지만 그는 진심으로 부인을 사랑했다. 그 후 18년 동안 샤 자한과 그의 아내 뭄타즈 마할은 어디든지 함께 여행을 다녔다. 안타깝게도 뭄타즈는 1630년에 열네 번째 아이를 낳고 숨졌다. 샤 자한은 아내를 위해 세상에서 가장 아름다운 무덤을 만들기로 결심했다. 2만 2천 명의 일꾼을 데리고도 작업에 22년 이상이 소요되었다. 1653년에 샤 자한은 마침내 아내의 무덤을 완성했다. 그것은 세상에서 가장 아름다운 건축물이자 아내를 향한 샤의 사랑의 상징이었다.

/ 해 / 설 /

1. 글에 여러 연도가 나오기 때문에 혼란스러울 수 있으나, 그 중에서 타지 마할이 완성된 연도는 7-8째 줄의 "Finally, in 1653, Shah Jahan completed his wife's tomb."에 나온다.

2. 5-6째 줄의 "Sadly, Mumtaz died after having her 14th child in 1630."에 나와 있다.

3. 타지 마할은 왕이 죽은 부인을 위해 지은 묘이다.

## Reading Practice ❹    p.44

1. (A)    2. (B)    3. (C)

### 평화 안에서 하나된 세계

국제연합은 세계 각국의 문제들을 해결하고 전쟁을 막기 위해 협력하는 각국 정부의 모임이다. 때로는 국제연합이 성공적인 역할을 하지만 때로는 그렇지 않다. 국제연합과 비슷한 국제연맹이라는 단체가 있었다. 미국의 대통령 우드로 윌슨은 1차 세계대전 후 또 다른 대규모 살상 전쟁이 발생하지 않도록 하기 위해 국제연맹을 설립했다. 그는 세계가 전쟁 없이 문제를 해결할 방법이 필요하다는 것을 알았다. 불행하게도 국제연맹은 거의 힘이 없었다. 회원국들은 종종 규칙을 어겼고, 국제연맹은 다음 전쟁인 2차 세계대전을 막지 못했다. 2차 세계대전 후 세계는 국제연맹을 없애고 국제연합을 창설했다.

/ 해 / 설 /

1. 첫 번째 문장에 유엔의 목적이 제시되어 있다.

2. 4-5째 줄의 "U.S. President Woodrow Wilson started the League of Nations after World War I"에 나와 있다.

3. 8째 줄의 "Its members often broke its rules, and it did

not stop the next big war"에서 국제연맹은 전쟁 방지에 실패했음을 알 수 있다.

## iBT Practice 1
p.45

1. (B)  2. (B)  3. (B)  4. (A)  5. (C)
6. **A**

### 산호초

대부분의 대륙 연안과 섬 주변에서 발견되는 산호초는 해양 환경을 구성하는 중요한 부분이다. 산호초는 사실 생물이다. 폴립이라는 작은 생물은 몸 주변에 단단한 껍질을 만든다. 폴립이 죽으면 그 껍질이 남고 새로운 폴립이 오래된 껍질 위에 자신의 껍질을 만든다. 수천 년에 걸쳐 폴립은 산호초를 만든다.

산호초는 여러 이유에서 중요하다. 산호초는 25%의 해양 생물에게 살아갈 환경을 제공한다. 작은 물고기들은 몸을 숨기기 위해 산호초로 모인다. 그들은 또 산호초 속의 식물을 먹는다. 산호초는 작은 물고기들을 먹는 큰 물고기들에게 사냥터 역할을 한다. 산호초는 해변을 보호하는 데에도 중요한 역할을 한다. 산호초는 파도의 힘을 완화시켜 파도를 작게 만든다. 산호초가 없다면 파도는 섬을 망가뜨릴 수 있다.

전 세계의 많은 산호초들이 사람들 때문에 위험에 처해 있다. 공해, 지나친 조업, 그리고 너무 많은 배가 산호초를 파괴한다. 우리는 산호초를 보호하기 위해 더 열심히 노력해야 한다, 새로운 산호초가 만들어지려면 수천 년이 걸리기 때문이다.

/ 해 / 설 /

1. 첫 번째 단락의 후반부에 산호초가 만들어지는 과정이 설명되어 있다.

2. 일반적으로 대명사는 바로 앞에 나온 주어를 가리키는 경우가 가장 많다. 앞 문장의 주어인 "polyps"를 "they"의 자리에 넣어 보고 뜻이 통하는지 확인한다.

3. 8-9째 줄의 "They provide a home for about 25% of all the life in the ocean."에서 알 수 있다.

4. 마지막 단락에 해당되는 내용이다. (B), (C), (D)는 모두 산호초를 없애는 원인으로 나와 있으나 (A)는 언급되어 있지 않다. 17째 줄의 "Many reefs around the world are in danger because of people."의 의미는 사람들(의 활동) 때문에 산호초가 위기에 처해 있다는 것이지, 사람이 너무 많아서 그렇다는 의미가 아님에 주의한다.

5. 산호초를 보호하도록 노력해야 한다는 말에서 "replace"의 의미가 무엇일지 유추해 본다.

6. "these fish"가 가리키는 것이 무엇인지 생각해 보고 "food"에 대한 내용이 나오는 부분을 찾아본다.

## iBT Practice 2
p.47

1. (A)  2. (C)  3. (B)  4. (B)  5. (B)
6. **B**

### 루이스와 클락의 대탐험

1803년 프랑스 정부는 미대륙에 있는 프랑스 영토를 미국 정부에 팔았다. 매우 큰 면적의 땅이었고 천5백만 달러를 약간 넘는 가격도 훌륭했다. 미국인들에게는 단 한 가지 문제가 있었다. 그들은 구입한 땅에 대해 거의 아는 것이 없었다. 제퍼슨 대통령은 재빨리 두 명의 탐험가, 메리웨더 루이스와 윌리엄 클락을 찾아서 신대륙을 탐험하도록 했다.

어렵고 위험한 여행이었지만 루이스와 클락은 전문 탐험가들이었다. 그들은 출발하기 전에 몇 개월에 걸쳐 계획을 세웠다. 그들의 임무에서 중요했던 것 중 하나는 새로운 영토에 살고 있는 원주민 부족들과 친구가 되는 것이었다. 그래서 그들은 많은 선물을 가져갔다. 루이스와 클락은 1804년에 출발했다. 그들은 대부분 강을 통해 여행했다. 하지만 서부의 록키 산맥에 다다르자 그것은 불가능해졌다.

루이스와 클락은 마침내 태평양에 다다랐다. 오랜 여행 동안 그들은 여러 놀라운 광경을 보았고 많은 어려움을 헤쳐나갔다. 하지만 그들의 여행은 시작에 불과했다. 두 사람의 여행은 많은 미국인들의 흥미를 끌었다. 곧 수천 명의 사람들이 부와 모험을 찾아 서부로 떠났다.

/ 해 / 설 /

1. 7째 줄에서 루이스와 클락을 보낸 이유가 "to explore the new land"라고 나와 있다. 만약 "explore"의 의미를 모르더라도, 그 앞 문장인 "They knew almost nothing about the land they had just bought."을 보면 땅을 조사하기 위해 그들을 보낸 것임을 짐작알 수 있다.

2. 보기 중 "They"의 앞에 나온 복수 명사는 "The Americans" 뿐이다.

3. 10-11째 줄의 "An important part of their job was to become friends with the Native American tribes... so they took many gifts with them."이라는 문장에 설명되어 있다.

4. 문맥상으로는 (A), (B), (D) 모두 뜻이 통하나 가장 적합한 것은 (B)이다.

5. 마지막 단락에 설명되어 있다.

6. 우선 "the mountains"가 가리키는 산이 앞에 나와야 하므로 록키 산맥이 언급되어 있는 (B)에 넣어 본다. 그러면 산이 너무 높아서 강으로 여행할 수 없었다는 뜻이 되므로 자연스럽다.

## Word Review p.49

1. (B)  2. (C)  3. (A)  4. (C)  5. (C)
6. (B)  7. (A)  8. (A)

## Sentence Review p.50

1. (C)  2. (B)  3. (C)  4. (C)  5. (B)

# Chapter 3
# Sentence Simplification

## 06 _ Sentence Simplification Questions

### Basic Drills 1 p.56

1. (C)  2. (B)  3. (B)  4. (C)

### Basic Drills 2 p.57

1. (C)  2. (B)  3. (A)  4. (C)  5. (B)

### Basic Drills 3 p.58

1. (C)  2. (B)  3. (B)  4. (C)  5. (A)

### Basic Drills 4 p.59

1. (B)  2. (C)  3. (B)  4. (B)

### Reading Practice ❶ p.60

1. (A)  2. (C)

#### 로봇 기수

사우디아라비아나 아랍에미리트를 비롯한 많은 중동 지역에서 낙타 경주는 매우 인기 있는 스포츠이다. 대부분의 낙타 경주에서 경주자, 즉 기수는 어린이인데, 이는 낙타가 어른을 태우고 달리는 것보다 어린이를 태우고 달릴 때 더 빠르기 때문이다. 불행히도 낙타 경주는 매우 위험하기도 하다. 해마다 어린이 기수들이 낙타 경주에서 부상을 당하며 어떤 경우에는 매우 심한 부상을 입는다.

하지만 머지않아 상황은 달라질 것이다. 과학자들은 낙타에 태울 로봇 기수를 만들고 있다. 로봇은 어린이만큼 작고 가볍고, 리모컨으로 조종할 수 있다. 향후 몇 년간 대부분의 중동 국가는 로봇 기수를 사용하는 쪽으로 방향을 전환할 것이다. 이렇게 하면 더 이상 아이들을 위험하게 하지 않으면서 경기를 즐길 수 있다.

/ 해 / 설 /

1. (A): 낙타가 어른을 실었을 때보다 아이를 실었을 때 빨리 달릴 수 있는 것은 아이가 몸집이 작기 때문이므로, 아이를 "a smaller person"으로 바꾼 것은 올바른 paraphrase이다.
   (B): 지문에서는 대부분의 경우에 기수가 아이들이라고 했지, 어른은 기수가 될 수 없다고는 하지 않았다.
   (C): 아이들이 어른보다 빠른 것이 아니라 아이들을 태운 낙타가 빠른 것이다.
   (D): 원래 문장의 의미를 왜곡하지는 않았지만, 부분적인 내용만 담고 있다.

2. (A): 로봇은 아이들만큼 작고 빠르다고 했지 아이들보다 작고 빠른 것은 아니다.
   (B): 아이들이 로봇을 조종하는 것이 아니므로 잘못된 paraphrase이다.
   (C): 문장의 순서가 바뀌어 있지만 같은 내용을 전달하고 있으므로 올바른 paraphrase이다.
   (D): 부분적인 정보만 담고 있다.

## Reading Practice ❷     p.61

1. (C)    2. (B)

### 벌레들아, 조심해!

대부분의 식물은 토양과 태양으로부터 양분을 섭취한다. 그들은 우리와 같이 '먹는' 행위를 하지 않는다. 하지만 어떤 식물들은 우리처럼 먹이를 먹는다. 끈끈이주걱은 곤충을 먹는다. 이 식물은 자잘한 털이 달린 크고 벌어진 잎을 갖고 있다.

곤충이 털을 건드리면 끈끈이주걱은 그 위에 곤충이 있다는 것을 알아차리고 곤충 주변의 잎을 닫아버린다. 곤충이 안에 갇히면 끈끈이주걱은 곤충을 먹기 시작한다. 끈끈이주걱에는 입이 없기 때문에 먹는 데 일주일이 걸린다. 대신 끈끈이주걱은 산성 물질을 이용해 곤충을 녹인다. 끈끈이주걱은 주로 척박한 토양에 살기 때문에 땅으로부터 양분을 취하기 어려워서 곤충을 먹어야 한다.

/ 해 / 설 /

1. (A): 원래 문장의 뒷부분인 "and the leaf closes…"의 내용이 빠져 있으므로 불완전한 paraphrase이다.
   (B): 털은 곤충에 있는 것이 아니라 끈끈이주걱에 있는 것이므로 잘못된 paraphrase이다.
   (C): 문장의 순서가 바뀌어 있지만 같은 내용을 전달하고 있으므로 올바른 paraphrase이다.
   (D): (B)와 마찬가지로 원문의 의미를 왜곡시킨 잘못된 paraphrase이다.

2. (A): 원문의 내용은 끈끈이주걱이 척박한 땅에 살고 있다는 것이지, 척박한 땅에 사는 곤충을 잡아먹는 것이 아니므로 잘못된 paraphrase이다.
   (B): 문장의 순서가 바뀌어 있지만 같은 내용을 전달하고 있으므로 올바른 paraphrase이다.
   (C): 원문의 because 대신 when이 쓰여 원문과 의미가 달라졌다. When과 같은 의미로 쓰일 수 있는 접속사는 as, while, if 등이 있다.
   (D): (B)가 없다면 답일 수 있으나 (B)에 비해 부분적인 정보만을 담고 있다.

## Reading Practice ❸     p.62

1. (A)    2. (C)

### 벤자민 프랭클린

초기 미국 역사에서 가장 유명한 사람 중 하나로 벤자민 프랭클린을 꼽을 수 있다. 프랭클린은 재주가 많은 사람이었다. 그는 인쇄업자로 출발했다. 처음에 그는 작은 인쇄소 하나를 갖고 있었지만, 그의 성실함과 재능으로 가게는 급속히 성장했다. 프랭클린이 43살이 되었을 때 그는 부자였다. 더 이상 돈이 필요하지 않았던 그는 은퇴를 했지만 일을 멈추지 않았다. 그는 여러 해 동안 과학자이자 발명가로 일하면서 많은 중요한 발명을 했다.

하지만 프랭클린의 가장 중요한 업적은 식민지 미국이 영국의 식민지배에 염증을 느끼던 1770년대에 이루어졌다. 프랭클린은 이주민들에게 커다란 영향력을 갖고 있던 지도자였다. 그는 독립선언문의 작성을 도왔다. 독립혁명 기간 동안 그는 대부분의 시간을 프랑스에서 보내며 프랑스가 전쟁에서 미국을 돕도록 설득했다.

/ 해 / 설 /

1. (A): "At first" 대신 "To begin with", "it quickly grew" 대신 "it got bigger"가 쓰이는 등 표현이 다르지만 의미

는 같으므로 올바른 paraphrase이다.
- (B): "his hard work and intelligence"가 커진 것이 아니라 사업이 커진 것이므로 잘못된 paraphrase이다.
- (C): 부분적인 내용만을 담고 있다. 사업이 번창했다는 내용이 빠져 있다.
- (D): 원문과 전혀 다른 내용이다.

2. (A): 1770년대에 프랭클린이 일을 했다는 것이 아니라 그의 가장 중요한 업적이 그때 이루어졌다는 것이므로 의미가 다르다.
- (B): 원문의 when 대신 because를 씀으로써 의미가 왜곡되었다.
- (C): 원문의 의미를 요약해서 전달하고 있는 올바른 paraphrase이다.
- (D): 문장 뒷부분의 의미가 원문과 다르므로 올바른 paraphrase가 아니다.

## Reading Practice ❹    p.63

1. (B)    2. (D)

### 신비의 묘석

영국 남부의 윌트셔에는 세계의 가장 큰 불가사의 중 하나가 있다. 그것은 거대한 돌들이 원형으로 놓여있는 것으로 스톤헨지라고 불린다. 스톤헨지가 기원전 2900년에서 기원전 1600년 사이에 만들어졌다는 것 외에 우리가 알고 있는 것은 별로 없다.

스톤헨지에는 거대한 돌덩이들이 있는데 그 중 어떤 것들은 무게가 50톤 가까이 나간다. 스톤헨지를 만든 사람들은 어떻게 이토록 거대한 돌덩이들을 옮길 수 있었을까? 놀라운 점은 그 돌들이 그 주변에 있던 것이 아니라 수 마일 떨어진 곳에서 가져온 것이라는 사실이다. 또 한 가지 놀라운 점은 그 돌들이 특별한 위치에 놓여있다는 것이다. 일년 중 하지나 동지가 되면 태양은 특별한 방법으로 그 돌들을 비춘다. 이 때문에 과학자들은 스톤헨지가 달력의 일종으로 사용되지 않았을까 생각한다.

/ 해 / 설 /

1. (A): 내용을 지나치게 단순화시켰다.
- (B): 문장 구조가 바뀌어 있지만 같은 내용을 전달하므로 올바른 paraphrase이다.
- (C): 스톤헨지의 돌이 신비로운 것이 아니라, 그 돌이 멀리서 옮겨왔다는 사실이 신비로운 것이므로 의미가 다르다.
- (D): (B)가 없다면 정답이 될 수 있으나 (B)에 비해서 원문의 내용이 많이 축소되어 있다.

2. (A): 원문에서는 여름 중 가장 긴 날과 겨울 중 가장 짧은 날을 언급하고 있으나 여기서는 "여름과 겨울의 가장 긴 날"이라고 했으므로 잘못된 paraphrase이다.
- (B): "여름과 겨울"이라고만 언급했으므로 잘못된 paraphrase이다.
- (C): 마찬가지로 "긴 여름날과 겨울날"이라고 되어 있으므로 불충분하다.
- (D): 원문의 "hits"가 "shines on"으로 바뀌었을 뿐 나머지는 동일한 문장이므로 올바른 paraphrase이다.

## iBT Practice ①    p.64

1. (B)    2. (C)    3. (C)    4. (A)    5. (C)

### 투탕카멘의 저주

파라오 투탕카멘 혹은 투트왕은 아마 이집트의 파라오 중에서 가장 유명할 것이다. 이것에는 여러 가지 이유가 있는데 첫째로 투탕카멘은 이집트가 가장 강성했을 때의 파라오였다. 또 다른 이유는 그의 무덤에 많은 금은보화가 묻혀 있었기 때문이다. 아마도 이집트의 어떤 다른 파라오 보다도 많은 보물이 묻혀 있었을 것이다. 하지만 투트왕을 유명하게 만든 가장 흥미로운 이유는 그의 저주일 것이다.

그가 죽자 이집트 사람들은 다른 파라오들처럼 투탕카멘을 미라로 만들고 무덤을 금은보화로 채웠다. 그리고 그들은 무덤을 봉인했다. 일부의 이야기에 따르면 이집트인들은 사람들이 무덤 안의 금은보화를 훔쳐가지 못하게 하기 위해 무덤에 저주를 걸었다고 한다. 1922년, 영국인 카나본 경은 투트왕의 무덤을 발견하고 안으로 들어가 금은보화를 가지고 나왔다. 며칠 후, 카나본경은 갑자기 죽었다.

투트왕의 저주 탓이었을까? 많은 사람들은 그렇다고 생각했다. 하지만 오늘날 우리는 투트왕의 무덤에 대해 더 많이 알고 있고, 저주 이야기는 더 이상 그럴듯한 이야기가 아니다. 투트왕의 무덤은 수천 년이나 되었고 그 안의 공기는 매우 나빴다. 그 안의 먼지에는 위험한 세균이 있었고 아마 그 때문에 카나본 경이 병에 걸렸을 것이다. 하지만 여전히 많은 사람들이 투트왕의 저주를 믿는다.

/ 해 / 설 /

1. 지문을 읽어보면 투탕카멘이 이집트의 왕이었음을 알 수 있으며, 첫째 줄에도 "King Tut"이라고 되어 있다.

2. 2-3째 줄의 "There are several reasons for this." 뒷 부분을 보면 투탕카멘이 유명한 이유가 세 가지로 제시되어 있다.

3. 일반적으로는 대명사는 앞에 나온 말을 가리키나, 간혹 뒤에 나오는 말을 받기도 하는데 이것이 그러한 경우이다. 여기서 "their"는 문장 내의 주어인 "Egyptians"를 지칭한다.

4. (A): 표현은 다르지만 같은 뜻을 전달하고 있는 올바른 paraphrase이다.
   (B): 원문의 내용은 사람들이 보물을 가져가지 못하도록 하기 위해 저주를 했다는 것인데, 이 문장에서는 사람들이 보물을 가져가면 저주했다는 것이므로 의미가 다르다.
   (C): "사람들을 무덤 속에 가두기 위해서"라는 것은 원문과 의미가 전혀 다르다.
   (D): 원문의 key word인 저주 이야기가 빠져 있으므로 불완전한 paraphrase이다.

5. 20-21째 줄의 "The dust inside held dangerous germs, and they were probably what made Lord Carnarvon sick."에서 글쓴이의 견해를 알 수 있다.

## iBT Practice 2    p.66

1. (A)   2. (C)   3. (A)   4. (C)   5. (B)

**소몰이 축제**

매년 스페인의 도시 팜플로나에서 젊은 남자들은 매우 특이하고 위험한 행위를 한다. 그들은 황소들을 거리에 풀어놓고 그 앞에서 달린다. 그들은 왜 이렇게 위험한 짓을 하는 것일까? 이것은 '소몰이 축제(the Running of the Bulls)'로 팜플로나 지방의 전통이다. 소몰이 축제는 산 페르민 축제(La Fiesta de San Fermin)의 일부이다. 이 축제는 1952년에 시작되었고 투우는 축제의 일부였다. 그런데 팜플로나의 사람들은 황소를 마구간에서 반 마일 이상 떨어진 경기장으로 옮겨야 했다. 그래서 매년 용감한 젊은 남자들이 황소들 앞에 서게 되었다. 황소들은 경기장으로 달려가는 젊은이들을 쫓아갔다. 그들은 이런 방법으로 투우경기에 쓸 소들을 경기장으로 데려갔던 것이다.

시간이 지나면서 소몰이 축제는 유명해졌다. 소몰이 축제는 남자들이 자신의 용기를 시험하는 방법이었다. 황소와 달리기 위해서 스페인 각지로부터 사람들이 모여들었고, 점차 유럽의 다른 지방에서, 심지어는 미대륙에서도 사람들이 오기 시작했다. 소몰이 축제는 매우 위험해서 매년 사람들이 다치거나 심지어 죽기도 한다. 비록 위험하기는 해도 소몰이 축제의 인기는 대단하다. 황소와 함께 달릴 기회는 누구에게나 있다. 그렇지만 굉장히 빨리 달려야 할 것이다.

/ 해 / 설 /

1. 글의 맨 처음에 "Each year"라고 나와 있다.

2. "festival"의 뜻은 "축제"이지만 보통 축제기간에는 사람들이 일을 하지 않으므로 "holiday"와 의미가 통한다고 볼 수 있다.

3. 17-18째 줄의 "Running with the bulls is very dangerous. ... and sometimes people even die."에서 사람이 죽기도 한다고 언급되어 있다.

4. 일반적으로 대명사는 바로 앞에 나온 주어를 가리키는 경우가 가장 많다. 앞 문장의 주어인 "the Running of the Bulls"를 대입해 본다.

5. (A): (B)가 없으면 답이 될 수 있지만, 부상당하는 내용이 빠져 있어 정확한 paraphrase는 아니다.
   (B): 표현은 다르지만 같은 내용을 전달하고 있는 올바른 paraphrase이다.
   (C): 문장의 의미가 원문과 다르고 every year의 위치가 적절하지 않다.
   (D): 역시 every year의 위치가 적절하지 않고 죽는 경우가 빠져 있다.

## Word Review    p.68

1. except         2. seriously
3. intelligence   4. appear
5. control        6. endanger
7. temperature    8. aspect

## Sentence Review    p.69

1. than it could carrying an adult
2. With the insect trapped inside
3. No longer in need of money
4. some of which weigh as much as
5. This makes scientists think that

# Chapter 4
# Inference and Purpose

## 07 _ Inference Questions

### Basic Drills 1 p.74

1. (C)  2. (A)  3. (B)  4. (C)

WORDS  p.74  flood, rarely, exercise
       p.75  rate, disease, habit

1. 황하는 중국에 있는 거대한 강이다. 오래 전, 황하는 매년 범람했었다. 그러나 현대적인 댐을 이용하면 범람을 막을 수 있다. 황하는 이제 거의 범람하지 않는다.

2. 많이 달리는 운동 경기는 심장을 튼튼하게 만들어주기 때문에 건강에 가장 좋은 경기이다. 축구 경기를 하는 동안 선수들은 거의 8마일을 달린다. 농구 선수들은 한 게임 동안 5마일 정도를 달릴 것이다. 미식축구 선수들은 한 게임 동안 2-3마일 정도만 달린다.

3. 미국은 세계에서 심장 질환의 발생율이 가장 높은 나라 가운데 하나이다. 미국인들의 식생활이 주된 원인이다. 과학자들은 육류와 튀긴 음식을 너무 많이 섭취하면 심장질환의 발생을 돕는다는 사실을 밝혀냈다.

4. 육식동물만이 위험한 동물은 아니다. 아마도 하마는 아프리카에서 가장 위험한 동물일 것이다. 하마는 매년 사자나 다른 커다란 고양이와 동물들보다 더 많은 사람을 죽인다. 하마는 아프리카의 강가에서 사람들과 더 자주 접촉하기 때문이다.

### Basic Drills 2 p.76

1. (C)  2. (B)

서기 2세기경, 유명한 과학자인 클라우디우스 프톨레마이오스는 지구가 우주의 중심이라고 말했다. 카톨릭 교회는 프톨레마이오스의 생각이 천주교의 천국과 지옥에 대한 생각과 비슷했기 때문에 마음에 들어 했다. 그 후 천 2백 년 동안 모든 사람들은 프톨레마이오스의 생각이 옳다고 믿었다.

1500년 초에 젊은 폴란드인 니콜라우스 코페르니쿠스가 프톨레마이오스의 생각에 의문을 품기 시작했다. 그는 새로운 우주의 지도를 만들었다. 하지만 프톨레마이오스의 지도와는 다르게 지구가 아닌 태양이 우주의 중심에 있었다. 코페르니쿠스는 그의 생각을 사람에게 말하기 위해 죽기 직전까지 기다렸다.

약 백 년 후에 이탈리아인 갈릴레오 갈릴레이는 최초의 망원경 중 하나로 행성을 관측했다. 그의 연구는 코페르니쿠스의 생각이 옳다는 첫 번째 증거를 제공했다. 교회 측은 분노했다. 그들은 코페르니쿠스의 책을 출판하는 것을 누구에게도 허락하지 않았고 갈릴레이에게 그의 생각을 번복하도록 강요했다. 그럼에도 불구하고 갈릴레이의 생각은 퍼져나갔다. 곧 전 세계 대부분의 사람들이 태양이 우주의 중심이라는 것을 믿게 되었다.

## 08 _ Rhetorical Purpose Questions

### Basic Drills 1 p.78

1. (C)  2. (C)  3. (B)  4. (C)

WORDS  p.78  valuable, award, championship, security
       p.79  electronics, already, career, earning(s)

1. 닉은 훌륭한 축구 선수이다. 그는 매우 빠르고 강하며 주장으로서 팀원들을 격려한다. 작년에 그는 팀에서 최우수선수상을 받았다. 그는 또한 팀을 주 대항 대회로 이끌었다.

2. 잭이 학교에 다닐 때 학교는 매우 안전한 곳이었다. 그는 학교 가는 것을 전혀 걱정하지 않았고 학교 안에는 범죄가 전혀 없었다. 하지만 지금의 학교는 다르다. 그가 다니던 학교에는 이제 보안 카메라와 경비원이 있다.

3. 해가 갈수록 가전제품은 점점 크기가 작아지고 속도는 빨라진다. 과거에 컴퓨터는 커다란 기계였다. 최초의 컴퓨터는 자동차만큼 컸고 굉장히 느렸다. 오늘날 대부분의 PDA는 주머니 속에 충분히 들어갈 수 있을 만큼 작아졌고 최초의 컴퓨터보다 훨씬 성능이 뛰어나다.

**4.** 타이거 우즈는 역사상 가장 위대한 골프선수이다. 그는 1996년, 모든 기록을 경신하겠다는 선언을 하며 미국 PGA 투어에 데뷔했다. 그로부터 14년이 흐른 지금, 우리는 그가 이미 그 약속을 지켰다고 말할 수 있다. 그는 PGA 투어에서 71회 우승했으며 14개의 메이저 대회 타이틀을 차지했다. 또한 그는 세계에서 가장 돈을 많이 버는 프로 운동선수이다. 그리고 그는 이제 겨우 30대이다!

## Basic Drills 2            p.80

> 1. (B)    2. (B)

**1.** 에베레스트 산은 세계에서 가장 높은 산이다. 또한 등반하기 가장 어려운 산이기도 하다. 수천 년 동안 아무도 에베레스트 산을 등반하지 않았다. 그 이유 중 하나는 그 지역 사람들인 셰르파들이 그곳을 신성한 곳이라고 믿어서 올라가려 하지 않았기 때문이었다. 그 믿음은 1950년과 60년대에 관광객들이 에베레스트 산에 오르기 위해 모여들자 변하기 시작했다. 관광객들이 가난한 셰르파 공동체에게 수입을 제공하면서 셰르파들은 서서히 사람들이 그들의 신성한 산을 오르는 것을 받아들이기 시작했다. 오늘날 아파 셰르파 같은 몇몇 셰르파들은 심지어 등산객들을 위한 호텔을 운영한다.

**2.** 2만 년 전에 세상은 지금보다 훨씬 추운 곳이었다. 얼음이 지구의 대부분을 뒤덮었고, 거대한 얼음 강과 빙하가 산으로부터 뻗어있었다. 빙하는 매우 느린 속도로 움직였지만 대단히 무거웠다. 빙하는 땅에 거대한 구멍을 내며 움직이면서 지형을 변화시켰다. 나중에 지구가 따뜻해지자 빙하는 녹았고 녹은 얼음은 구멍을 물로 채웠다. 이렇게 해서 새로운 거대 수역들이 만들어졌다. 미대륙에서는 바다처럼 넓은 오대호를 볼 수 있다.

## Reading Practice ❶        p.81

> 1. (A)    2. (C)

### 핵시대

1945년 여름, 미국이 나가사키와 히로시마에 원자폭탄을 떨어뜨리면서 2차 세계대전은 끝이 났다. 하지만 종전은 지구를 안전한 곳으로 만들지 않았다. 핵시대가 열린 것이다. 핵시대는 이후에 벌어질 전쟁에서 원자폭탄을 사용할지도 모르기에 매우 불안한 시대였다. 두 강대국인 미국과 러시아는 지구를 파괴하기에 충분한 양의 원자 폭탄을 갖고 있었다. 1950년대와 60년대 사람들은 이를 잘 알고 있었기 때문에 핵전쟁의 공포 속에서 살았다.

그 당시 많은 미국인들은 방공호를 만들었다. 방공호란 핵 전쟁에서 자신을 보호하기 위해 지하에 만들어놓은 방이었다. 핵 전쟁 직후에 식물을 먹는 것은 안전하지 않을 것이었기 때문에 사람들은 방공호 안에 몇 달치 식량과 물을 비축해놓았다. 대부분의 방공호는 너무 작아서 실제로 핵전쟁이 발생할 때 사람들을 구할 수 없을 것이었지만, 많은 사람들이 방공호의 존재로 인해 자신들이 조금은 안전하다고 느꼈다.

/ 해 / 설 /

**1.** 글 전체의 내용을 파악해야 풀 수 있는 문제이다. 이 글의 중심 내용은 2차대전 이후 사람들이 핵전쟁에 대한 두려움 속에서 살았다는 것이며, 방공호는 그러한 두려움을 보여주는 예로 사용되었다.

**2.** 13-14째 줄의 "because it would not be safe to eat plants after a nuclear war"를 통해, 핵무기가 식물을 오염시킨다는 사실을 추론할 수 있다.

## Reading Practice ❷        p.82

> 1. (C)    2. (C)

### 토네이도

토네이도는 아마도 지상에서 가장 강력한 폭풍일 것이다. 토네이도는 속력이 시속 300마일에 이르는 바람으로 막대한 피해를 가져온다. 미국에서는 매년 평균 800건의 토네이도가 발생한다. 대부분은 텍사스와 네브라스카 사이에 있는 낮은 평야인 '토네이도 앨리(tornado alley)'에서 발생한다. 미국은 지리적 위치 때문에 다른 어떤 나라들보다 토네이도의 발생이 잦다. 멕시코의 온난하고 습윤한 공기가 위로 이동하고 캐나다에서 차가운 공기가 아래로 이동하다가 토네이도 앨리 위에서 만난다.

토네이도는 매우 위험하다. 왜냐하면 경고가 거의 없고, 사람들이 안전한 곳을 찾을 시간이 별로 없기 때문이다. TV 방송국에서 종종 토네이도 경보를 내보내지만 현대 기술로도 그 경보 시간은 12분 정도에 불과하다.

/ 해 / 설 /

1. 첫 단락 후반부에서 미국에서 토네이도가 많이 발생하는 원인에 대해 이야기하고 있다. 멕시코에서 오는 따뜻하고 습한 공기와 캐나다에서 오는 찬 공기가 만나서 토네이도가 발생한다고 한다. 이로부터 토네이도는 찬 공기와 따뜻한 공기가 만날 때 발생한다는 것을 추론할 수 있다.

2. TV에서 토네이도 경보를 발령하는데도 시간이 12분밖에 되지 않아 촉박하다는 이야기를 하고 있다.

## Reading Practice ③ p.83

1. (A)   2. (B)

### 최후의 체펠린 비행선

역사상 가장 큰 비행물체가 비행기가 아니라는 사실을 알고 있는가? 역사상 가장 큰 비행물체는 비행선이었다. 체펠린으로 더 잘 알려진 비행선은 소형 연식 비행선처럼 생겼지만 그것보다 훨씬 크다. 역사상 가장 큰 비행선은 힌덴부르크였다. 힌덴부르크는 거대했고 타이타닉보다 약간 작았다. 타이타닉처럼 이 비행선에도 슬픈 이야기가 얽혀 있다.

1930년대 독일인들이 힌덴부르크를 만들었을 때 그들은 힌덴부르크를 비인화성 기체인 헬륨으로 채우고 싶었다. 그러나 세계에서 상당량의 헬륨을 보유하고 있는 나라는 미국뿐인데, 미국은 독일에게 헬륨을 팔지 않으려고 했다. 미국은 독일이 1차 세계대전에서 체펠린 비행선을 사용했기 때문에 힌덴부르크를 전쟁무기로 사용할까봐 두려워했다. 그래서 독일은 대신 수소를 사용해야 했다. 독일인들은 수소는 헬륨보다 훨씬 더 주의해야 한다는 것을 알았다. 그들은 승객들로부터 모든 성냥과 라이터를 압수하고 비행을 시작했다. 그렇게 조심했음에도 불구하고 힌덴부르크의 첫 비행에서 화재가 일어나 36명의 사망자를 냈다. 그 이후로는 아무도 비행선을 타려 하지 않았다.

/ 해 / 설 /

1. 헬륨은 인화성이 없으나 구할 수 없어서 수소를 썼다는 것에서 수소는 인화성이 있다는 것을 짐작할 수 있다. 또 글의 마지막 부분에서 수소를 사용했다가 화재가 발생하는 사고가 일어난 이야기를 통해서도 알 수 있다.

2. 배에서 모든 성냥과 라이터를 버렸다는 것은 독일인들이 얼마나 주의깊게 화재에 대비했는가를 보여준다.

## Reading Practice ④ p.84

1. (C)   2. (C)

### 마라톤의 기원

가장 길고 유명한 달리기 경주인 마라톤에는 길고도 흥미로운 이야기가 있다. 기원전 4세기경 페르시아인들은 그리스의 유명한 도시인 아테네를 공격하기로 했다. 아테네는 도움이 필요했다. 그래서 그들은 달리기를 가장 잘하는 피디피데스를 또 다른 그리스 도시인 스파르타로 보냈다. 그 도시는 140마일 정도 떨어져 있었지만 피디피데스는 36시간 동안 그 거리를 달렸다. 불행하게도 스파르타인들은 아테네인들을 도울 수 없었다. 그래서 피디피데스는 나쁜 소식을 전하기 위해 140마일을 더 달려서 아테네로 돌아왔다. 아무런 도움도 없이, 승리에 대한 실낱 같은 희망만을 가지고, 아테네 사람들은 아테네에서 26마일 떨어진 마라톤에서 페르시아와 싸웠다. 놀랍게도 아테네는 전투에서 승리했다. 피디피데스는 왕에게 기쁜 소식을 전하기 위해 아테네로 달렸다. 그 이후 그리스인들은 피디피데스의 놀라운 달리기를 기리기 위해서 매년 마라톤에서 아테네까지 달리기 대회를 개최했다. 오늘날까지도 그 경주는 이어지고 있다.

하지만 모든 사람들이 피디피데스의 이야기를 믿는 것은 아니다. 역사의 모든 이야기가 사실은 아니다. 헤라클레스 이야기는 그리스의 유명한 이야기 중 하나이다. 우리는 피디피데스의 이야기가 사실인지 확인할 수 없겠지만 마라톤은 언제나 유명하고 인기 있는 경주로 남을 것이다.

/ 해 / 설 /

1. 세부적인 사항을 찾아 종합해야 하는 다소 까다로운 문제이다. 여러 가지 거리가 나와 혼란스러울 수 있으나 차근차근 읽어보면 답을 알 수 있다. 첫 단락 마지막에 "After that, the Greeks held a race from Marathon to Athens each year ..."을 보면 마라톤 경주의 거리는 마라톤에서 아테네까지임을 알 수 있다. 마라톤은 아테네에서 26마일 떨어져 있다고 했으므로 마라톤 경주 거리는 26마일이 된다.

2. 헤라클레스의 이야기는 바로 앞 문장인 "Not all stories from history are true."를 뒷받침하는 예로 사용되었다.

## iBT Practice 1
p.85

1. (B)  2. (C)  3. (C)  4. (B)  5. (C)
6. (B), (D), (E)

---

### 초기의 유럽 탐험가들

1400년대 말과 1500년대 초, 유럽인들이 미 대륙에 대해 알고 있던 정보 중 많은 것들이 매우 부정확하거나 완전히 틀린 것이었다. 콜럼버스가 첫 번째 탐험을 마치고 돌아온 후, 황금도시에 대한 황당한 이야기들이 유럽 전역에 퍼졌다. 그리하여 많은 사람들이 신대륙을 탐험하고 싶어했다.

스페인의 후안 폰세 데 레온도 그런 사람들 중 하나였다. 그는 젊음의 샘에 관한 이야기를 들었다. 그 이야기에 따르면 그 샘물에서 목욕을 하면 영원히 늙지 않고 젊어진다는 것이다. 그 이야기에 의하면 그 샘물은 비미니섬에 있다고 했지만 아무도 그 섬을 찾을 수 없었다. 후안은 스페인을 떠나 신대륙으로 젊음의 샘을 찾으러 떠났다. 후안은 그의 여생을 비미니섬과 젊음의 샘을 찾기 위해 보냈다. 그는 카리브해에서 수많은 새로운 섬을 발견했다. 그는 플로리다에 간 최초의 유럽인이었다. 그는 모든 땅을 스페인 영토로 만들었고 스페인 왕은 매우 기뻐했다. 하지만 젊음의 샘은 그저 전설일 뿐이었다.

또 하나의 황당한 이야기 때문에 유명한 탐험가인 월터 롤리 경은 신대륙으로 떠났다. 그 이야기는 전설 속의 원주민 왕인 엘도라도에 관한 것이었다. 전설에 따르면 그는 매일 금가루로 목욕을 하고 황금으로 된 도시에서 살았다고 한다. 롤리 경은 남미 대부분 지역을 탐험하며 엘도라도와 그의 황금도시를 찾아 다녔지만 결국 찾지 못했다. 엘도라도는 또 하나의 젊음의 샘이었다.

/ 해 / 설 /

1. Juan Ponce de Leon이 탐험을 떠난 목적은 젊음의 샘을 찾기 위해서였으나, 16-17째 줄의 "but the fountain of youth was just a legend"을 통해 결국 젊음의 샘을 찾지 못했음을 알 수 있다.

2. 15째 줄의 "He took all of these lands for Spain"에서, Juan Ponce de Leon의 탐험을 통해 카리브해의 많은 섬을 스페인의 식민지로 확보했음을 짐작할 수 있다.

3. "El Dorado" 바로 뒤에 "a legendary Native American king"이라고 설명되어 있다.

4. 젊음의 샘이 "legend"에 불과했다는 말을 통해 "legend"의 의미를 이해할 수 있다.

5. 글쓴이는 앞 단락에서 젊음의 샘이 실제로 존재하지 않았다는 이야기를 하였다. 그렇다면 엘도라도를 "또 하나의 젊음의 샘"이라고 비유한 것은 엘도라도 역시 존재하지 않는다는 것을 말하려는 의도이다.

6. 중심 내용을 뒷받침하는 major idea와, 세부적인 내용만을 언급하는 minor idea를 구별할 수 있어야 한다. 이 글의 중심 내용은 유럽의 많은 탐험가들이 전설 때문에 신세계로 떠났다는 것이고, Juan Ponce de Leon과 Sir Walter Raleigh의 이야기는 그에 대한 두 가지 예이다. 그러므로 (B)와 (D)는 반드시 포함되어야 한다. 나머지 보기 중 (C)와 (F)는 각각 (B)와 (D)에 대한 세부적인 내용이며, (A) 역시 중요하지 않은 내용이다. (E)는 이러한 탐험이 대부분 실패하였다는 것이므로 글의 종합적인 결론에 해당된다.

## iBT Practice 2
p.88

1. (C)  2. (B)  3. (A)  4. ■B  5. (C)
6. (A)  7. (A), (C), (E)

---

### 사람의 심장

인체의 모든 기관 중 가장 강한 곳은 바로 심장이다. 심장은 놀라운 근육이다. 다른 근육들과 달리 심장은 지치지 않고 평생 멈추지 않는다. 인간의 심장은 얼마나 강할까? 한번 테니스 공을 꽉 쥐어보자. 당신의 심장은 이 정도의 힘으로 혈액을 온몸으로 보낸다. 당신은 몇 번이나 테니스 공을 쥘 수 있는가? 당신의 심장은 이런 일을 하루에 10만 번이나 한다!

심장에는 네 개의 '방'이 있다. 각각의 '방'에는 '문', 즉 판막이 있다. 위쪽의 방은 심방이라고 하고 아래쪽의 방은 심실이라고 한다. 심장의 기본 역할은 혈액을 온몸으로 보내는 것이다. 먼저 혈액은 우심방에서 시작해서 심장 속을 흐른다. 그리고 나서 아래쪽 우심실로 내려갔다 나와서 폐로 들어간다. 혈액은 다시 심장의 좌심방으로 돌아왔다가 좌심실로 내려간다. 마지막으로 심장은 혈액을 다시 온몸에 공급한다.

운동을 하면 심장은 더 빨리 뛴다. 그 이유는 근육이 더 많은 산소를 소비하기 때문이다. 당신의 건강한 최고 심박수는 220에서 나이를 뺀 숫자로 알 수 있다. 예를 들어 20세에 적절한 최고 심박수는 분당 200회이다. 당신의 심장은 이보다 빨리 뛸 수 있지만 그것은 건강한 것이 아니다.

/ 해 / 설 /

1. 테니스공의 예는 4째 줄의 "How strong is the human heart?"를 설명하기 위한 비유이다.

2. 두 번째 단락에서 심장에는 4개의 방이 있다고 하였다.

3. 12-13째 줄의 "Then, it moves down into the right ventricle and out into the lungs"에서 알 수 있다.

4. 운동을 할 때는 심장박동수가 증가하는 것을 이야기한 후, 참고적으로 평균 심장박동수를 말해주는 것이 자연스럽다. 다른 곳은 모두 어색하다.

5. "maximum"이 들어있는 문장은 그 앞 문장에 대한 예이다. 그러므로 "your fastest, healthy heartbeat"가 "the maximum heartbeat"와 같은 의미임을 알 수 있다.

6. 마지막 단락에서, 운동을 하면 심장박동이 빨라지는 것은 산소가 더 많이 필요하기 때문이라고 나와 있다. 그러므로 피가 근육에 산소를 공급한다는 사실을 추론할 수 있다.

7. 이 글은 세 단락으로 구성되어 있다. 주어진 요약문의 첫 문장은 글 전체의 주제(main idea)를 담고 있다. 그러므로 나머지 세 문장은 각 단락의 중심 내용으로 이루어져야 한다. 중심 내용과 세부사항을 구별하도록 한다. 보기 (A), (C), (E)는 각 단락의 중심 내용인 반면, (B), (D), (F)는 세부적인 내용이다.

## Word Review                          p.91

1. order
2. underground
3. location
4. infer
5. accept
6. mention
7. Technology
8. purpose

## Sentence Review                      p.92

1. make the Earth a safer place
2. any new war could include
3. but even with modern technology
4. they would not sell any to
5. the most famous and longest running race (또는 the longest and most famous running race)

# Chapter 5
# Insert Text

## 09 _ Insert Text Questions

### Basic Drills 1                      p.98

1. (C)-(D)-(A)-(B)    2. (B)-(D)-(A)-(C)
3. (C)-(A)-(D)-(B)    4. (A)-(D)-(B)-(C)
5. (C)-(B)-(A)-(D)

### Basic Drills 2                      p.99

1. (1) ⑤    (2) ① - ⑤ - ② - ③ - ④
2. (1) ⑦    (2) ① - ⑦ - ② - ③ - ④ - ⑤ - ⑥

**WORDS**  jungle, fur, several, break (broke)

1. ① 재규어는 몸집이 큰 고양이다. ② 그들은 주로 남아메리카 정글에 산다. ③ 하지만 사람들이 정글의 나무들을 베어 내서 재규어들은 살 곳을 잃어가고 있다. ④ 얼마 후면 재규어가 한 마리도 남아있지 않을지도 모른다. ⑤ 재규어는 표범처럼 생겼지만 털이 검다.

2. ① 요즘 MP3플레이어는 큰 인기를 얻고 있다. ② 하지만 CD플레이어에는 몇 가지 문제점이 있었다. ③ CD플레이어는 너무 커서 대부분의 사람들이 주머니에 넣고 다닐 수 없었다. ④ 또한 너무 쉽게 망가졌다. ⑤ 게다가 사람들은 CD를 모두 가지고 다니고 싶어하지 않았다. ⑥ MP3플레이어는 CD를 가지고 다닐 필요가 없기 때문에 더 편리하다. ⑦ MP3플레이어가 나오기 이전에 사람들은 CD플레이어를 사용했다.

### Basic Drills 3                      p.100

1. (A)    2. (C)

**WORDS**  probably, sail, average

1. 미국에서 수상스포츠는 인기가 높다. 수상스키가 아마 가장 인기 있는 수상스포츠이겠지만 다른 스포츠도 많이 있다. 예를 들어 윈드서핑은 매우 인기 있는 스포츠이다. 윈드서핑용 보드는 위에 돛이 달린 서핑보드처럼 생겼다. 사람들은 바람이 많이 부는 곳에서 윈드서핑을 한다. 강한 바람이 불면 보드가 매우 빨리 갈 수 있어서 아주 재미있다.

2. 흰긴수염고래는 지구에서 가장 큰 동물이다. 그들은 가장 큰 공룡보다도 훨씬 크다. 흰긴수염고래의 평균 몸길이는 80피트 정도이다. 흰긴수염고래는 지구상에서 가장 시끄러운 동물이기도 하다. 그들의 목소리는 제트엔진보다도 크다! 비록 흰긴수염고래가 크기 하지만 그들은 지구에서 가장 작은 동물들을 먹는다. 흰긴수염고래는 플랑크톤을 먹는다. 플랑크톤은 먼지만큼 작다. 흰긴수염고래는 매일 수백만 마리의 플랑크톤을 먹는다.

## Basic Drills 4  p.101

1. (D)　2. (C)

WORDS  temperature, protect, cartoon, character

1. 우주는 작업하기 위험한 곳이다. 그곳에는 공기도 없고 기온의 변화도 크다. 기온은 화씨 250도까지 올라갔다가 화씨 -250도까지 떨어진다. 이렇게 위험한 조건에서 일을 하려면 우주비행사들은 우주복이 필요하다. 우주복은 우주비행사들에게 공기를 공급하고 매우 높거나 매우 낮은 온도로부터 우주비행사들을 보호한다. NASA는 몇 년에 걸쳐 우주복을 제작했다. 이 우주복의 성능은 매우 좋다.

2. 월트 디즈니는 굉장한 만화들로 유명하다. 전 세계 사람들은 그의 캐릭터들을 잘 알고 있고 특히 미키마우스를 좋아한다. 월트 디즈니는 1920년대에 만화를 그리기 시작했다. 그는 많은 새로운 것들을 만화에 도입했다. 월트 디즈니는 사람들을 돕기 위해 여러 가지 일을 했다. 그는 만화 이외에 학교를 위한 영화도 만들었다. 이 영화는 아이들에게 안전 규칙과 다른 중요한 것들을 가르쳤다.

## Reading Practice ❶  p.102

1. C　2. B

### 브라질의 위험한 스포츠

브라질 리우데자네이루의 젊은이들은 종종 매우 위험한 경기를 한다. 그들은 그 경기를 '트레인서핑(train surfing)'이라고 부른다. 트레인서핑을 하는 젊은이들은 움직이는 열차 위에 서 있는데, 이것은 매우 위험하다. '서피스타(surfista)', 즉 트레인서핑을 하는 사람은 기차에서 떨어질 수도 있다. 또한 기차의 전선에 부딪힐 수도 있다. 매년 많은 서피스타들이 이 위험한 경기를 하다 죽는다.

서피스타들은 이 경기가 위험하다는 것을 안다. 하지만 서피스타는 주로 도시의 매우 가난한 지역 출신이기 때문에 삶에 대한 희망이 거의 없다. 경찰과 열차 회사들은 서피스타들을 막으려 하지만 그것은 매우 어려운 일이다. 브라질은 부유한 나라도 아니고 열차를 지킬 만큼 많은 경찰도 없다. 대신 브라질은 젊은이들에게 트레인서핑의 위험성에 대해 가르친다. 안타깝게도 서피스타들은 삶이 나아질 때까지 트레인서핑을 멈추지 않을 것이다.

/ 해 / 설 /

1. "Both of these accidents"가 무엇인지 확인한다. 두 가지 사고는 열차에서 떨어지는 것과 전선을 건드리는 것이므로, 주어진 문장은 그 두 가지가 언급된 후 들어가는 것이 적절하다.

2. "this"가 가리키는 것이 무엇인지 찾아야 한다. 브라질 젊은이들이 죽음을 두려워하지 않는 이유가 무엇인지 찾아 그 문장 뒤에 주어진 문장을 넣는다.

## Reading Practice ❷  p.103

1. C　2. B

### 로데오의 영웅들

로데오는 미국 남서부에서 인기 있는 경기이다. 로데오를 할 때 카우보이들은 커다란 수컷 황소에 탄다. 황소는 매우 힘이 세고 난폭하다. 카우보이는 황소의 등 위에 머물러 있는 초 수만큼 점수를 얻지만 보통 몇 초 후에 떨어진다. 이때 경기는 정말 위험해진다. 말에서 사람이 떨어지면 말들은 사람을 밟지 않으려고 애쓴다. 실제로 황소들은 사람을 밟으려 하거나 뿔로 찌르려고 한다. 카우보이들은 황소에서 떨어지고 나면 큰 위험에 노출된다.

하지만 카우보이들이 혼자 경기를 하는 것은 아니다. 그들이 떨어지면 광대들이 나타나 그들을 돕는다. 로데오광대들은 서커스의 일반 광대와는 전혀 다르다. 로데오

광대들은 황소의 주의를 끈다. 황소가 로데오 광대를 뒤쫓을 때 카우보이는 안전하게 빠져나올 수 있다. 물론 로데오 광대가 되는 것은 매우 위험한 일이다. 하지만 대부분의 광대들은 자신의 일을 사랑한다.

/ 해 / 설 /

1. 주어진 문장에서 "this"가 가리키는 것이 무엇인지 생각해 본다.

2. 일단 "they"가 무엇인지 생각해 본다. "the same funny clothes"를 입는다는 것에서 광대라는 것을 알 수 있다. 같은 옷을 입지만 훨씬 중요한 역할을 한다는 것은 그들이 보통의 광대와 다르다는 것을 의미한다.

## Reading Practice ❸   p.104

1. **D**   2. **C**

### 좀비는 영화에만 있는 것이 아니다

걸어 다니는 시체인 좀비는 공포영화에서 매우 인기가 있다. 하지만 영화가 만들어지기 오래 전부터 좀비에 관한 이야기들이 존재했다. 좀비에 관한 최초의 이야기는 1500년대와 1600년대 경에 카리브해에서 시작됐다. 아프리카의 노예들은 새로운 종교인 부두교를 만들었다. 그들의 종교에는 '보코(bokor)'라고 하는 주술사들이 있었다. 보코는 죽은 자들을 살릴 수 있다고 주장했다. 이런 좀비들은 보코의 노예가 된다. 과학자들은 보코들이 죽은 자를 일으킬 수 있다는 것을 믿지 않았다. 하지만 많은 보코들은 좀비 노예들을 갖고 있었다. 어떻게 이런 일이 가능했던 것일까?

오늘날 과학자들은 '좀비'에 대해 더 많이 안다고 생각한다. 좀비는 죽은 것이 아니었다. 그들은 보통 사람들이었다. 보코는 사람을 죽이지 않았지만 죽은 것처럼 보이게 하는 특별한 독약을 만드는 법을 배웠다. 보코가 사람들에게 독약을 먹이면 '죽은' 사람의 가족들은 그들이 정말 죽었다고 믿고 땅에 묻는다. 나중에 보코는 그들을 땅에서 파낸다. 독약의 약효가 멈추고 사람들은 깨어난다. 이 과정이 너무 무서웠기 때문에 대부분의 '좀비'들은 자신이 정말 죽었다고 생각해서 보코의 노예가 되었던 것이다!

/ 해 / 설 /

1. 주어진 문장에서 "this"가 가리키는 내용이 무엇인지 생각해 본다.

2. 주어진 문장에는 지시어나 연결어와 같은 signal words가 없으므로 내용으로 판단해야 한다. 논리적으로 내용이 자연스럽게 이어지는 곳을 찾는다. 주술사들이 땅에 묻었던 사람들에게 이런 내용을 말해주기 위해서는 땅에서 다시 파낸 후여야 한다는 점을 생각해 본다.

## Reading Practice ❹   p.105

1. **D**   2. **A**

### 물거미집

거미는 매우 재미있는 생물이지만 물거미는 특히 더 흥미롭다. 물거미는 물속에 살지만 공기로 숨을 쉰다. 물거미는 풍선처럼 안에 공기를 담을 수 있는 특수한 그물을 만든다. 물거미의 몸에는 특수한 털이 나 있어서 그 털이 공기를 간직한다. 거미집을 다 지으면 거미는 물속에서 살 수 있다.

물거미는 뛰어난 수영 선수이다. 대부분의 거미는 거미집을 이용해서 먹이를 잡지만 물거미는 그렇게 할 수 없다. 이미 거미집을 공기를 담아놓는 데 사용하기 때문이다. 작은 곤충들이 거미집 근처에서 헤엄치면 물거미는 재빨리 밖으로 헤엄쳐 나와 곤충을 문다. 거미의 독은 즉시 곤충을 죽인다. 그리고 나서 물거미는 그 곤충을 거미집으로 가져와서 먹는다.

/ 해 / 설 /

1. "these"가 가리키는 것이 무엇인지 생각해 본다. 지문에서 물거미가 공기를 얻기 위해 이용하는 것이 두 가지 나오는데 "a special web"과 "hairs"이다. 그런데 "these"는 복수형이므로 "a special web"은 답이 될 수 없다. 그러므로 주어진 문장은 "hairs"가 나오는 문장 뒤에 들어가야 알맞다.

2. "They"가 무엇인지, 그리고 "have to be." 뒤에 생략된 말이 무엇인지 생각해 본다. 단락의 내용을 읽어 보면 물거미가 먹이를 얻기 위해서는 재빨리 헤엄쳐야 한다는 것을 알 수 있다. 그러므로 "They have to be."의 의미는 "They have to be excellent swimmers."임을 짐작할 수 있다.

## iBT Practice 1

p.106

1. (C)  2. (C)  3. (C)  4. (A)  5. (C)
6. **B**  7. (B), (C), (E)

### 증기선의 탄생

1800년대 초 증기기관은 새로운 것이 아니었다. 스코틀랜드 출신의 제임스 와트가 1769년에 최초의 증기기관을 만들었다. 와트의 증기기관은 대부분 공장의 기계를 돌리는 데 사용되었다. 이것은 매우 유용했지만 증기기관이 정말로 유용해진 것은 1807년부터였다. 그해 로버트 풀턴이라는 미국인이 최초의 증기선을 만들었다. 그의 배 North River호는 증기기관을 이용해 강을 거슬러 올라갔다. 그전에는 강을 거슬러 올라가기가 매우 어려웠다. 사람들은 배를 젓거나 말과 밧줄을 이용하여 배를 끌었다. 이것은 속도가 매우 느렸다. North River호는 속도가 훨씬 빨랐다. 1860년대 무렵에는 수천 대의 증기선들이 미국의 강을 거슬러 올라갔다.

증기선은 미국을 변화시켰다. 증기선은 여행을 더 쉽게 만들었고 사업에도 유용했다. 이제 사업가들은 그들의 제품을 멀리 떨어진 도시에 팔 수 있었다. 하지만 증기선에도 문제는 있었다. 증기기관은 매우 위험했다. 때때로 증기기관은 폭발하곤 했다. 수년 후 사람들은 더 좋고 안전한 증기기관을 만들었지만 항상 위험했다. 그래도 증기기관은 1800년대를 살았던 사람들의 삶에 있어서 중요한 부분이었다.

/ 해 / 설 /

1. 증기기관을 만든 사람으로 James Watt와 Robert Fulton 두 사람이 소개되지만 최초로 증기기관을 만든 사람은 James Watt이다. (2째 줄 "James Watt ... made the first steam engines in 1769." 참조)

2. 10-11째 줄에서 1860년 경에는 수천 대의 증기선이 다녔다고 했으므로 (C)는 글의 내용과 반대되는 내용이다.

3. 증기선의 발명으로 강의 상류 지역으로의 이동이 원활해졌다는 사실에서, 그 지역 사람들이 증기선으로 인해 혜택을 받았음을 짐작할 수 있다.

4. "sell"의 목적어로 쓰일 수 있는 말이 무엇인지 생각해 본다.

5. 일반적으로 대명사는 바로 앞에 나온 주어를 가리키는 경우가 가장 많지만, 여기에서는 "they" 대신 "people"을 넣으면 뜻이 통하지 않는다. "they"는 내용상 "steam engines"를 가리키고 있다.

6. 많은 사람들이 증기선을 만들었다면 그 결과로 강에는 많은 증기선이 다녔을 것이다. 그러므로 주어진 문장은 "By 1860, ..." 앞에 들어가야 원인·결과로 자연스럽게 연결된다.

7. 이 글은 '증기선(steamboats)'에 대한 내용이다. 보기들은 모두 증기선에 대해 지문에 언급된 내용이지만 그 중에서 중요한 것이 있고 중요하지 않은 것이 있다. 너무 구체적이거나 단순한 사실은 요약문에 포함되지 않는다. 구체적인 사실을 종합하고 요약한 문장을 찾도록 한다.

## iBT Practice 2

p.109

1. (C)  2. (B)  3. (B)  4. (A)  5. **A**
6. (B), (D), (F)

### 시베리아의 수수께끼

1908년에 러시아의 추운 동부 지방인 시베리아에서 거대한 폭발이 일어났다. 그 폭발은 주변 수 마일 내에 있는 나무들을 파괴했다. 사람들은 수백 마일 밖에서도 그 폭발음을 들을 수 있었다. 오늘날 과학자들은 이 폭발이 얼마나 강력했는지 추측할 수 있다. 그것은 오늘날의 가장 큰 핵폭탄만큼이나 강력했다. 하지만 1908년에는 핵폭탄이 없었다. 폭발의 원인은 무엇이었을까?

오랫동안 이것은 수수께끼였다. 이제 과학자들은 해답을 알아낸 것으로 보인다. 소행성이 폭발한 것이었다. 매년 수백 개의 작은 소행성이 지구에 떨어진다. 하지만 실제로 그들 중 대부분은 지표면에 다다르지 않는다. 소행성은 초속 12km로 비행한다. 이 속도에서는 많은 열이 발생한다. 그래서 소행성들은 땅에 닿기 전에 타버리는 것이다. 커다란 소행성은 타서 없어질 수 없다. 그러한 소행성이 지표면을 강타해서 지표면에 커다란 구멍을 만든다. 하지만 시베리아에는 구멍이 없다. 과학자들은 이 소행성이 중간 크기여서 타 없어지기엔 너무 크지만 지표면을 강타하기엔 너무 작았다고 생각한다. 대신 지표면으로부터 6km 상공에서 폭발했기 때문에 지표면에 구멍을 만들지 않은 것이다.

과학자들은 이삼백 년마다 한 번씩 이와 비슷한 소행성이 지구를 강타한다고 한다. 이렇게 생각하면 역사상의 많은 수수께끼들이 해결된다. 초기의 과학자들은 하늘에서 불이 떨어진다고 이야기했다. 옛날 사람들은 신의 분노 때문에 불이 내려온 것이라고 생각했지만 현재 우리는 그렇게 생각하지 않는다.

/ 해 / 설 /

1. 지문에서 "nuclear bombs"가 언급되지만, 시베리아에서 일어난 폭발이 핵폭탄의 위력과 맞먹는다는 것을 말하기 위한 것일 뿐, 핵폭탄과 아무런 관계가 없다.

2. 두 번째 단락에서 설명되어 있다.

3. 일반적으로 대명사는 바로 앞에 나온 주어를 가리키는 경우가 가장 많다. 앞 문장의 주어인 "small asteroids"를 대입해 보고 뜻이 통하는지 확인한다.

4. 소행성이 땅에 부딪힐 때 무엇이 생기는지 생각해 본다.

5. 주어진 문장은 "asteroid"라는 생소한 용어를 설명하고 있다. 이 용어가 처음 사용된 직후에 설명이 나오는 것이 적절하다.

6. 보기 중 (B), (D), (F)는 주제와 관련된 중요한 내용이지만 (A), (C), (E)는 중요하지 않은 내용이다. 요약문에 포함되려면 이 글의 주제인 폭발과 직접적으로 관계가 있어야 하는데, (A), (C), (E)는 시베리아나 소행성에 대한 세부적인 내용일 뿐 시베리아에서 발생한 폭발과는 무관하다.

### Word Review                           p.112

1. (A)   2. (B)   3. (A)   4. (C)   5. (C)
6. (A)   7. (A)   8. (C)

### Sentence Review                       p.113

1. (B)   2. (A)   3. (C)   4. (C)   5. (A)

# Chapter 6
# Classifying, Categorizing, and Organizing Information

## 10 _ Classifying, Categorizing, and Organizing Information Questions

### Basic Drills 1                        p.118

**Contrast/Change Subject**
on the other hand, while, as opposed to

**Same Subject**
Furthermore, Finally

|                | Whales | Fish |
|----------------|--------|------|
| Breathe water  |        | ✔    |
| Eggs           |        | ✔    |
| Live babies    | ✔      |      |
| Warm-blooded   | ✔      |      |
| Cold-blooded   |        | ✔    |

바다에 있는 모든 동물이 다 물고기는 아니다. 고래는 물고기처럼 보이지만 전혀 다르다. 물고기는 육지 동물처럼 숨을 쉬지 않는다. 물고기는 허파가 없고 아가미가 있다. 물고기는 아가미를 통해 물로 숨을 쉰다. 반면 고래는 허파가 있다. 고래는 육지 동물처럼 공기로 숨을 쉰다. 게다가 물고기는 냉혈동물인 반면 고래는 온혈동물이다. 마지막으로 물고기는 알을 낳는 반면 고래는 새끼를 낳는다.

## Basic Drills 2
p.119

**Contrast/Change Subject**
however, on the other hand

**Same Subject**
Furthermore

|  | Southern States | Northern States |
|---|---|---|
| More money |  | ✔ |
| More people |  | ✔ |
| Farm states | ✔ |  |
| Wanted slavery | ✔ |  |
| Factory states |  | ✔ |

남북전쟁은 미국 역사상 최악의 전쟁이었다. 대부분의 사람들이 노예제도가 전쟁의 원인이라고 생각했지만 그것은 부분적인 원인일 뿐이다. 미국 북부와 남부 사이에는 중요한 차이가 있었고 이 차이들 때문에 전쟁이 일어났다. 노예제도도 물론 중요한 차이 중 하나였다. 남부는 노예를 부려 농장에서 일을 시키기 위해 노예제도를 원했다. 그러나 북부는 노예제도를 원하지 않았다. 남부와 북부의 또 다른 차이는 돈이었다. 남부의 주들은 농장을 운영하는 주들이다. 반면 북부의 주들은 공장을 운영했다. 공장은 농장보다 더 많은 돈을 벌기 때문에 북부의 주들이 더 부유했다. 또한 북부에는 남부보다 인구가 많았다. 미국 인구의 3분의 2 이상이 북부에 살았다. 그 때문에 북부는 정치적으로 더 큰 힘을 얻을 수 있었다.

## Basic Drills 3
p.120

Many people love boats. Going out on the water on a warm summer day is a lot of fun. But different people like different kinds of boats. Two of the most popular kinds of boats are sailboats and speedboats. Sailboats use the wind to give them power. They only have small engines. In contrast, speedboats have large engines and go very fast. Furthermore, speedboats are usually not as big as sailboats. Speedboats are small so that they can go fast. Sailboats, on the other hand are big so that they are more comfortable. In addition, sailboats can travel into the ocean, but this would be very dangerous in a speedboat. You can only use most speedboats on rivers and lakes.

|  | Sailboats | Speedboats |
|---|---|---|
| Wind power | ✔ |  |
| Large engines |  | ✔ |
| Small and fast |  | ✔ |
| Large and comfortable | ✔ |  |
| For lakes and rivers |  | ✔ |

많은 사람들이 배를 좋아한다. 따뜻한 여름날 물가로 나가는 것은 정말 재미있다. 하지만 사람마다 좋아하는 배가 다르다. 가장 인기 있는 두 가지 종류의 배는 요트와 모터보트이다. 요트는 바람을 이용해 동력을 얻는다. 거기에는 소형 엔진이 있을 뿐이다. 반면 모터보트는 큰 엔진이 있어서 매우 빠르다. 게다가 모터보트는 요트만큼 크지 않다. 모터보트는 작아서 빠르게 갈 수 있다. 반면 요트는 넓어서 더 편안하다. 게다가 요트로는 바다까지 갈 수 있다. 하지만 모터보트로 바다에 가는 것은 매우 위험하다. 모터보트는 대체로 강이나 호수에서 사용된다.

## Basic Drills 4
p.121

Running is a big sport in the summer Olympics. Running was one of the first Olympic sports. There are two kinds of runners in the Olympics. Sprinters run for short distances, usually less than 400 meters. Distance runners run for long distances, sometimes up to 10,000 meters! Distances runners and sprinters have very different training programs. Sprinters need very strong, powerful legs. This is because they must go very fast, but only for a short time. They usually lift a lot of weights with their legs to make their muscles bigger. Distance runners, on the other hand, do not need to run as fast, but they must run for much longer. They do not need very large leg muscles and usually do not lift many weights. Furthermore, distance runners must have very strong hearts, because their heart must work hard for a long time.

|  | Sprinters | Distance Runners |
|---|---|---|
| Large leg muscles | ✓ |  |
| Strong hearts |  | ✓ |
| Run short distances | ✓ |  |
| Do not lift weights |  | ✓ |
| Run for a long time |  | ✓ |

달리기는 하계 올림픽에서 매우 중요한 경기이다. 달리기는 최초의 올림픽 종목 중 하나이다. 올림픽에는 두 가지 종류의 달리기 선수가 있다. 주로 400미터 이하의 짧은 거리를 달리는 단거리 선수와 때로 10,000미터나 되는 긴 거리를 달리는 장거리 선수가 있다. 장거리 선수와 단거리 선수는 훈련 방식이 다르다. 단거리 선수들은 매우 강한 다리를 갖고 있다. 짧은 시간 동안만 매우 빠르게 달리기 위해서이다. 그들은 보통 다리 근육을 키우기 위해 다리로 웨이트 트레이닝을 한다. 반면 장거리 선수는 빨리 달릴 필요가 없다. 하지만 훨씬 더 오래 달려야 한다. 그들에게는 튼튼한 다리 근육이 필요 없어서 대개 웨이트 트레이닝을 하지 않는다. 또한 장거리 선수들은 매우 튼튼한 심장을 가져야 한다. 왜냐하면 심장이 오랜 시간 동안 활발히 움직여야 하기 때문이다.

## Reading Practice ❶   p.122

**South American Tribes:**
- Large temples
- Large armies
- Powerful kings

**North American Tribes:**
- Chiefs
- Small communities

**북미와 남미의 부족들**

유럽인들이 미대륙에 도착했을 때 그들은 그곳에 이미 사람이 살고 있다는 것을 알았다. 하지만 북미와 남미의 원주민들은 서로 전혀 달랐다. 아즈텍과 잉카 같은 남미의 원주민들은 어떤 면에서 유럽의 왕국과 비슷한 거대한 왕국에서 살았다. 그들은 왕 혹은 황제, 거대한 정부, 그리고 강력한 군대를 갖고 있었다. 그러나 북미의 부족들은 일반적으로 훨씬 규모가 작았다. 그들은 왕국을 형성하지 않았다. 대신 각각의 부족에는 추장이나 추장단이 있었다. 추장들은 남미 부족의 왕만큼 강력한 권한을 갖지 못했다. 게다가 북미와 남미의 부족은 집도 전혀 달랐다. 남미 부족은 거대한 도시를 지었는데 어떤 것들은 유럽의 가장 큰 도시들 같았다. 게다가 그들은 커다란 궁전이나 사원을 지었다. 반면 북미 부족들은 더 작은 공동체로 살았다. 그들은 남미 부족들보다 이동이 잦았기 때문에 큰 건물을 짓지 않았다.

/ 해 / 설 /

- Large temples: 12째 줄 참조
- Chiefs: 8째 줄 참조
- Fought against Europeans: 언급되지 않은 내용
- Large armies: 6째 줄 참조
- Powerful kings: 5째 줄 참조
- Excellent hunters: 언급되지 않은 내용
- Small communities: 13째 줄 참조

## Reading Practice ❷   p.123

**Athens:**
- Great thinkers
- People chose leaders

**Sparta:**
- Powerful army
- Many rules
- Long time in army

### 위대한 도시들: 스파르타와 아테네

4세기와 5세기에 그리스는 매우 중요한 곳이었다. 이집트나 고대 페르시아와 달리 그리스는 단일왕국이 아니었다. 그리스는 독립된 도시의 모임이었다. 때때로 이 도시들은 협력하기도 했고 서로 싸우기도 했다. 그 도시들 중에서 가장 중요하고 막강한 두 도시는 아테네와 스파르타였다.

스파르타와 아테네는 전혀 다른 도시였다. 아테네는 문화와 예술로 유명했다. 소크라테스나 플라톤 같은 많은 위대한 사상가들이 아테네 출신이다. 반면 스파르타는 주로 군대로 유명했다. 스파르타 군대는 도시를 통제했으며 그리스에서 가장 강력한 군대였다. 모든 스파르타인 남자는 군복무를 해야 했다. 소년들은 7살 때부터 훈련을 시작해서 30살까지 군대에 있었다. 스파르타는 규율이 많아서 사람들이 별로 자유롭지 못했다. 군복무를 해도 매우 단기간에 끝나는 아테네의 생활과는 전혀 달랐다. 게다가 아테네 사람들은 군사 정부 대신 스스로 그들의 지도자를 뽑았다.

### 두보이스와 워싱턴: 미국의 위대한 흑인 지도자들

20세기 초, 미국의 흑인들은 미국 사회의 동등한 구성원이 아니었다. 예를 들면 그들은 백인들과 같은 학교에 다닐 수 없었고 투표도 할 수 없었다. 그 당시 많은 흑인 지도자들은 흑인들이 더 많은 자유와 더 나은 삶을 갖길 원했다. 그 당시 가장 영향력 있는 두 명의 흑인 지도자로 W.E.B 두보이스와 부커 T. 워싱턴을 들 수 있다.

두보이스와 워싱턴 모두 흑인들을 돕고 싶어했지만, 그들은 전혀 다른 계획과 생각을 갖고 있었다. 워싱턴은 많은 흑인들에게 직업 기술을 가르치길 원했다. 일례로 그는 흑인들이 목수나 기술자 같은 직업을 갖도록 훈련을 시키고 싶어했다. 반면 두보이스는 가장 똑똑한 소수의 흑인들을 대학에 보내 의사나 변호사를 만들고 싶어했다. 두보이스는 그의 계획을 '재능있는 소수'라고 불렀다. 그는 미국을 변화시키기 위해서 흑인들이 의사나 변호사 같은 영향력 있는 직업을 가져야 한다고 믿었다. 반면 워싱턴은 미국이 스스로 서서히 변화할 거라 믿었으며, 백인과 흑인이 자연스럽게 함께 사는 방법을 터득할 것이라 생각했다.

/ 해 / 설 /

- Great thinkers: 7째 줄 참조
- Powerful army: 8-10째 줄 참조
- First Greek city: 언급되지 않은 내용
- Many rules: 11째 줄 참조
- People chose leaders: 13째 줄 참조
- Fought many wars: 언급되지 않은 내용
- Long time in army: 13-14째 줄 참조

/ 해 / 설 /

- Wanted to teach many people job skills: 7째 줄 참조
- Did not trust whites: 언급되지 않은 내용
- Wanted to send most intelligent African-Americans to college: 9-10째 줄 참조
- Thought African-Americans must change America: 13-14째 줄 참조
- Thought African-Americans could not change America: 언급되지 않은 내용
- Thought America would change naturally: 11-12째 줄 참조
- Thought African-Americans needed powerful jobs: 11-12째 줄 참조

## Reading Practice ❸  p.124

**Booker T. Washington:**
- Wanted to teach many people job skills
- Thought America would change naturally

**W.E.B. Dubois:**
- Wanted to send most intelligent African-Americans to college
- Thought African-Americans must change America
- Thought African-Americans needed powerful jobs

## Reading Practice ❹  p.125

**Colonists:**
- Better guns
- Attacked in small groups

**British:**
- Fought far from home
- Larger army
- Fought in European style

### 미국이 전쟁에서 승리한 이유

미국 혁명이 시작됐을 때 영국인들은 이주자들이 이길 확률이 거의 없다고 생각했다. 영국은 더 큰 군대를 보유하고 있었고 이주자들보다 훨씬 부유했기 때문이다. 그때 비록 영국인들은 모르고 있었지만 이주자들은 많은 유리한 점을 갖고 있었다.

영국군은 대규모 군대가 전쟁터에서 만나 개방된 곳에서 서로 공격하는 유럽식 전쟁에 매우 능숙했다. 그러나 이주자들은 이런 식으로 싸우지 않았다. 그들은 작은 규모로 공격을 하고 숨어 버렸다. 게다가 이주자들은 영국인들보다 더 좋은 총을 갖고 있었다. 그들은 영국군이 반격할 수 있을 만큼 가까이 오기 전에 영국군을 공격할 수 있었다. 게다가 영국군은 모든 장비와 총, 식량 등을 영국에서 가져와야 했다. 반면 이주자들은 자신의 땅에서 싸우기 때문에 많은 장비를 더 쉽게 구할 수 있었다. 마지막으로 영국 군인들은 좋은 훈련을 받았지만 신대륙에 대해서는 잘 몰랐다. 이주자들은 지형을 잘 알고 있었고 이것이 그들에게 큰 도움이 되었다.

/ 해 / 설 /

- Help from Native Americans: 언급되지 않은 내용
- Better guns: 8째 줄 참조
- Fought far from home: 9-10째 줄 참조
- Larger army: 2째 줄 참조
- Attacked in small groups: 7째 줄 참조
- Smarter leaders: 언급되지 않은 내용
- Fought in European style: 5째 줄 참조

## iBT Practice 1   p.126

1. (B)   2. (B)   3. (B)   4. (D)   5. (C)
6. Space Capsules:
   - Large metal ball
   - Cheaper to build
   - Perfect safety record
   - Still used by Russians

   Space Shuttles:
   - Fly back to Earth

### 우주캡슐과 우주왕복선

우주여행은 1960년에 시작되었다. 당시에 우주로 사람을 보낸 나라는 미국과 러시아뿐이었다. 비록 두 나라는 독자적으로 계획을 진행했지만 그들의 우주선은 매우 비슷했다. 두 나라 모두 우주캡슐을 사용했는데, 그것은 로켓으로 우주에 발사되는 거대한 금속 구슬 같은 것이었다. 우주캡슐이 지구로 돌아올 때에는 낙하산을 이용해 속도를 늦추어 땅으로 떨어진다. 러시아인들이 여전히 캡슐을 쓰는 동안 미국인들은 1980년대에 캡슐 사용을 중단했다. 대신, 비행기와 더 흡사한 우주왕복선을 만들었다. 우주왕복선은 날개가 있어서 지구로 비행해서 돌아왔다. 우주캡슐과 우주왕복선은 둘 다 장단점이 있다.

우주왕복선의 가장 좋은 점은 우주로 여러 번 왕복할 수 있다는 것이다. 그러나 우주캡슐은 한 번만 갔다 올 수 있다. 그리고 나서 다시 새로 우주캡슐을 만들어야 한다. 우주왕복선은 제작 비용이 더 많이 들지만 우주 여행을 할 때마다 새로운 비행선을 만들지 않기 때문에 여러 번 비행하면 비용을 절약할 수 있다. 우주왕복선은 많은 이점이 있는 반면 만들기가 어렵다. 그렇기 때문에 더 위험하기도 하다. 1986년과 2003년에 일어난 두 번의 미국 우주왕복선 실종 사고는 이 점을 증명했다. 반면 러시아의 우주캡슐은 더 나은 안전 기록을 보유하고 있다.

/ 해 / 설 /

1. 마지막 문장에 나와 있듯이, 깨끗한 안전 기록을 보유하고 있는 것은 러시아의 우주캡슐이다.

2. 7-8째 줄에 "…the U.S. stopped using space capsules in the early 1980s"라고 나와 있다.

3. 16-17째 줄의 "…over time, space shuttles save money because you don't build a new one for each trip into space"라는 문장을 통해 우주왕복선은 여러 번 사용가능하다는 것을 알 수 있다.

4. "advantage"의 뜻을 모를 경우에도 문맥을 통해 뜻을 짐작할 수 있는 문제이다. "While space shuttles have many advantages, they are harder to build."에서 "while"은 "although"와 같은 의미를 갖는 접속사이다. 즉, 우주왕복선이 많은 "advantage"를 갖고 있기는 하지만 만들기가 어려운 단점이 있다는 내용이므로 "advantage"가 '장점'을 의미함을 알 수 있다.

5. 1986년과 2003년에 발생한 사고는 미국의 우주왕복선이 폭발한 예이다.

6. (A) Most trips into space: 언급되지 않은 내용

(B) Large metal ball: 4째 줄 참조
(C) Fly back to Earth: 10째 줄 참조
(D) Very easy to build: 언급되지 않은 내용
(E) Cheaper to build: 16-17째 줄 참조
(F) Perfect safety record: 21-22째 줄 참조
(G) Still used by Russians: 7째 줄 참조

## iBT Practice 2
p.129

1. (B)   2. (C)   3. C   4. (A)   5. (C)
6. **Hunter-Gatherer Groups:**
   - Small groups
   
   **Farming Groups:**
   - Had soldiers
   - Took land
   - More people
   - Built permanent homes

### 수렵 채집 집단과 농경 집단

수천 년 전 초기 인류는 수렵 채집 집단과 농경 집단이라는 두 종류의 사회에서 살았다. 수렵 채집 집단은 이동을 많이 했다. 그들은 사냥과 채집 생활을 했기 때문이다. 농경 집단은 주로 한곳에 정착해서 영구적인 가옥을 지었다. 농경 집단도 사냥을 하긴 했지만 대부분의 시간을 농사와 식량 재배에 소비했다.

시간이 지나자 농경 집단은 점점 세력이 강해졌고 수렵 채집 집단으로부터 땅을 빼앗았다. 여기엔 여러 가지 이유가 있다. 먼저 수렵 채집 집단은 소규모였다. 대규모의 수렵 채집 집단은 모든 구성원에게 충분한 식량을 공급할 수 없기 때문에 대개 100명 이하의 사람들로 구성되었다. 반면 농경 집단은 많은 양의 식량을 재배할 수 있었기 때문에 더 많은 사람을 먹일 수 있었다. 그들은 더 많은 사람들에게 식량을 제공할 수 있었기 때문에 농경 집단의 모든 구성원이 다 농사를 지을 필요는 없었다. 몇몇 사람들은 군인과 같은 다른 직업을 가질 수 있었다. 수렵 채집 집단에서는 모든 구성원이 식량을 찾아야 했다. 그래서 그들은 따로 전문 군인을 두지 않았다. 이로 인해 농경 집단이 수렵 채집 집단으로부터 땅을 빼앗기가 쉬웠다.

/ 해 / 설 /

1. 6째 줄의 "Although farming groups did hunt animals,...."에서 농경 집단도 사냥을 했다는 사실이 언급되어 있다.

2. 일반적으로 대명사는 바로 앞에 나온 주어를 가리키는 경우가 가장 많다. 앞 절의 주어인 "farming groups"를 대입하여 뜻이 통하는지 살펴본다.

3. 앞에는 "Having many people"에 대한 내용이 나오고, 뒤에는 "many advantages"에 대한 내용이 나오는 곳을 찾아보도록 한다.

4. 등위접속사 so로 연결되어 있는 문장을 paraphrase할 경우, so 대신 종속접속사인 because를 사용하는 경우가 많다. 한편 but으로 연결된 문장은 흔히 though, although, while 등을 사용하여 paraphrase한다.

5. 두 번째 문단의 마지막 부분을 읽어 보면 농경 집단에는 "soldier"가 있어서 수렵 채집 집단으로부터 땅을 빼앗을 수 있었다는 것을 알 수 있다. 이러한 사실로부터 "soldier"의 의미를 짐작해 보도록 한다.

6. (A) Small groups: 10째 줄 참조
   (B) Often hungry: 언급되지 않은 내용
   (C) Had soldiers: 17째 줄 참조
   (D) Took land: 19째 줄 참조
   (E) Lived in tents: 언급되지 않은 내용
   (F) More people: 15째 줄 참조
   (G) Built permanent homes: 5-6째 줄 참조

## Word Review
p.132

1. (A)   2. (A)   3. (C)   4. (B)   5. (A)
6. (A)   7. (C)   8. (B)

## Sentence Review
p.133

1. (A)   2. (C)   3. (B)   4. (A)   5. (C)

# Chapter 7
# Prose Summary

## 1_ Prose Summary Questions

### Basic Drills 1   p.139

1. When a hornet attacks a honeybee nest, the honeybees have an interesting way of fighting.
2. They started the colonies in America for religious freedom, but they started other colonies for different reasons.
3. The invention of the electric guitar greatly changed music.

**WORDS**  spice, electric, invention

1. 호박벌은 꿀벌의 천적이다. 호박벌이 꿀벌의 벌집을 공격하면 꿀벌은 흥미로운 방법으로 대응한다. 꿀벌은 너무 작기 때문에 침으로 호박벌을 죽일 수 없다. 대신 많은 꿀벌들이 호박벌 위에 앉아서 몸으로 호박벌을 덮는다. 그리고 나서 다같이 몸을 비빈다. 그렇게 하면 열이 발생한다. 호박벌은 벌떼와 함께 점점 더 뜨거워진다. 꿀벌은 호박벌보다 높은 온도에서도 살 수 있다. 몇 분이 지나면 호박벌은 죽고 꿀벌들은 다시 안전해진다.

2. 영국은 전 세계에 식민지를 건설하기 시작했다. 그들이 미대륙에 식민지를 건설한 것은 종교의 자유 때문이었지만, 또 다른 여러 이유에서 다른 지역에 식민지를 건설하기 시작했다. 예를 들어 호주는 영국 범죄자들을 위한 식민지였다. 영국은 더 많은 감옥을 짓는 대신 범죄자들을 호주로 보냈다. 반면 인도는 상업적인 목적으로 영국의 식민지가 되었다. 영국은 인도에 있는 차와 값비싼 향신료들을 원했다.

3. 악기로서 기타의 역사는 500년이나 된다. 하지만 1930년대에 사람들은 전자기타를 만들기 시작했다. 전자 기타의 발명으로 음악은 급변하게 된다. 이전까지 음악에서 기타가 차지하는 비중은 작았다. 하지만 전자 기타는 곧 밴드에서 가장 중요한 악기가 되었다. 또한 전자기타는 많은 다양한 소리를 낼 수 있었고 이로 인해 음악도 변화했다. 블루스와 로큰롤은 모두 전자 기타의 산물이다.

### Basic Drills 2   p.140

2  Humans are the main cause of shrinking forests.
3  Shrinking forests cause problems for the Earth and for people.
X  Shrinking forests are causing pollution.
1  Modern technology brought attention to shrinking forests.

1. 세계의 숲은 점점 줄어들고 있다. 아마존 우림 같은 거대한 숲은 50년 전보다 20% 감소했다. 오랫동안 누구도 이 사실을 알아차리지 못했다. 숲은 거대하고 측정하기가 어려웠기 때문에 아무도 숲의 실제 크기를 알지 못했다. 하지만 이제는 비행기나 인공위성에서 찍은 사진이 있다. 이 사진들은 매년 숲이 점점 줄어드는 것을 명확히 보여준다.

2. 세계의 숲이 줄어드는 원인에는 여러 가지가 있다. 벌목 회사는 많은 나무를 베어 낸다. 종종 그들은 새 나무를 심는다. 하지만 새 나무들이 자라려면 시간이 많이 걸리고 그 기간 동안 벌목 회사는 더 많은 나무들을 베어 낸다. 농부들 역시 농지를 확보하기 위해 나무를 벤다. 이는 가난한 나라에서 특히 그렇다.

3. 세계의 숲은 점점 줄어들고 이로 인해 많은 문제들이 발생한다. 세계의 거대한 숲은 우리가 숨쉬는 신선한 공기를 배출한다. 이 숲이 점점 작아지면 공기는 더 나빠진다. 나쁜 공기는 사람들에게 여러 가지 건강상의 문제를 일으킨다. 게다가 숲은 수많은 동물들의 집이다. 숲이 줄어들면서 이런 동물들이 많이 죽어가고 있다. 이들 중 상당수는 인간에게 유익해서 이들이 사라지는 것은 인간에게 좋지 않다.

# Basic Drills 3      p.141

1. **Early humans used dead animals for many things.** They used animal skins as clothing. The animal skins were tough and strong. They were also warm and were very important during the cold winters. Early humans also used the animal bones to make tools and weapons. Early humans made some of the first knives from animal bones. They also made arrows and other weapons from animal bones.

2. Female black widow spiders are very poisonous, but male black widow spiders are not. **You can tell a male black widow from a female black widow in many ways.** Female black widows look different from male black widows. A female black widow is about twice the size of a male. In addition, female black widows have a red spot on their bellies. Males are completely black and have no spots. Moreover, females usually build larger webs than males. A female's web may be several feet across. Males usually do not build webs as large as this.

3. Tattoos are very popular these days. Most parents don't like tattoos because they are permanent. Once a child gets a tattoo, they can never take it off. **Some kinds of tattoos, however, are not permanent.** Henna tattoos use a special ink to color the skin. The ink stays on the skin for about a month and then washes off. Henna tattoos originally come from India. Young people can also get temporary tattoos. Temporary tattoos are like stickers for you skin. They usually come off in about two weeks.

**WORDS**  clothing, completely, permanent

1. 초기에 인간들은 죽은 동물을 여러 가지로 이용했다. 그들은 동물의 가죽을 옷으로 썼다. 동물의 가죽은 질기고 튼튼하며 또한 따뜻해서 추운 겨울 동안 매우 중요한 역할을 한다. 더욱이 초기 인간들은 동물의 뼈를 사용해서 연장과 무기를 만들었다. 최초의 칼 중 몇 개는 동물의 뼈로 만들었다. 그들은 또 동물의 뼈로 화살과 다른 무기들을 만들었다.

2. 암컷 검은과부거미의 독은 굉장히 강하다. 하지만 수컷 검은과부거미는 그렇지 않다. 검은과부거미의 암수를 구분하는 방법에는 여러 가지가 있다. 암컷 검은과부거미는 수컷 검은과부거미와 생김새가 다르다. 암컷이 수컷의 약 두 배 정도이다. 그리고 암컷은 배에 빨간 점이 있다. 수컷은 전체적으로 검은색이고 점이 없다. 또한 암컷은 주로 수컷보다 더 큰 집을 짓는다. 암컷은 지름이 몇 피트씩 되는 집을 짓는다. 수컷은 이렇게 크게 집을 짓지 않는다.

3. 요즘 문신이 유행이다. 부모들 대부분은 문신이 영구적이기 때문에 별로 좋아하지 않는다. 일단 문신을 하면 절대로 지울 수 없다. 하지만 어떤 문신은 영구적이지 않다. 헤나 문신은 특수한 잉크를 사용하여 피부에 물을 들인다. 그 잉크는 한 달 정도 피부에 남다가 지워진다. 헤나 문신은 원래 인도에서 온 것이다. 젊은이들은 일회용 문신을 할 수도 있다. 일회용 문신은 피부에 붙이는 스티커 같은 것이다. 그것은 2주 정도가 지나면 떨어진다.

## Reading Practice ❶      p.142

(B), (E), (F)

### 생명수

피는 생명수이다. 피가 없으면 사람은 살 수 없다. 사람의 몸에는 평균 5리터의 피가 있다. 비록 눈으로 볼 수 없지만 피는 세 가지 다른 부분으로 구성되어 있다. 적혈구는 크기가 작은 세포이다. 그것은 인체의 각 기관에 산소와 양분을 운반한다. 적혈구는 동그란 베개처럼 생겼다. 적혈구는 너무 작아서 육안으로 볼 수는 없지만 몸속에 많이 들어 있다. 한 방울의 피에는 2억 5천만 개의 적혈구가 있다.

백혈구는 적혈구보다 크기가 크다. 백혈구는 세균과 싸우기 때문에 병에 걸렸을 때 매우 중요한 역할을 한다. 백혈구는 적혈구만큼 많지 않다. 피 한 방울에는 백만 개 정도의 백혈구가 있다. 사실 백혈구에도 다섯 가지 종류가 있는데 각각의 혈구가 다른 종류의 세균과 싸운다. 마지막으로 피의 55%는 혈장이 구성하고 있다. 혈장은 물과 비슷하다. 혈장의 임무는 적혈구와 백혈구를 몸속에서 운반하는 것이다.

/ 해 / 설 /

요약문 첫 문장에 제시된 것처럼 이 글은 혈액의 세 가지 구성 요소에 대해 이야기하고 있다. 세 구성 요소는 적혈구와 백혈구, 그리고 혈장이다. 그러므로 각각의 구성 요소에 대해 설명하고 있는 보기를 고르면 된다.

## Reading Practice ❷  p.143

(B), (D), (F)

### 흑사병

1347년, 끔찍한 병이 유럽 전역에 퍼지기 시작했다. 그 병에 걸리면 피부가 까맣게 되기 때문에 사람들은 그 병을 흑사병이라고 불렀다. 불과 5년 동안 흑사병으로 2천 5백만 명의 사람이 죽었다. 그것은 거의 유럽 인구의 3분의 1이었다. 유럽인들은 흑사병을 멈추게 하려고 노력했지만 모든 시도는 병을 더 빠르게 확산시킬 뿐이었다.

이 병은 유럽인들을 극심한 공포에 몰아넣었다. 일단 마을에서 한 사람이 병에 걸리면 나머지 사람들은 다른 마을로 도망가려고 했다. 이들 중 많은 사람들이 이미 병에 걸렸기 때문에 병은 더욱 확산되었다. 다만 그들이 여태 모르고 있었을 뿐이었다. 도망 다니면서 그들은 병을 새로운 지역으로 옮겼다. 게다가 유럽 사람들은 고양이가 그 병을 옮긴다고 생각했다. 그 당시 유럽 사람들은 고양이를 악마적인 동물이라고 생각했기 때문에 수백만 마리의 고양이를 죽였다. 불행하게도 흑사병을 옮긴 것은 쥐였기 때문에 유럽 사람들은 고양이를 죽임으로써 병의 확산을 도울 뿐이었다.

/ 해 / 설 /

이 글은 첫 단락에서는 흑사병의 피해에 대해, 두 번째 단락에서는 흑사병이 더 널리 퍼지게 된 것에 대해 이야기하고 있으며, 그 원인을 두 가지로 분석하고 있다. 주어진 첫 문장은 글의 첫 번째 단락을 요약하고 있다. 그러나 이 글은 두 번째 단락의 내용이 더 중요하다. 두 번째 단락의 중심 내용은 (B)이며, (D)와 (F)는 (B)를 뒷받침하는 내용이다. 나머지 보기들은 중요하지 않은 내용이다.

## Reading Practice ❸  p.144

(B), (E), (F)

### 기울어진 탑

대부분의 유명한 건축물은 뛰어난 축조술 때문에 유명하다. 그런데 제작자의 형편없는 작업 때문에 유명한 건축물도 있다. 피사의 사탑은 이탈리아 피사에 있는 유명한 탑이다. 모든 건물들은 똑바로 서 있지만 피사의 사탑은 그렇지 않다. 그것은 기울어져 있다! 피사의 사탑은 남쪽으로 10도 정도 기울어져 있다. 어떻게 이런 일이 일어났을까?

피사의 사탑은 1173년에 지어지기 시작했는데 거의 시작하자마자 문제가 발생했다. 탑 아래에 있는 지면이 매우 부드러워서 탑의 한쪽 면이 바닥으로 가라앉기 시작했다. 그 당시 기술로는 이 문제를 수정할 수 없었지만 피사 사람들은 포기하지 않았다. 그들은 탑이 계속 기우는데도 불구하고 계속해서 탑을 지었다.

놀랍게도 그 탑은 쓰러지지 않았고 몇 년 후 매우 유명한 건축물이 되었다. 사람들은 유럽 각지에서 피사의 사탑을 보러 왔다. 몇 년 동안 사람들은 탑에 많은 작업을 하였다. 초기 수리공들은 탑을 똑바로 세우는 데 중점을 두었다. 하지만 피사의 사람들은 "기울어진" 탑이 똑바로 서 있는 탑보다 더 인기가 있다는 것을 깨닫기 시작했고 탑을 똑바로 세우려는 노력을 중단했다.

/ 해 / 설 /

이 글은 피사의 사탑이 기울어져서 유명하다는 사실과 그렇게 지어지게 된 과정을 설명하고 있다. 보기들의 중요성을 비교하여 보다 중요한 내용을 고르도록 한다.

## Reading Practice ❹  p.145

(A), (C), (D)

### 황제의 군대

　중국의 도시 시안에서는 세계에서 가장 오래된 군대를 볼 수 있다. 각각의 군사들은 2천 살이고 아직도 싸울 준비가 되어 있다! 그 군사들이 조각상이기 때문이다. 그리고 이 군대는 역사상 가장 거대한 규모의 예술 작품 중 하나이기도 하다.

　기원전 2세기에 진시황은 중국 전체를 지배한 최초의 왕이 되었다. 그는 만리장성을 쌓기 시작한 왕이기도 하다. 황제는 크고 강한 군사를 갖고 있었는데 죽으면 그들을 모두 데려가고 싶어했다. 그래서 그는 조각가들에게 그 군대를 똑같이 만들어 줄 것을 명령했다. 그것은 방대한 작업이었다. 그들은 6천 개 이상의 석재 군사를 만들어야 했다. 그리고 군대를 위한 말까지 만들어야 했다. 황제의 군대를 만드는 데 수천 명의 일꾼과 6년 이상의 시간이 걸렸다. 황제가 죽자 조각가들은 군대를 그의 무덤 옆에 묻어서 영원히 황제를 지킬 수 있도록 했다.

/ 해 / 설 /

　이 글은 진시황의 지하 군단에 대한 내용이다. 그러므로 진시황의 지하 군단과 직접 관련있는 내용을 고르도록 한다. (A)는 첫 단락의 중심 내용이며 지하 군단의 예술작품으로서의 가치를 말해주므로 중요한 내용이다. (B)는 지하 군단과 관계없는 내용이다. (C)와 (D)는 지하 군단에 대한 중요한 내용이지만 (E)는 중요하지 않은 내용이고 (F)는 본문의 내용과 다른 의미를 전달하고 있다.

## iBT Practice 1    p.146

1. (B)   2. (B)   3. (C)   4. (B)   5. (B)
6. (A), (C), (E)

### 파나마 운하

　수백 년 동안 대서양에서 태평양으로 가려면 배는 남미 끝까지 돌아서 가야 했다. 이렇게 하려면 많은 시간이 걸렸고 또한 매우 위험하기도 했다. 남미의 최남단은 심한 폭풍우로 유명했다. 그 후 1800년대 후반에 프랑스는 파나마에 운하를 건설하기로 했다. 운하는 두 개의 수역을 연결하는 인공 강과 같은 것이다. 이 경우에 운하는 대서양과 태평양을 연결하게 될 것이었다.

　프랑스의 계획에는 시작부터 문제가 발생했다. 계획은 훌륭했지만 장비가 열악했으며, 그들은 50마일의 운하를 파야 했다. 그들은 거대한 굴착기가 필요했지만 그 작업에 적합한 기계는 미국만이 갖고 있었다. 게다가 파나마는 정글이다. 그곳에는 많은 벌레가 있고 그 중 어떤 것은 프랑스인에게 익숙하지 않은 질병을 옮기기도 했다. 그 결과, 프랑스의 인부들은 빈번하게 병에 걸렸고 작업은 매우 느려졌다.

　1888년에 프랑스는 운하 건설을 중단했다. 1904년에 미국이 운하의 건설을 이어받았다. 처음에 미국은 질병을 막기 위해 벌레들을 죽였다. 그리고 커다란 굴착기를 동원했다. 그 좋은 장비로도 운하를 완공하는 데에는 3만 9천명의 인부가 동원되었고 10년이 소요되었다.

/ 해 / 설 /

1. 6째 줄의 "A canal is like an artificial river that connects two other bodies of water."라는 설명과 일치하는 보기를 고른다.

2. (A), (C)는 본문에 직접 언급되어 있고, (D)는 10째 줄의 "their equipment was too small, while they had over 50 miles of canal to dig"이라는 부분에서 운하의 길이가 매우 길었음을 짐작할 수 있다.

3. 마지막 단락에 설명되어 있다.

4. 문맥상으로는 (A)와 (D)도 가능하나, "constantly"의 의미와 가장 가까운 것은 (B)이다.

5. 첫 번째 단락에서 파나마 운하가 생기기 전에 남미를 돌아가야 했을 때는 폭풍 때문에 매우 위험했다고 설명되어 있다.

6. 이 글은 프랑스가 파나마 운하 건설을 시도했다가 실패한 것과 그 후에 미국이 운하를 완성한 이야기를 하고 있다. 그러므로 (C)와 (E)는 반드시 포함되어야 한다. (B)는 (A)를 설명하는 것으로, 중요하지 않은 내용이며 (D)도 중요하지 않은 내용이다. 남은 (A)와 (F) 중에서 (F)는 미국이 공사를 하던 과정을 구체적으로 설명한 내용이고 (A)는 첫 단락의 중심 내용이므로 (A)가 상대적으로 더 중요하다고 볼 수 있다.

## iBT Practice 2    p.149

1. (C)   2. **B**   3. (C)   4. (A)   5. (A)
6. (A), (C), (E)

### 라브레아 타르 광산

　어떤 과학자들에게는 캘리포니아의 라브레아만큼 좋은 곳이 없을 것이다. 수천 년 전에 살던 동물에 대해 연구하고 싶다면 라브레아는 세계에서 최적의 장소일 것이다. 라브레아에는 라브레아 타르 구덩이가 있기 때문이다. 타르는 기름에서 나온다. 타르는 도로를 만들 때 쓰이기 때문에 오늘날 많은 타르 공장이 있지만 자연에서도 얻을 수 있다.

4만년 전부터 8천년 전까지 라브레아에는 거대한 타르 구덩이가 있었다. 동물들은 타르 안으로 걸어 들어갔지만 나올 수 없었다. 타르 속에 가라앉아 죽었기 때문이다. 그러나 타르는 동물의 시체를 온전한 상태로 보존했다. 나중에 타르를 채굴하면서 사람들은 동물의 시체를 발견했다. 과학자들은 타르 구덩이에서 59종의 육지 동물과 135종의 조류를 발견했다.

이 시체들은 수천 년 전에 이미 멸종한 동물들이기 때문에 과학자들에게 매우 유용하다. 일례로 과학자들은 타르 광산에서 검치호랑이라는 거대한 고양이의 몸을 발견했다. 이 동물은 만년 전에 멸종한 것이었다. 과학자들은 타르 광산으로부터 많은 것들을 알아냈다. 그들은 타르 광산을 발견하기 전보다 북미 대륙에 대해 더 많은 사실을 알게 되었다. 우리는 이제 미대륙에 검치호랑이 같은 크고 사나운 동물이 살았다는 것을 알고 있다. 하지만 이 동물들 중 대부분은 만오천 년 전에 인류가 출현하기 전에 멸종되었다.

## Word Review p.152

1. summary
2. average
3. notice
4. spread
5. colony
6. electric
7. invention
8. minor

## Sentence Review p.153

1. each kind of which
2. it turned the skin black
3. helped the disease spread faster
4. had a great deal of work done to it
5. It took thousands of workers over thirty-six years

/ 해 / 설 /

1. 2째 줄의 "If you want to study animals from thousands of years ago, La Brea may be the best place in the world."에서 알 수 있다.

2. 주어진 문장은 "tar"에 대해 설명하고 있으므로 "tar"가 처음 언급된 문장 바로 뒤에 들어가는 것이 자연스럽다.

3. 라브레아에서 발견된 동물들은 이미 수천 년 전에 사라진 동물들이다.

4. "discovered"의 자리에 단어들을 대입해 본다.

5. 라브레아에서 발견된 동물들은 수천 년 전에 멸종되었으므로 현재 북미에 살고 있는 동물들은 4만년 전과 전혀 다르리라는 것을 짐작할 수 있다.

6. 요약문을 작성할 때는, 원문을 보지 못한 사람들이 요약문만 읽고서도 중요한 내용을 파악할 수 있어야 한다. 주어진 첫 문장은 라브레아가 과학자들에게 중요한 장소라는 사실을 이야기하고 있다. 그러므로 나머지 문장들은 라브레아가 어떤 곳이며 왜 중요한지를 설명해야 한다. 각각의 보기에 대해서 이러한 질문을 해보도록 한다. 예를 들어 (B)와 같은 내용은 라브레아가 왜 중요한지에 대해 아무것도 말해주지 않는다. 주제와 직접적으로 관계 있는 보기를 선택해야 한다.

# Mini Test

## Mini Test ①      p.154 - 163

1. (A)  2. (C)  3. (B)  4. (D)  5. C
6. (B)  7. (C)  8. (B)  9. (A), (C), (E)
10. (B)  11. (B)  12. (C)  13. (C)  14. (C)
15. B  16. (B)
17. **North Pole:**
- Sea of ice
- Large animals
- Not as cold

**South Pole:**
- Huge continent
- Almost no plants

18. (B)  19. (C)  20. (A)  21. (C)  22. (B)
23. (B)  24. (B)  25. (B), (E), (F)

### Passage 1      p.155

**후버와 FBI**

연방수사국, 즉 FBI는 미국에서 가장 유명한 수사기관이다. FBI 요원은 일반 경찰관과 다르다. 일반 경찰관은 관할 주에서만 사법권을 행사할 수 있다. 즉 그들은 자신의 주 내에서만 일할 수 있고, 사람들을 체포할 수 있다. 그러나 FBI 요원은 미국 전역에서 사법권을 행사한다. 가장 유명한 FBI 요원은 J. 에드가 후버였다.

후버는 정부를 위해 일하는 변호사로 그의 경력을 시작했다. 그는 여러 중요한 사건을 다루었지만, 그 중에서도 가장 유명한 사건은 파머 습격 사건이다. 파머 습격 사건에서 미국 정부는 수천 명의 사람들을 체포했는데, 이는 그들이 정부에 대항하여 활동했다고 후버가 생각했기 때문이었다. 사실은 그들 중 대부분이 무죄였지만 후버는 그들이 미국의 적이라고 생각했다.

1924년, 후버는 연방 수사국의 국장이 되었다. 그 당시에 수사국은 작은 기관이어서 거의 힘이 없었다. 몇 년이 지나면서 후버는 FBI를 크고 막강한 권력을 가진 기관으로 만들었다. 1930년대에 FBI는 알 카포네와 베이비 페이스 넬슨처럼 유명한 갱단을 체포하면서 유명해졌다. 그는 또한 경찰 수사에 과학을 도입했다. 예를 들어 후버는 처음으로 지문 연구소를 시작했다.

그러나 후버가 한 모든 일이 훌륭했던 것은 아니다. 그는 많은 사람들이 미국의 적이라고 생각했다. 1940년대와 1950년대 동안 후버는 수많은 사람들을 잡아들였다. 그는 그들이 공산주의자라고 생각했지만 사실은 파머 습격 사건 때와 다를 바가 없었다.

### / 해 / 설 /

1. 첫 단락에서 FBI는 미국 전역에 걸쳐 사법권을 행사할 수 있다고 설명되어 있다(5째 줄 "In contrast, FBI agents have jurisdiction all across the United States.").

2. 8째 줄의 "Hoover started his career as a lawyer for the government."에 설명되어 있다.

3. 13째 줄의 "Actually, most of the people were innocent"와 "Hoover thought they were the enemies of the United States"가 "but"으로 연결되어 있으므로 "innocent"의 의미는 '미국의 적'이 아니라는 의미여야 한다.

4. 일반적으로 대명사는 바로 앞에 나온 주어를 가리키는 경우가 가장 많다. 앞 절의 주어인 "people"을 대입해 본다.

5. "that"이 가리키는 내용이 무엇인지, 즉 후버가 변화시킨 것이 무엇인지 생각해 본다. FBI에 일어난 변화를 설명하는 부분을 찾아 변화 이전과 이후의 사이에 주어진 문장이 들어가야 자연스럽다.

6. "gangsters"의 자리에 단어들을 대입해 보고 가장 자연스러운 것을 찾는다.

7. 18째 줄의 "the FBI became famous for arresting gangsters like…"하는 부분에 나와 있다.

8. "Palmer Raids"에 대해서는 두 번째 단락에 나와 있다. 이 사건은 후버가 죄 없는 사람들을 수천 명이나 체포했던 사건이다. 1940-50년대에 후버가 사람들을 공산주의자 혐의로 체포한 것과 이 "Palmer Raids" 사건의 공통점을 생각해 본다.

9. 지문은 후버라는 인물에 초점이 맞추어져 있으므로, 그의 경력에서 중요한 사항들을 선택한다. 각 단락의 중심이 되는 내용과 세부사항을 구별하도록 한다. (A)는 지문의 두 번째 단락 전체가 후버의 변호사 활동에 대한 것이므로 포함되어야 한다. (B)는 후버가 변호사로 일할 때 있었던 사건에 대한 세부적인 내용이므로 포함되지 않아야 한다. (C)는 세 번째 단락의 중심 내용이다. (D)는 후버가 과학적인 방법을 수사에 도입한 예이다(일반적으로 예시에 해당되는 내용은 요약문에 포함되지 않는다). (E)는 마지막 단락의 중심 내용이다. (F)는 세 번째 단락에 언급된 세부사항이다.

## Passage 2
p.158

### 북극과 남극

북극과 남극은 지구상에서 가장 추운 두 곳이다. 지구의 가장 윗부분과 아랫부분인 이곳에서 기온은 한 번도 영상으로 올라가지 않고, 대체로 빙점의 훨씬 아래를 밑돈다. 거대한 얼음판이 육지를 덮고 있고 바다는 빙하로 가득하다. 그러나 극심한 추위와 수많은 얼음 외에 북극과 남극의 공통점은 거의 없다. 북극과 남극은 사실 서로 전혀 다르다.

북극의 대부분이 실제로 드넓은 얼음 바다임에도 불구하고, 북극에는 많은 생물이 존재한다. 많은 식물이 추운 날씨에서도 살아갈 수 있다. 사실은 눈이 식물이 살 수 있도록 돕는다. 눈 아래의 온도는 눈 위의 온도보다 25℃나 더 따뜻할 수 있다. 눈은 식물을 덮어서 그들을 따뜻하게 유지한다. 북극에는 동물도 많이 있다. 어떤 동물은 추운 겨울 동안 북극을 떠나기도 하지만 북극여우 같은 동물은 1년 내내 추위 속에서 살아간다.

남극은 사실 광활한 대륙이지만, 땅은 수천 피트의 얼음 아래에 있다. 남극이 북극보다 훨씬 고도가 높기 때문에 날씨도 더 춥다. 남극의 생물은 북극과 많이 다르다. 식물이 거의 없고, 남극 중심부에는 생명체가 전혀 없다. 바닷가에만 생물이 존재한다. 남극에는 새와 물고기가 많이 있지만 북극의 북극곰 같은 큰 동물은 살지 않는다.

/ 해 / 설 /

**10.** 앞에서 북극과 남극이 지구에서 가장 추운 두 곳이라는 이야기를 하였으므로 "extreme cold"가 매우 심한 추위를 뜻한다는 것을 짐작할 수 있다.

**11.** 13째 줄의 "The snow covers the plants and keeps them warm." 문장에 설명되어 있다.

**12.** 8째 줄의 "Although most of the North Pole is actually a huge sea of ice ..."를 보면 북극은 얼음으로 이루어져 있고 땅은 거의 없다는 사실을 알 수 있다.

**13.** 17째 줄의 "Because the South Pole is much higher than the North Pole, it is also colder."에 설명되어 있다.

**14.** 일반적으로 대명사는 바로 앞에 나온 주어를 가리키는 경우가 가장 많다. 앞 절의 주어인 "the South Pole"을 대입해 보고 뜻이 통하는지 확인한다.

**15.** 주어진 문장은 남극이 북극보다 높다는 내용 앞에 들어가야 적절하다.

**16.** "coasts" 바로 뒤에 "near the sea"라고 설명이 되어 있다. 이처럼 어려운 단어가 나올 때는 쉼표 후에 그 설명이 따라 나오는 경우가 있다. 때로는 쉼표 뒤에 '즉'이라는 뜻으로 "or"가 삽입되기도 한다.

**17.** (A) Huge continent: 16째 줄 참조
(B) No animals: 언급되지 않은 내용
(C) Sea of ice: 19째 줄 참조
(D) Almost no plants: 19-20째 줄 참조
(E) Large animals: 22째 줄 참조
(F) Not as cold: 18째 줄 참조
(G) Snow all year: 언급되지 않은 내용

## Passage 3
p.161

### 올바른 식생활

당신은 오늘 점심으로 무엇을 먹을 것인가? 이것은 매우 중요한 질문이다. 음식은 우리의 몸을 '만든다'. 당신은 종이로 집을 지으려고 하지는 않을 것이다. 그렇지 않은가? 물론 아니다! 그 집은 튼튼하지 않을 것이다. 만약 몸이 건강하기를 원한다면 음식을 신중하게 고를 필요가 있다.

가장 기본적인 음식은 쌀과 빵 같은 곡물이다. 이러한 음식은 우리 몸의 기본 연료인 탄수화물을 많이 함유하고 있다. 탄수화물은 에너지를 공급한다. 쌀과 빵을 충분히 섭취하지 않으면 쉽게 피로를 느끼게 된다.

그 다음으로 중요한 음식군은 과일과 채소이다. 우리 몸은 하루에 약 4-5개 종류의 과일과 야채를 필요로 한다. 과일과 야채는 우리 몸에 중요한 비타민을 제공한다. 예를 들어, 오렌지나 다른 과일에 들어있는 비타민 C는 병을 물리치도록 도와준다.

한 걸음 앞으로 움직여 보라. 그러면 54개의 근육을 사용한 것이다. 근육을 보다 강하고 튼튼하게 만들고자 한다면 단백질이 필요하다. 대부분의 단백질은 고기에 들어있지만 콩과 견과류에서도 섭취할 수 있다.

한 걸음 움직였을 때 당신은 16개의 뼈를 움직인 것이다. 그러나 그것은 작은 수에 불과하다. 우리 몸에는 206개의 뼈가 있기 때문이다. 각각의 뼈를 튼튼하게 유지하려면 칼슘이 필요하다. 칼슘은 주로 치즈, 요구르트와 같은 유제품, 그리고 물론 우유에서 얻을 수 있다. 올바른 식생활을 하면 우리는 훨씬 더 건강해질 것이다.

/ 해 / 설 /

**18.** 글쓴이는 비유의 방법을 사용하여, 종이로 집을 지으면 집이 약하게 되듯이 우리가 먹는 음식에 따라 우리 몸이 강해질 수 있다는 이야기를 하고 있다.

**19.** 탄수화물이 우리 몸에 에너지를 준다는 사실로부터 탄수화물이 포함된 음식이 우리 몸에 매우 중요하다는 것을 알 수 있다.

**20.** 19번 문제에서 설명한 것처럼 탄수화물이 포함된 음식이 가장 중요하다.

**21.** 12째 줄의 "Fruits and vegetables give your body important vitamins."에 설명되어 있다.

**22.** "them"은 복수이므로 (A), (C), (D)는 답이 될 수 없다.

**23.** "remain"은 '…한 상태로 남아 있다'는 의미이다.

**24.** 마지막 단락에서 '칼슘이 뼈를 튼튼하게 한다'는 내용과 '칼슘은 치즈, 요구르트와 같은 유제품과 우유에 들어 있다'는 내용을 종합하여 추론한다.

**25.** 이 글은 건강한 몸을 유지하기 위해서는 적절한 음식을 먹어야 한다는 것이 주제이며, 탄수화물과 비타민, 단백질, 칼슘의 섭취에 대해 한 단락씩 설명하고 있다. 보기 중 (B)는 탄수화물에 대해, (E)는 비타민에 대해, (F)는 단백질과 칼슘에 대해 이야기하고 있으므로 이 세 가지를 선택해야 한다.

## Mini Test 2
p.164 - 173

1. (C)   2. (D)   3. D   4. (C)   5. (C)
6. (B)   7. (C), (D), (F)   8. (B)   9. (B)
10. (C)   11. (D)   12. (A)   13. (C)   14. (B)
15. (B), (D), (F)   16. (D)   17. (B)   18. (B)
19. (B)   20. (A)   21. (C)   22. (D)
23. United States:
- Mercury program
- Changed launch plan
- Used monkeys in space program

Russia:
- First man in space
- Sputnik

### Passage 1
p.165

**허리케인 미치(Mitch)**

허리케인은 매우 강력한 폭풍이다. 역사상 최악의 허리케인은 허리케인 미치였다. 1998년 10월 말과 11월 초, 허리케인 미치는 11,000명이 넘는 사람들을 죽이고 수천 명의 사람들의 집 수백 채를 파괴하며 수십억 달러에 이르는 피해를 발생시켰다. 미치는 온두라스와 니카라과 두 나라를 가장 심하게 강타했고, 가장 큰 규모의 피해와 가장 많은 수의 사망자를 낳았다. 미치는 왜 유독 이 두 나라에서 그렇게 많은 사람들을 죽인 것일까? 여기에는 몇 가지 원인이 있다.

첫째, 허리케인은 보통 빠르게 이동하지만, 미치는 이상 기후 조건 때문에 온두라스와 니카라과를 아주 느린 속도로 지나갔다. 그래서 온두라스와 니카라과는 다른 나라보다 강수량이 훨씬 많았다. 3일 동안 3피트에 달하는 비가 내렸다. 두 나라에는 끔찍한 홍수가 일어났고 불어난 물에 많은 사람이 죽었다.

둘째, 니카라과와 온두라스는 모두 가난한 나라이다. 많은 주택이 허술하게 지어졌고 튼튼하지 못했다. 이러한 집은 허리케인의 강풍에 쉽게 파괴되었다.

끝으로, 두 나라는 작은 나라이다. 더 큰 나라에서는 사람들이 허리케인이 지나가는 동안 안전한 장소로 대피할 수 있다. 예를 들어, 미국인들은 허리케인이 왔을 때 플로리다를 떠나 조지아로 이동했다. 허리케인이 조지아를 치지 않아서 사람들은 안전했다. 온두라스와 니카라과는 나라 전역이 미치의 사정권에 들었다. 그래서 사람들이 피할 만한 안전한 장소가 없었다.

/ 해 / 설 /

1. 3째 줄의 "hurricane Mitch killed over 11,000 people"에 설명되어 있다. 여기서 "over"는 "more than"의 뜻이다.

2. 두 번째 단락의 첫 번째 문장과 두 번째 문장(11-13줄)에 설명되어 있다.

3. 주어진 문장은 집이 무너져서 사람들이 죽었다는 이야기를 하고 있으므로, 그 원인에 해당되는 문장을 찾아 주어진 문장의 앞에 오도록 배치한다.

4. 일반적으로 대명사는 바로 앞에 나온 주어를 가리키는 경우가 가장 많다. 앞 문장의 주어인 "Nicaragua and Honduras"를 대입해 보고 뜻이 통하는지 확인한다.

5. 글의 마지막 문장인 "In Honduras and Nicaragua, hurricane Mitch hit the whole country, so there was no safe place for people to go."에 설명되어 있다.

6. 사람들이 플로리다를 떠나 안전한 지역인 조지아로 대피했던 사례는 전국이 허리케인의 세력권에 들어 대피할 곳이 없었던 온두라스와 니카라과의 사례와 대조를 이룬다.

7. 주어진 첫 문장은 글 전체의 주제를 담고 있다. 그리고 지문의 2, 3, 4번째 단락은 그 주제를 뒷받침하는 세 가지 이유를 각각 설명하고 있다. 각 단락의 내용을 요약하는 보기 세 가지를 찾도록 한다.

## Passage 2    p.168

### 브라질의 축구 스타

축구는 영웅과 슈퍼스타로 가득하다. 오늘날, 브라질의 호나우두와 영국의 데이비드 베컴은 세계적으로 잘 알려져 있고 팬들에게 사랑받고 있다. 그러나 이들보다 훨씬 더 유명한 축구 선수가 있다. 그의 이름은 에드손 아란테스 도 나시멘토이지만, 펠레로 더 널리 알려져 있다.

펠레는 1940년에 브라질에서 태어났다. 브라질에서는 축구가 국민적 스포츠로, 펠레는 축구를 하며 자랐다. 그의 아버지는 재능 있는 축구 선수였으나 다리 부상을 입게 되었다. 그 후, 그는 축구를 할 수 없어서 아들에게 축구를 가르치는 데 시간을 보냈다. 1956년, 펠레는 처음으로 프로축구 클럽인 산토스 축구클럽에 가입한다. 펠레가 들어온 후 산토스 클럽은 남미의 최고 축구팀 중 하나가 되었고, 펠레는 남미에서 순식간에 유명해졌다.

그리고 마법의 해인 1958년이 왔다. 1958년은 펠레의 선수 생활 중 가장 위대한 해일 것이다. 그 해에 그는 158골을 넣어 브라질을 월드컵 우승으로 이끌었다. 펠레의 진두 하에 브라질은 1962년과 1970년에도 월드컵에서 우승했다.

펠레는 팀을 위대한 승리로 이끌었을 뿐 아니라 개인적으로도 놀라운 것들을 성취했다. 1969년에 그는 천 번째 골을 기록했다. 축구 생활을 마감할 때까지 그는 1,363개 게임에서 1,282골을 넣었다. 거의 한 게임당 한 골을 넣은 셈이다. 지금까지 다른 어떤 선수도 이 기록에 근접하지조차 못했다.

/ 해 / 설 /

8. 호나우두와 베컴의 이야기를 하고 있지만 이들보다 더 유명한 선수는 펠레라고 이야기하고 있다.

9. 일반적으로 대명사는 바로 앞에 나온 주어를 가리키는 경우가 가장 많다. 앞 문장의 주어를 찾아 대입해 본다.

10. 7째 줄의 "Pelé was born in 1940 in Brazil, where soccer is a national passion, and Pelé grew up playing the game."에서 알 수 있다.

11. 8-11째 줄에 설명되어 있다.

12. 15째 줄의 "Then came the magical year of 1958." 이하에서 설명되어 있다.

13. "victories"의 자리에 다른 단어들을 대입해 보고 가장 적절한 것을 찾는다.

14. 23째 줄에서 "This is almost one goal for every game." 이라고 한 것은 펠레가 평균적으로 경기당 약 1골을 기록했다는 것인 반면, (B)는 실제로 매 게임마다 1골을 넣었다는 것이므로 의미가 다르다.

15. 각각의 보기에 해당되는 단락을 찾은 후, 그 중요성을 비교해 본다.
    ● (A)는 첫 단락의 세부사항이다.
    ● (B)는 두 번째 단락의 중심내용이다.
    ● (C)는 두 번째 단락의 세부사항이다.
    ● (D)는 세 번째 단락의 중심내용이다.
    ● (E)는 세 번째 단락의 세부사항이다.
    ● (F)는 마지막 단락의 중심내용이다.
    그러므로 답은 (B), (D), (F)가 된다.

## Passage 3    p.171

### 우주 경쟁

1957년, 러시아는 작은 금속 공인 스푸트니크 호를 우주로 쏘아올렸다. 스푸트니크 호는 지구 주위를 돌면서 하나의 무선 메시지를 지구로 보냈다. 하지만 그 발신음은 미국인들을 놀래키기에 충분했다. 러시아가 우주 경쟁에서 이기고 있었던 것이다. 우주 경쟁이란 무엇인가? 아주 간단하다. 어느 나라가 우주로 처음 진출하는지를 판가름하는 경쟁이었다. 러시아와 미국 모두 굉장히 이기고 싶어했다. 이 경쟁에서 러시아는 스푸트니크 호로 첫 승리를 거머쥐었으나, 다음 단계, 즉 사람을 우주로 보내는 것이 두 나라 모두에게 훨씬 더 중요한 일이었다.

우주로 사람을 보내려는 미국의 계획은 '머큐리 프로그램(Mercury program)'이었다. 미국인은 첫 우주 비행사로 해군의 테스트 조종사인 앨런 셰퍼드를 선택했다. 사람들은 그의 임무를 '머큐리 프리덤 7(Mercury Freedom 7)'이라고 불렀다. 셰퍼드는 임무를 위해 몇 달 동안 훈련을 받았다. 그 동안 기술자와 과학자들은 우주선의 모든 부품을 테스트하며 안전을 진단했다. 마침내 1961년, 원숭이를 우주로 안전하게 보낸 후, 미국인은 셰퍼드를 보낼 준비를 끝마쳤다. 2월 마지막 주에 셰퍼드의 레드스톤 로켓은 발사대 위에 놓였지만, 마지막 순간에 발생한 문제로 로켓을 발사할 수 없었다. 그들은 발사일을 5월 5일로 다시 조정했다. 그리고 나서 4월 12일, 미국인들은 끔찍한 소식을 듣게 되었다. 러시아인인 유리 가가린이 우주에 있다는 것이었다. 러시아가 또 한 번 미국을 이긴 것이었다.

/ 해 / 설 /

16. 첫 단락에 의하면 1957년에 발사된 스푸트니크 호가 최초로

우주에 보내진 물체였다.

17. 5째 줄의 "But what was the space race? Very simply, it was a race to see which country could get into space first."에 설명되어 있다.

18. 일반적으로 대명사는 바로 앞에 나온 주어를 가리키는 경우가 가장 많다. 앞 문장의 주어를 찾아 대입해 본다.

19. 20째 줄에 설명되어 있다("but a last minute problem meant that they could not launch").

20. 사람을 태우지 않고 원숭이를 태워 보낸 것은 혹시라도 발생할 수 있는 사고에 대비한 것임을 짐작할 수 있다.

21. 두 번째 단락에 나와 있는 정보를 종합해 보면 최초로 인간이 우주에 보내진 날짜는 러시아의 유리 가가린이 우주에 나간 날짜이다.

22. 마지막에 발생한 문제 때문에 발사일을 어떻게 했을지 생각해 본다.

23. (A) Mercury program: 12째 줄 참조
    (B) First man in space: 23-24째 줄 참조
    (C) Changed launch plan: 21째 줄 참조
    (D) Used monkeys in space program: 17째 줄 참조
    (E) Better scientists: 언급되지 않은 내용
    (F) Sputnik: 1째 줄 참조
    (G) First man on moon: 언급되지 않은 내용

## Mini Test 3     p.174 - 183

1. (A)  2. (C)  3. (B)  4. (A)  5. (A)
6. C   7. (C)
8. **John Wilkes Booth:**
   - Good childhood
   - Helped U.S. enemies secretly
   - Took a long time to catch
   
   **Lee Harvey Oswald:**
   - Killed President Kennedy
   - Never had a good job

9. (D)  10. (A)  11. C  12. (B)  13. (C)
14. (C)  15. (B)  16. (A)  17. (C), (D), (E)
18. (A)  19. (B)  20. (C)  21. (A)  22. (D)
23. (A)  24. A  25. (B), (D), (E)

### Passage 1     p.175

**대통령의 암살자들**

존 윌크스 부스와 리 하비 오스왈드는 미국 역사상 가장 유명한 두 살인자일 것이다. 존 윌크스 부스는 1865년에 링컨 대통령을 죽였고, 오스왈드는 약 100년 후에 케네디 대통령을 죽였다. 이 두 살인자 사이에는 흥미로운 유사점과 차이점이 있다.

부스와 오스왈드는 대통령뿐 아니라 미국의 적이기도 했다. 남북전쟁 중 오랜 기간 동안 부스는 남군에게 식량과 의약품을 몰래 가져다 주었다. 반대로 오스왈드는 공공연한 미국의 적이었다. 1959년에 그는 미국을 떠나 소련에서 살았다. 후에 그는 미국으로 돌아와 미국의 또 다른 적인 쿠바를 지원하는 활동을 했다.

두 사람 모두 미국 정부를 싫어했지만 둘의 삶은 판이하게 달랐다. 부스는 좋은 가정에서 자랐다. 그는 배우가 되었고 크게 성공했다. 오스왈드의 삶은 그다지 행복하지 않았다. 그의 아버지는 그가 태어나기도 전에 죽었다. 그는 평생 정신적 문제로 어려움을 겪었고, 변변한 직업을 가져본 적이 없었다.

마지막으로, 두 사람은 모두 재판을 받기 전에 죽었지만 전혀 다른 방법으로 죽었다. 오스왈드는 케네디 대통령을 쏘고 나서 몇 시간 후에 경찰에게 붙잡혔다. 그는 감옥에서 법원으로 가는 길에 잭 루비가 쏜 총탄에 맞아 죽었다. 반면, 부스는 그와 마찬가지로 미국 정부를 싫어한 친구들로부터 도움을 받았기 때문에 12일이 지나서야 잡혔다. 그는 체포되었을 때, 순순히 응하지 않았다. 그는 연합군과의 총격전 중 사망했다.

/ 해 / 설 /

1. 두 사람 다 재판을 받기도 전에 죽었으므로 감옥살이를 하지 않았다.

2. 일반적으로 대명사는 바로 앞에 나온 주어를 가리키는 경우가 가장 많다. 앞 문장의 주어를 찾아 대입해 본다.

3. 13째 줄에서 쿠바를 "another enemy of the U.S."라고 표현한 것을 보면 그 바로 앞에 언급된 소련 역시 미국의 적이었음을 짐작할 수 있다.

4. "support"의 자리에 단어들을 대입해 보고 가장 적절한 것을 찾는다.

5. 8째 줄의 "For much of the Civil War, Booth worked to secretly bring food and medicines to the Southern Army."를 올바르게 요약한 보기를 찾는다.

6. 오스왈드가 불행한 어린시절을 보낸 원인이 되는 문장을 찾아 주어진 문장을 그 뒤에 넣는다.

7. 오스왈드가 법정에 가는 길에 죽었다는 사실로부터 "trials"가 재판을 의미한다는 것을 짐작할 수 있다.

8. (A) Killed President Kennedy: 3-4째 줄 참조
   (B) Good childhood: 15째 줄 참조
   (C) Helped U.S. enemies secretly: 9-13째 줄 참조
   (D) Killed president for money: 언급되지 않은 내용
   (E) Took a long time to catch: 24째 줄 참조
   (F) Never had a good job: 18-19째 줄 참조
   (G) Was never caught: 두 사람 모두 붙잡혔음

## Passage 2
p.178

### 미국으로 망명한 과학자들

알버트 아인슈타인은 역사상 가장 위대한 과학자 중 한 명이었다. 처음에 아인슈타인은 전문적인 과학자가 아니었다. 그는 스위스 정부에서 일했고 여가 시간에 과학을 연구했다. 1905년에 아인슈타인은 그의 가장 중요한 과학 논문 중 하나인 '특수 상대성 이론'을 썼다. 아인슈타인은 순식간에 세계에서 가장 중요한 과학자 중 한 명이 되었다. 1916년, 아인슈타인은 '일반 상대성 이론'을 집필했다. 이 두 이론은 우주에 대한 많은 것을 설명했다.

1930년대에 나치는 독일에서 정권을 장악했다. 나치 정부는 매우 잔인했다. 아인슈타인은 나치를 좋아하지 않았고 독일을 떠나 미국으로 망명했다. 이는 독일에게는 엄청난 손실이었고 미국에게는 커다란 이득이었다. 아인슈타인은 미국 대학에서 강의를 하고 젊은 과학자들을 가르치기 시작했다. 그들 중 많은 과학자가 나중에 NASA의 우주 계획에서 일하게 되었다. 아인슈타인 외에도 고국을 떠나 미국으로 온 위대한 과학자들이 있었다. 엔리코 페르미는 유명한 이탈리아의 과학자였다. 1930년대의 이탈리아 정부도 나치처럼 매우 잔혹했기에, 페르미는 1939년에 이탈리아를 떠났다. 미국에서 페르미는 최초의 원자폭탄이 만들어지는 데 기여했다. 페르미와 아인슈타인 두 사람 모두 미국에 지대한 공헌을 했다. 그들은 젊은 과학자들을 가르쳤을 뿐만 아니라, 그들의 연구로 인해 미국은 세계 최고 강대국의 위치에 오를 수 있었다.

/ 해 / 설 /

9. 아인슈타인은 독일을 떠나 미국을 위해 일했다.

10. 13-14째 줄에 아인슈타인이 독일을 떠나 미국으로 온 사실이 언급되어 있고, 18-19째 줄에는 '조국을 떠나 미국으로 온 위대한 과학자가 아인슈타인뿐만이 아니었다'고 되어 있으므로 아인슈타인의 조국이 독일임을 추론할 수 있다.

11. 아인슈타인은 원래 직업이 과학자가 아니었으나 상대성 이론을 발표하면서 갑자기 유명한 과학자가 되었다. 이러한 변화가 일어나기 전후의 문장을 찾아 본다.

12. 문맥상으로는 "wrong"도 답이 될 수 있으나 "unkind"가 "cruel"의 의미에 더 가깝다.

13. 12-13째 줄의 "Einstein did not like the Nazis and left Germany for America."에 설명되어 있다.

14. 여기서 "whom"은 관계대명사 목적격으로서 앞에 나온 "a new generation of scientists"를 가리키고 있다.

15. 21-22째 줄의 "In the United States, Fermi helped to build the first atomic bombs."에 나와 있다.

16. 사역동사 let, make, have 중에서 allow의 의미와 가장 가까운 것은 let이다.

17. 주어진 첫 문장은 글 전체의 주제를 담고 있다. 주제를 직접 뒷받침하는 문장을 보기 중에서 선택하도록 한다.

## Passage 3
p.181

### 사람의 뇌

뇌는 아마 우리 몸에서 가장 복잡한 부분일 것이다. 우리는 뇌에 대해 별로 아는 것이 없다. 예를 들어, 보통 사람은 자기 뇌의 15%만 사용한다. 그렇다면 나머지 85%는 왜 있는 것일까? 과학자들은 이것에 대해 아는 바가 없다. 뇌에 대한 우리 지식의 대부분은 뇌를 다친 사람들을 연구함으로써 얻어진 것이다. 사람들이 뇌를 다칠 때 그들은 종종 어떤 능력을 상실한다. 뇌의 손상된 부위와 상실된 능력을 연결함으로써 우리는 뇌의 각 부분이 무엇에 사용되는 것인지 추측할 수 있다.

오늘날 우리는 뇌가 대뇌, 소뇌, 뇌간 이렇게 세 부분으로 이루어져 있다는 것을 알고 있다. 대뇌는 뇌의 가장 큰 부분으로 두개골의 앞쪽에 위치한다. 대뇌는 뇌에서 가장 발달된 부위이다. 대뇌는 어학 능력과 문제 해결 능력 같은 고도의 사고 능력을 통제한다. 대뇌는 두 부분으로 되어 있다. 우뇌는 예술적이고 창의적인 능력을 통제하고, 좌뇌는 언어와 수리 능력을 통제한다.

소뇌는 두개골의 뒤쪽 아래 부분에 있고, 대개 신체의 움직임을 통제한다. 뇌간은 대뇌와 뇌의 중심부에 위치해 있고 대뇌와 소뇌 바로 아래에 있다. 뇌간은 몸의 여러 부

분으로부터 뇌로 신호를 전달하는 메신저 역할을 한다. 또한 호흡과 심장박동과 같은 중요한 생명 기능을 통제한다.

/ 해 / 설 /

**18.** 3째 줄의 "the average person only uses 15% of their brain"에 설명되어 있다.

**19.** 12째 줄의 "The cerebrum is the largest part of the brain"에 설명되어 있다.

**20.** "advanced" 대신 다른 보기들을 대입해 본다. 대뇌(cerebrum)가 언어 능력과 문제 해결 능력 같은 높은 차원의 사고를 조절한다는 뒷 문장의 내용과 연결시켜 생각해 본다.

**21.** 심장박동은 뇌간(brain stem)에서 조절한다(마지막 줄 참조).

**22.** 추론 문제이다. 두 번째 단락에서 대뇌의 왼쪽 부분이 언어와 수학 능력을 조절한다고 설명되어 있으므로 (D)가 답이 된다.

**23.** "skull"의 뜻은 '두개골'이므로 (C)를 답으로 고르기 쉬우나 문맥상 (A)에 더 가깝다.

**24.** 주어진 문장에서 "Still"은 '그럼에도'라는 뜻으로 사용된 부사이다. 따라서 주어진 문장과 상반되는 문장이 앞에 와야 한다.

**25.** 이 문제에서는 주어진 요약문의 첫 문장이 글의 주제와 일치한다. 그러므로 주어진 문장에 제시된 "three basic parts", 즉 "cerebrum", "cerebellum", "brain stem"에 해당되는 내용을 각각 찾으면 된다.

## LinguaForum TOEFL® *i*BT Series eBasic - e - b - m - i - Hooked On

**Junior Series**
- *i*BT eBasic TOEFL® Reading / Listening
- *i*BT e TOEFL® Reading / Listening / Grammar
- *i*BT b TOEFL® Reading / Listening / Writing / Grammar

**Test Prep.**

### Intermediate Level
- TOEFL® *i*BT m-Reading / m-Listening / m-Writing / m-Speaking
- New Edition TOEFL® *i*BT i-Reading / i-Listening / i-Writing / i-Speaking
- TOEFL® *i*BT Core Topic Guide Series / Intro Vocabulary

### Advanced Level
- New Edition Hooked On TOEFL® Reading / Listening / Writing / Speaking
- Frequency#1 TOEFL® Vocabulary
- TOEFL® *i*BT INSIDER - The Super Guide / TOEFL® *i*BT Test Book I

---

**LinguaForum™**

우06153, 서울특별시 강남구 봉은사로 442,75th(Avenue빌딩)
교재주문 1588-6066 팩스 (02) 390-0251
- www.linguaforum.com 회사소개·도서문의및상담

## 🔍 시험 상세 : 시험 화면은 다음과 같이 구성되었습니다.

### Reading
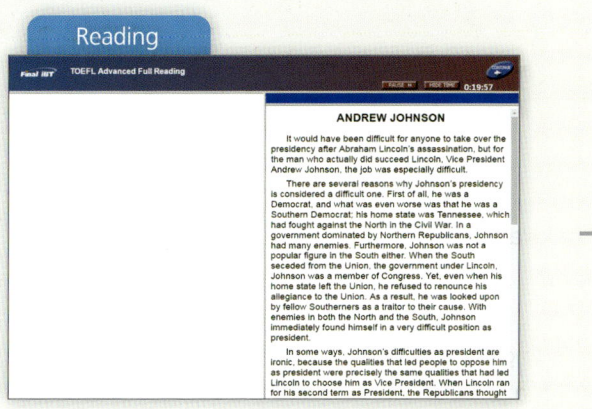

학술적인 내용의 지문을 이해하는 능력을 평가합니다.

### Listening

강의, 교실 토론 및 대화를 듣고 이해하는 능력을 평가합니다.

### Speaking
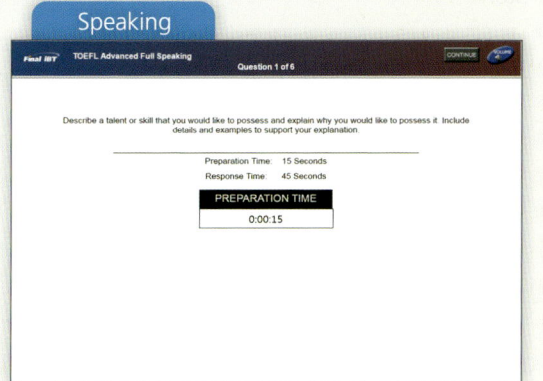

다양한 주제에 대해 말할 수 있는 능력을 평가합니다.

### Writing
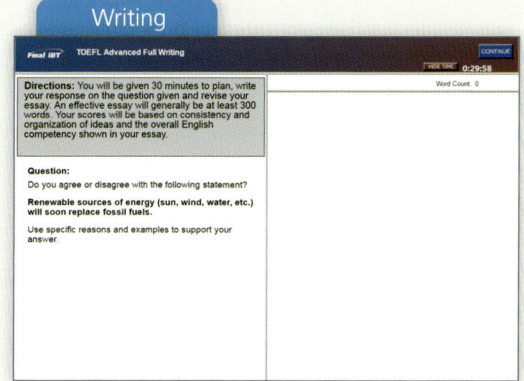

강의내용을 요약하고 자신의 의견을 정리하는 작문능력을 평가합니다.

### 성적표

각각의 모의 테스트를 마친 후 **예상점수를 확인**할 수 있습니다. SPEAKING과 WRITING 점수는 **채점 전문 인력**에 의해 매겨집니다.

## 시험 준비 세팅

먼저, 마이크가 있는 헤드셋을 준비해주세요.
그리고 인터넷이 연결된 상태에서 크롬브라우저로 접속하여 시험에 응시하시면 됩니다.

📞 시험 응시 및 문의 사항 Tel : 02-3483-2786

## 초급부터 실전까지 토플교재의 바이블
# 링구아포럼 TOEFL Series

- 아시아 최초로 2003년부터 미국은 물론 전 세계로 영어 교재와 판권 수출
- 온라인 서점 아마존닷컴 토플 판매 1위 (2003년, 2004년)
- 주니어 토플 개념 정의
- 최초 6단계별 토플 시리즈 개발

**링구아포럼의 6단계별 토플 교재 eBASIC / e / b / m / i / Hooked on / Insider / Test Book**
- eBasic 시리즈를 시작으로 e, b, m, i, Hooked On 순으로 단계가 올라갑니다. 영문 종합서 Insider 와 모의고사집 Test Book이 있습니다.

### 1 단계 — New Edition eBasic Series
중학교 1~2학년 수준으로 토플을 처음 접하는 학습자를 위한 입문 단계로, iBT의 주제와 형식, 문제유형에 입문 수준의 어휘와 문법으로 구성되었습니다.
<개정판>

### 2 단계 — New Edition e Series
중학교 2~3학년 수준의 토플 학습자를 위해 개발된 두번째 초급 단계이며, iBT의 주제와 형식, 문제유형에 입문 수준의 어휘와 문법으로 구성되었습니다.
<개정판>

### 3 단계 — b Series
중학교 3학년 이상의 영어능력을 가진 학습자를 대상으로 개발. 링구아포럼 eBasic, e 시리즈를 학습한 학습자에서부터, 토플을 처음 접하는 대학생/성인들 모두 토플에 적응하고 중급~고급 단계로 진입할 수 있도록 구성 되었습니다.

### 4 단계 — m Series
중급 수준(성인 입문)의 토플 학습자를 대상으로 개발. iBT에 등장하는 모든 주제와 문제유형 등을 모두 다루었으며, 실전보다 조금 쉬운 수준으로 연습할 수 있습니다.
<개정판>

### 5 단계 — New Edition i Series
실제 토플 시험을 준비하는 학습자를 대상으로 개발. 링구아포럼 토플 시리즈의 중/고급단계로, iBT에 등장하는 모든 주제와 문제유형 등을 모두 다루었으며, 실전과 거의 유사한 수준으로 연습할 수 있습니다.

### 6 단계 — New Edition Hooked On Series
실제 토플 시험을 준비하는 학습자를 대상으로 한 고급단계로, iBT에 등장하는 모든 주제와 문제유형등을 모두 다루어,실전과 동일한 수준으로 연습할 수 있습니다.